THE SOUTHWEST REVIEW READER

THE
SOUTHWEST
REVIEW
READER

EDITED BY
MARGARET L. HARTLEY

Foreword by
ALLEN MAXWELL

SMU PRESS · DALLAS

Material in this volume was drawn from the Autumn 1974 Fiftieth Anniversary Issue of the *Southwest Review*, which was published with the support of the Texas Commission on the Arts and Humanities and the National Endowment for the Arts, a Federal Agency.

Contents

Foreword

IN A POEM WRITTEN a decade before she came to work for the SMU Press in 1947, Margaret Lohlker Hartley wrote, "We must learn how to say this word Yes. . . . The Yes that encircles time, being life itself." She brought to the Press and the *Southwest Review* the same vitality, commitment, and optimism expressed in those lines.

Before coming to Dallas, Margaret lived for some years in Santa Fe, New Mexico, where in the course of working on the staff of the *Santa Fe New Mexican* and acting as editor and copublisher of the *Santa Féan* magazine, she came to know many of the writers of that particular part of the Southwest.

One year after I returned to SMU from naval service in World War II and became director of the SMU Press and editor of the *Southwest Review*, Margaret came aboard, bringing her knowledge and love of the region to the service of the Press and the magazine—first as editorial assistant, but soon as assistant editor of the *Review* and later as managing editor. Since 1965 she has been editor, continuing at the same time to work on the book program of the Press, of which she is now associate director and editor.

Margaret has referred to *The Southwest Review Reader* as her crowning achievement but, while it is a shining example of her skills as an editor, it is only one of her many outstanding literary accomplishments. For almost three decades now as writer, critic (particularly as puncturer of bigotry balloons), and editor she has maintained the magazine's reputation as "the Southwest's most distinguished literary quarterly." Among many gratifying recognitions of her preeminence in her profession was the presentation to her of the 1974 Matrix Special Award for Literary Achievement by the Dallas chapter of Women in Communications, which cited her as "an editor of rare perception, grace and courage" and a writer whose work blends "compassion and honesty."

To the authors whose work appears in this volume, and to the hundreds of others with whom she has talked and corresponded, Margaret has been a source of sound advice and encouragement—in many cases the first to say Yes to their literary efforts. As for myself, without her energy and dedication it would have been difficult indeed for me to have maintained a steady course.

The rich diversity of selections in the *Reader* reflects the clear and honest judgments of its editor. But behind that keen professionalism, and most obvious to those of us who have worked with her through the years, is a warm and generous spirit, one that has learned well how to say Yes to life.

ALLEN MAXWELL

Southern Methodist University
November, 1974

Introduction

THE OCCASION for the publication of this *Reader* is the fiftieth anniversary of the *Southwest Review*—under its present name, that is, and in its present location. The magazine was actually established in 1915, but at the University of Texas and under the name of the *Texas Review*. With the Autumn 1924 issue the same magazine, under new editorship but with no break in continuity of publication, moved from Austin to Dallas, from the University of Texas to Southern Methodist University, and was renamed the *Southwest Review*. The move and rechristening made a new beginning, and it is the fiftieth anniversary of this event that we are celebrating with the publication of this anthology.

We shall not attempt to write a history of the *Southwest Review* in these pages. The historically minded will find reprinted statements by earlier editors and fresh reminiscences by various people connected with the magazine in its Autumn 1955 issue, supplemented by John Chapman's "Afterthoughts on an Anniversary" in the Summer 1956 issue and Jay B. Hubbell's "Southwest Review, 1924-1927" in the Winter 1965 issue. For anyone interested in going more deeply into the subject there are Thomas F. Gossett's "A History of the *Southwest Review*: 1915-1942," his unpublished Master's thesis at Southern Methodist University (1948), and *A History of the Southwest Review: Toward an Understanding of Regionalism*, Mary Maud Trippet's Ph.D. dissertation at the University of Illinois in 1966 (published on demand by University Microfilms, Ann Arbor, Michigan).

I suspect, however, that the historically minded are a rather small minority. For everyone else who reads a magazine such as the *Southwest Review*—whose special Fiftieth Anniversary Issue has metamorphosed into this *Reader*—the question is not so much what trials and tribulations its editors have encountered over the years as whether the result of their struggles has been an interesting and valuable journal, one worth anthologizing. Not unnaturally, the present editors believe that it has.

By no means all the forms these qualities of interest and value have assumed over a period of fifty years—two hundred issues—could be exemplified in the pages put at our disposal for the special issue and thus for this *Reader* with the aid of the Texas Commission on the Arts and Humanities and the National Endowment for the Arts. So problems of choice have arisen, our solutions to which will not, we realize, satisfy everyone. As is true with every such selective presentation, there will be those who will ask why a favorite article, story, or poem has not been included. Very many of our own favorites have had to be omitted, so we can only ask for tolerance on everyone's part and an assessment of what is here rather than what is not.

As we thought about these questions of choice, several possible criteria suggested themselves. First, we might select the best from each decade, say, of the *Southwest Review*'s fifty years. But as we studied the early issues we realized anew the speed with which changes in the world of taste, as in the worlds of economics, politics, and technology, have come about. Contributions that were splendid for their time now have a strangely antique ring to them. And this issue is to be read in the space age, not that of the years soon after World War I, or even of the years immediately before, during, and after World War II.

Another possible criterion was the importance of the names represented. Naturally, the great triumvirate of J. Frank Dobie, Roy Bedichek, and Walter Prescott Webb are here, as are others such as Paul Horgan and Mary Austin. Had we followed this standard rigidly, however, though our table of contents might have been more impressive, the contents themselves, alas, would not. When a magazine is small and new, some "great names" will occasionally throw it a few crumbs. But too often they *are* crumbs, not the full nourishing loaf. They helped, in their time, to keep the magazine alive. But to include them here would do honor neither to the authors nor to the *Southwest Review*.

There are, however, many other names prominent in the history of southwestern writing and of the *Southwest Review* that are absent from these pages for an entirely different reason. One of the great satisfactions of the editors has always been the discovery of new writers and the opportunity to give them a hearing. An anniversary issue which attempts to be somehow representative must, we feel, include a good proportion of these—whether, like William Goyen, they have gone on to distinguish themselves since they first appeared with us, or whether they have not yet had time to become widely known. Including them has meant omitting some of our old and dear friends and contributors—people of wisdom and graciousness who, if they are still among us, like Henry Nash Smith, William A. Owens, Charles W. Ferguson, Paul F. Boller, Jr., H. E. Francis, Lon Tinkle, Leonard Casper, Victor White, Levi A. Olan, to name just a few, we know will understand. We salute them all here, as we do the memory of others such as Mody C. Boatright, John A. Lomax, Fred Gipson, and Erna Fergusson.

The editors of the *Southwest Review* have always been proud of the fact that the journal has been a voice for freedom when that freedom has been threatened in any area of the life of the nation and the region. An anthology could be made solely of contributions in this area, but its interest would be principally historical. One thinks, for example, of the McCarthy era (Joe McCarthy, that is) and the *Southwest Review*'s Autumn 1953 special issue, "Freedom in America." In order to understand the real significance of that issue (of which a book, *The Present Danger*, was later made) and the courage *Southwest Review* editor Allen Maxwell showed by publishing it, one must be able to remember and reexperience the mood of that time. People who were then too young to be fully aware are, I have found in conversation with them, unable to believe that one junior senator from Wisconsin could actually have succeeded in casting a heavy pall of fear over America, affecting every aspect of its life. And yet it was true. A record, "The Investigator," which now seems nothing but a mild enough satire on McCarthy, was sold only under the counter; and I remember listening to it with a carefully screened academic group at the country home of a professor, with no neighbors close enough to eavesdrop, and the sense we all had of doing a forbidden and dangerous thing. I am sure few would disagree with the articles by Richard H. Rovere, Paul G. Hoffman, Kenneth C. Royall, Henry M. Wriston, and Gerald W. Johnson in that Freedom Issue; but there would be no way to make a reprinting of them now convey the urgent, the almost desperate importance which they had in the context of their time.

The same would be true of such discussions in the magazine's pages as that of the controversy about "leftism" and academic freedom at the University of Texas in the late forties, or of the admission of Heman Marion Sweatt, a black, to the law school of the same university, or of an instance of antisemitism that afflicted SMU in the early fifties. We are proud to have published what we did concerning these things, but the country and we have gone on to fight other wars. So for our present purposes we have omitted the essays, exciting in their time, that deal too closely with ". . . old, unhappy, far-off things,/And battles long ago."

One of the most difficult questions of choice, one which has been constantly discussed and indeed argued with some heat over the years, concerns regionalism. In the first issue of his editorship, when the *Southwest Review* entered the new phase of its existence at SMU in 1924, Jay B. Hubbell wrote:

We purpose to follow Carl Sandburg's advice and get into the pages of the *Southwest Review* the five-gallon hat of the cowboy as well as the skyscrapers of Dallas and Denver.

The *Southwest Review*, then, will be national in its outlook, and its pages will be open to all who write well; but it will especially encourage those who write on Western themes, for it is a magazine for the Southwest.

Following the appearance of the Autumn 1940 issue, J. Frank Dobie wrote to editor John H. McGinnis objecting to the prominence given in that issue to an article so far from regional as Lon Tinkle's "France's Undeclared Civil War." McGinnis replied:

I'm not upset at your objection to our international article. I defend my point of view by saying that *at the moment* not cotton, nor your Nueces County cows—certainly not recollections of Texas yesteryears can be considered as important to Texans—urban or rural—as whether we shall fall into the democratic confusion that finished France, and almost got England. I simply couldn't face the criticism—the potential criticism—that might be made now or years later: "The poor sand blind Regionalists didn't realize what was happening to them," or, "The nation's fate was at stake, and they were talking about little regional books and prints."

Rapid advances in transportation and communication that came with World War II brought the Southwest even more closely into the mainstream. In the Spring 1946 issue, his first as editor upon his return from service in the Pacific, Allen Maxwell expressed this change:

In a world shrunk to the size of an old lemon under the impact of jet propulsion and kindred marvels the Southwest can't afford to turn in upon itself and ruminate upon its past—however remarkable that past may have been. We must look outward to comprehend our present and plan our future.

And Dobie himself, having come to some different conclusions in the decade since his criticism of the Tinkle article (which, incidentally, he admitted he had not read at the time of his letter to McGinnis), wrote in "The Writer and His Region," which is reprinted here from the Spring 1950 issue:

No sharp line of time or space, like that separating one country from another or the territory of one nation from that of another, can delimit the boundaries of any region to which any regionalist lays claim. Mastership, for instance, of certain locutions peculiar to the Southwest will take their user to the Aztecs, to Spain, and to the border of ballads and Sir Walter Scott's romances. I found that I could not comprehend the coyote as animal hero of Pueblo and Plains Indians apart from the Reynard of Aesop and Chaucer.

In the same article Dobie quoted Robert Frost, who in his opinion "approached a satisfying conception" of the nature of regionalism, as saying, "I am not a regionalist. I am a realmist. I write about realms of democracy and realms of the spirit." This kind of regionalism, or "realmism," is, as I wrote in my first Editor's Notebook in the Spring 1965 issue, very different from provincialism, with its blinders narrowing the view to the immediate area. It can, and now indeed must, coincide with the broadest of worldviews. I quoted Lon Tinkle's words, which I still find good: "Nowadays, depth is inseparable from regionalism. All of us lead public lives on a very broad level of awareness of global events. For depth, we need the compensating awareness of our daily and manageable life. This is our concrete, not abstract, level of existence, our richest sense of life." And I concluded with an attempt to put into words the attitude we have, in the succeeding almost-decade, found most useful:

It is in this way that I believe SWR should be "regional"—expressing our awareness of our region and of the nation and the world, in writing originating in our area and also in a choice of writing from elsewhere that conveys, by the very nature of its selection, the way we see things from our "plot of earth," as Dobie called it.

So there we have our final choice of criterion for inclusion in this anthology—the only one, really, that I believe we could use: "the way we see things." For better or for worse, *The Southwest Review Reader* must represent the seeing of the present editors as they have looked back over the issues of the past fifty years. We hope, as we have hoped with every issue we have published, that our readers will find something to enjoy in these pages, and something in which they will find, as we do, the merit of lasting value.

MARGARET L. HARTLEY

Southern Methodist University
November, 1974

THE SOUTHWEST REVIEW READER

About the Southwest
A Panorama of Nueva Granada

PAUL HORGAN

THE LAND

A FRENCH MAP in the year 1679 showed the new land explored as far as the *terra incognita* of present-time Utah. The groaning wagons and horses had tried the terrain of Nueva Granada, that embraced everything we know now as New Mexico, Texas, Arizona, and part of Oklahoma. The Río Grande, according to the heroic cartographer who sent his map to Paris for engraving, flowed from the north into the Pacific Ocean. Mountains, in the light of later accuracies, were a little carelessly disposed. But the yellowing water-laid paper carried a fiber of mankind that was ambitious, tough, and wild enough to follow blind riverbeds to the north. The shifts of sunlight on our yellow horizons could easily dazzle a mapper and put his rivers and his mountains out of accuracy. But nothing made him turn back. His chart of what he found suggests that we use his name for the territory, since it so easily indicates the boundaries of the Southwest as we now regard it.

In area, then, Texas, New Mexico, Arizona, and Oklahoma will constitute the Southwest of our time. America's regions seem to divide themselves into those of New England, the East (Atlantic states), the South, the Middle West, the Southwest, the West (mountain states), the Northwest, and California.

The Southwest is large enough to include the widest varieties of terrain, and thus of weather and of human pursuits. It is a country of one of two characters: either there are immense plains, flat alike to the tempests and the endless days of sunlight, or there are mountains that challenge the zenith with the power of a legend. Only in the littlest local sense are there pastoral regions, with bounding green hills and sustained valleys. This meant that, looking for natural securities and havens, the early people found none; and the resultant exercise of human ingenuity and faith produced that crew of pioneers whose philosophy so often seemed almost geological in its simplicity and its strength. The great river, Río Grande, went slowly and widely down to the Gulf of Mexico, hardly oozing enough water in summer to slake a traveled animal train, going brown and reedy in the winter under its red banks, tearing away from the course of mountains in the spring, and changing the face of the deserts through which it went with the high breast of flood. So, either sleepy and endlessly peaceful, or sudden and terrible with storm and change, the life in the valley of the Río Grande affords an easy figure for the life of the entire region.

In a land where gold was the temptation from the first rumors of the cities of Cíbola, water was immensely more valuable. Its only sources were the mountain streams that made the rivers and the heavy thunderheads that gathered like a doom in El Greco. When the clouds broke and the plains were harried by the quick passing lines of the rain, the water sheeted down the brown spotted hills into the low runs where the arroyos were cut; and the sandy walls of the arroyos were dragged and broken by the red water as it flowed. A party of travelers, crossing such an arroyo to the south, where it might be sunny and dry, could hear a roar of mysterious quality and suddenly perceive the flood wall, dirt-red, advancing between the blue shadowed walls of the bed upon their fording party. The foam on the water would be light tan, whipped up from the surface mud. Yet the whisper of gravel, rolling under the pour, the scamper of prairie animals, the hurry of the travelers to mount the firm ground while the flood went by, and wait for the fall of the water, and the final seep of the red earth under the sun—these things marked the land but rarely. For the rest of the time, there was the sun overhead, and there lay the distance, changing in the heat and never dropping its challenge.

The surface of the ground was hard and resistant, with unfriendly plants and stones. The salty white of alkali was exposed, and the chalky sharp stone of gypsum. Under the shadow of the mountains, where they might be encountered, lay hills that offered protection. Safer from sunlight, they were neither baked nor blinding. Farms might be set up in such places, if the river country was too insecure with flood and shift.

To the south, near Mexico, the wild plants blossomed with furious color, scarlets and whites, high yellows and flashing greens. Over the whole of the territory when the spring had been soaked by the skies, the white and lavender verbena came to purfle the ground. It was one of the few times when a sense of something intimate, like a little wild flower, pervaded the land and gave it, besides its terrible beauty and mysterious wonder of distance and newness, some friendly aspect, much needed by men in a place where the only change from a flat brown plain was a sudden butte, hard and disdainful in its abrupt walls and unseen top.

The things that lived there required no conditions that were not common. Up the river valleys lived the Indians in houses built of the earth. Wild animals found their food in the endless life-process of stalking and killing, with the high vultures sailing until the feast was done and the refuse abandoned. Snakes dwelt with the secrecy of plants, and in the mountains the cat watched for the antelope, and the coyote whimpered after dark on the desert.

Buffalo wandered under the changing months, governed by solstices and the species of food. Their paths were never constant; nothing charted the huge spaces for the pioneers but the courses of rivers and the steadfast sign of stars. The interruption of a northward course by a canyon, long ago eaten down by an irresistible water, would cause weeks of search for a crossing or a ford. A mountain range, with flanks rearing back for miles of approach, must have been resistant to the search for a pass, over or around. There were dangers from everything, from the very distance, from the very passage of time. A young man could easily die from natural causes before a mission was completed. A climate, tropical in the daytime and cold at night because of the steady rise of the ground with the advance away from the sea, could of itself produce a need for a new philosophy. To the European eye, the eloquent strangeness of this country of Nueva Granada must have offered first fancy, and then fact, as a basis for legend. Travelers that return from new lands bring exactly enough information and have suffered exactly enough terror and hardship and excitement to let the several kinds of experience mingle in their reports. And so legend is born, is transmuted in passing from person to person, and a social force too strong to be resisted is put in motion. The quality of this sort of legend that makes it both dangerous and splendid is its constant change: while the serene legend from which myth grows, the legend that is devised without author and accepted without apostasy, is so slow to change that dogma seems really safe and the gods truly reliable.

But men put upon a new country at once bring about marvels too exciting for silence. So it is the combination of land and people that gives history its earliest point of departure.

THE HEROIC TRIAD

Against the land stand three great themes: the Indians, the Spaniards, and the American pioneers. The antiquity of the Indian balks us. How much of the Aztec went into the tribes that live in the pueblos, and how much of the Mongolian? When was Bering Strait an isthmus? What qualities has the life in mud houses on earthy plains in common with the oriental splendor of Indian dances and crafts?

The two Indian kinds, the Pueblo and the nomad, were profoundly established and differentiated in their religions, their cultures, and their arts long before the Spaniards came in the sixteenth century. Long before then, even, a whole nation of cliff dwellers had evolved, lived human lives, and perished in some ghostly fashion, leaving their habitations in perfect order, with no explanation of their tribal death. Only from the surviving Indians are we able to picture the people that watched the steel and silver helmets of the invaders spark with sunlght in the hot distance.

His dignity and his irony are the two traits of the Indian which impress the white man today. Certainly he watched the Spaniard approach with dignity. Perhaps his irony is the result of his conquest. But with immense pride in his ancestry, the Indian approached the Spaniard with severe passiveness. This severity marked his daily life. It infused his religious devotion with a passion out of the earth. It made him reliable in peace and stoical in war. The character of the Pueblo Indian was constant. It came out of the roots of his country as sturdily as the rocks on which he toiled and lived. The country and its temper, endless skies and spaciousness upon the earth, must have given him a lordliness and a humility which helped to keep him wise and simple.

In his religion, the Indian used mountains and clouds, the rain, the elements, the familiar animals of his hunt and his sustenance, all things which either nourish the earth or derive from it. The magnificent unity of the Indian conception of life demanded a religious joy which was bound to the ground in the dance. The deities were many, their functions as diverse as their characters. No one deity seems ever to have transcended the human conception of life and its universal embrace that the Indians held.

6

In the pueblos, religion and art mingled in a dance ritual, a theater of devotion. There were dances for the fecundation of the spring; dances for the growth of summer; dances for the blue rains that beat upon fields and pueblos and turned them wetly brown; dances for the harvest in the autumn when smoke from the clay chimneys smelled sharp and stood straight in the frosty air. There were dances for the sick, the dying, the possessed; for the blessing of new houses, whose earth was hardly dry upon the sunbaked bricks; for the hunt, with antelope bounding; for human fecundity, elaborate rituals of the phallus, conception, and new life; dances of the secret, hidden from women, danced in the ceremonial star chambers; all profoundly related to the Indian cosmos, explanatory of his character, as traditional as his warm family feeling and his tribal loyalty.

These symbols sufficed. The Indian had a culture of his own making, in which the social units were woven into the pueblo whole. The family, monogamous, prolific, separate, was the basis of the society. But gregarious and unselfish, the families, while dwelling alone as units, still lived in the great terraced house of the pueblo, contributing by presence and activity to the community, which in times of religious dance would act as a whole, as in times of war, harvest, and hunt. So, with family and religion and a passionate integrity of crafts and arts as his strongest tributes to life, the Indian was an epitome of the freedom of his country and the beauty of its terrain.

Any people which has found tradition a bulwark of happiness had better be allowed to retain that tradition. From it must flow a tribal consciousness of the past, and to it must be added the best works of the present. The Indians of the pueblos, peaceful and traditional in their outlook, have been robbed and put upon by their conquerors, as any weaker nation will be robbed and put upon. The things of their past are the things of peace and not of war. Their legends; their arts of the silversmith and weaver and potter; their dances, in which a sincerity of belief replaces the sincerity of the mime in sophisticated theater and ballet; their adherence to the amenities of Indian life: all impress us as attributes of a truly intelligent race, mysteriously powerful in its relation to its environment.

It is a race abounding in legends and themes. The very designs of the rugs and the jars made by Indians in their time of independence have significance of a legendary or religious character. A rug would be made with an intricate maze in its pattern, a channel which the eye would follow with difficulty. In this channel on the pattern a devil could travel. The rug would be put over a sick man. The devil would leap from the sick man to the rug, to the path of the maze, and take his way to the one corner of egress, which the weaver had left open for just such an exit of an evil spirit. The constant use of mythological symbols, such as the familiar thunderbird in jewelry, betrays the artist's concern with a moving canon of belief and opinion—what we should nowadays term a point of view—whose so-frequent absence from the works of our artists and authors is held to be a symptom of emotional and social bankruptcy. Certainly, if an artist is so possessed by his thoughts about life and the symbols he uses to think that these symbols enter into all his work, then that artist is fulfilling his function perfectly, regardless of his degree of talent.

And the legends of a physical character: the Enchanted Mesa—the great mesa that rises from the desert, a rock like a tree-trunk of gigantic girth, chopped off clean five hundred feet above the ground. Nearby is the other butte of Acoma, with gradual ascent to its summit from one side. It is declared that the dwellers of Acoma are the survivors of the race that used to live upon the Enchanted Mesa, who were swept from its top by war. In the valley below the mesa, the fields were waiting for tillage. The men and women went down, leaving children and the aged and the sick on top of the mesa, where their pueblo rose to the sky, and hawks and eagles flew upward to its edge. Great ladders reached from the ground to ledges on the way up, a terraced pathway to the city. Upon the workers in the fields below, hostile bands descended from the hills about; massacred them; and destroyed the ladders, leaving the few living Indians on top isolated and doomed. The legend says that the city crumbled before many weathers; thunderclouds rested on its brow and beat with rain. The few that lived after the massacre in the cornfields set up life on the mesa of Acoma, a mile away. In time, the top of the Enchanted Mesa was as wind-clean as a bone on the open desert.

The Indian has been so typical in his attitude to the conquerors that it is natural to think of him in uniform terms. For the student of his race who would use him in literature, to be sure, the Indian will present as many different traits, aptitudes, opinions, and characters as any comparable group of white people whose religion and allegiance to the earth are as strong. But the Indian's dignity may always be taken for granted;

and his irony, the only attitude which could follow the destruction of his integrity by a foe that still strives to improve him, must be counted the last defensive spark of the passion that consumed him when the silvery helmets first came winking over the sandy valleys.

In contrast to these pueblo dwellers of New Mexico and Arizona, the roaming tribes of Plains Indians put nothing permanent of their lives upon their land. Oklahoma and parts of Texas must have been visited and lived upon by such Indians, and even the border regions of the other states. But a nation that can uproot its capital, pack it upon squaws and horses, and trail onward to another water hole, can develop few refinements except in the arts of war. The Spaniards must have tilted first with the nomads. . . . What was this new material? this European force, hard like armor, and arrogant with faith?

The second element of the triad is the invader. Behind him were the brocaded values of Spain and the burning pyres of Aztec villages, a sense of conquest over the awful Atlantic; behind him, and thrusting him forward, were the two civilized impulses of gold and Rome. Arquebuses and ciboria: the scaling ladder and the miter: arm and soul set out together on Spain's trail of desire.

There was a remarkable simplicity regarding the men for such expeditions. To be sent to America could mean either a great honor from the king, or a disgrace visited upon a blackguard who would do better by all concerned in the colonies. The great gentlemen of the day (it was the sixteenth century) carried in their persons all those curious elements which fascinate and astound the student of the period. They had a sophisticated taste for the arts, and their manners were atrocious. They bought pearls from the oriental traders to edge their collars, and their clothing was often noisome. The glories of the mind and the pleasures of the body were wedded in an extraordinary appreciation of the values of both, and the product of the union was often a piece of loutish cruelty. A cardinal was a man in a red train with a diamond cross, a parcel of cynical children, and a masterly skill in diplomacy. Worldliness lay cheek by jowl with the zeal of St. Francis. The human spirit produced rich fruits; art lay ripening by the side of science. Nations warred lavishly. Symptoms of universal poverty began to appear. The zealot was appalled by the worldling. Gold and Christ were imperative needs. Spain answered the question with Mexico, where pagan priests adored odd gods before altars of gold and diamonds, and whole cities were beaten together from gold and there were mountains of precious stones.

Enthusiasm betrayed the mariners, the conquerors. Every lavish rumor was, instead of a sign for caution, an urge onward, regardless of the state of troops, the conveyancing, the unfriendly land. Decades were occupied in getting from the coast of Mexico to the Río Grande. Cities in imitation of Seville and Madrid came up in the jungles, where leaves were as big as a breastplate. With the first impulses of the conqueror, the Spaniard established his own civilization in miniature. Mexico City, built of mud, saw the mimic masses, courts, governors-general, and social usages of home. With the aid of friendly Indians of Mexico and a few directions from addled travelers full of stories about soft golden cities, they set out for the north. No country in their experience had had the qualities of this vast one they crawled across under the brassy sunlight. Exhaustion could come quickly; eyes peering into the boundless heaven at the horizon could water with despair of ever reaching any sort of goal. The usual desertions, collapses, rebellions occurred. Disease came and destroyed men and horses. The Indians became fickle, the itinerant priests would have to harangue them and persuade them with heroic examples. The military arm of the expeditions would sometimes grow impatient, there were words between Christ and General, the party would divide; perhaps never to meet again, perhaps to reunite some dusk under the suspicious regard of a watching pueblo. Bizarre as it was, and stupidly unorganized, childlike in its credulities and even more childlike in its disappointments, this northward move of the Spanish conquerors commands respect for its tenacity. Wave after wave of explorers and preachers set out from Mexico. The more the years passed, the more dogged these foreigners grew in the conquest of a land which, they now perceived, harbored neither gold, nor mountains of emerald, nor any race whose capture would glorify God particularly. With their original purposes rubbed out by the touch of experience, they nevertheless persisted; took the pueblos, planted crosses in the *placitas* of the towns, delivered proclamations of amnesty and fatherhood, and moved on, leaving the Indians polite and amazed at such energy and such goals. There were battles, the Indians would resent pillage and theft, but all resistance came to the common end: the planting of a bell in a tower, the ringing for mass, the beginning of the slow corruption of language and custom.

Long years were required for the movement northward from the landing-place of Mexico. The soldiers took Indians to wife, a new race began to evolve. It was presently noticed that the Río Grande did not flow from the north into the Pacific Ocean. It was discovered that farms could be made along the river and its tributaries. The wagon trains began moving up from the capital, where the king's governor-general lived in a palace hung with paintings from home. The toiling priests of the beginning were succeeded by prelates in purple, whose carriages were slung on springs and drawn by four horses topped with papal rosettes. Reproductions of the official and social life of Spain became constant in such cities as San Antonio and Santa Fé, though the latter saw several wars of conquest and reconquest before the Indians were reconciled. What could the conquerors have sent home that paid for their expeditions? Very little, surely, except the heartening indices of converts and descriptions of a truly magnificent country whose mountains and plateaus gave glory to the Creator. It was perhaps a wry enough substitute for bullion and gems. The indifference of the government at home was attested by the lack of intensity with which it governed the provinces. Grants of land from the king were frequent and prodigious. Governors-general and captains-general were appointed by letter from Spain, a confusing affair since in Nueva Granada a man could be elevated, reign, and die before his appointment could be confirmed or denied. No, there was little to justify the firm planting of Spanish culture and Spanish dominion. The invaders brought their hopes and their language, their firearms and their carved furniture and dark paintings, their society of courtiers and their ambitious priests. The accents of the Renaissance were imposed upon a more ancient culture, a culture that was adapted to the land of its emergence; and the changes that resulted betray the triumph of the spiritual enthusiasm of the church, and at the same time the superior force of the more ancient Indian culture. For it altered the Spaniards more than they knew, so that when the third occupation came, the occupation of the Americans, there was no organized life, there were no racial or communal bulwarks against the new invasion. The country had conquered the Latins.   .

Yet, the fiercer patriarchal families that came from Spain to govern in the new land preserved through the centuries their integrity of blood and bearing There were no palaces to be had here of marble and tile, with the luxuries familiar at home. But great rambling habitations of mud and wood could be built, and within the thick walls, furnished by shiploads of magnificence, the pattern of life was as severe as any ancestor could require. The men would have to soldier and defend in unsettled times. The women must sew, make vestments, discover the ingenuities which would turn the new foods into old excellencies, keep the altar lamps burning brightly crimson, and maintain the values of painting and literature in a place where they were scarce and forgettable. Hospitality was a creed, informed by the most exquisite of formalities: a double handful of gold laid out upon a table from which the departing guest could select as much as he might need. There were evenings of harp and violin in the earthen houses, with remotenesses of mountains and plains bringing memories of home and fears of the present. There was thick, heavy chocolate, frightfully hot, served in silver mugs. There were the guns standing in the freshly whitewashed corner, and the bills for the shipment of furs and taffetas and spices and Damascus blades and brass bolts for harness-making and a set of silver plates and assorted seeds for the vineyard and the kitchen garden. In the flash of the firelight, dancing up the wall even behind the steady little flames of the candles in their silver holders, there is a feeling that the pride and the courage of the family are beautiful things. God is adored in the remote earthen chapels, and the tales of past hardships and terrors go by like dreams of which the present is somehow compounded.

Up the valley of the great river the traders move, suffering in travel the things the first travelers told of. But the trails begin to be easier to follow. There is money at the end, where people live who want to buy as well as conquer and convert. The generations follow the cycle of their seasons. It is not long until men and women live here whose roots are now mingled with the new country. Spain? A place of which stories have been told. Civilization, with its local conventions, continues. The families that survive and descend from the conquistadores rule the land. The servants and the farmers, the private soldiers and the team-drivers of that old time now fall into place among the peasant farmers. Peonage is normal and satisfactory, as a system that serves the noble and houses and feeds the serf. Separate from all that, yet subject in official allegiance, the Indians continue their tribal and communal life, changing more profoundly than they can be aware, adopting new gods, yet in the process remaining closer to the life engendered of the country than their conquerors, who also change: more rapidly, perhaps, and more obviously. Soldiering, as a profession, has little to sustain its importance now; gentlemen are not farmers in Spain, what is there to give a core to the new life?

But (strong are the ties, and haunting the proprieties of home) society with carriages, chocolate parties, and balls with harps and violins, the formalities of government, the weightiness of the Church proclaim the character of the land and its dwellers, as mountains and plains do, and as Indians with hostility and guile do. In the face of the third known occupation of the country, there were two races full of resentment instead of one. Yet the Americans from the East, with superior vitality, well-organized forces, and an almost fanatical impulse for the westward experience, came relentlessly and cleverly over the whole country, and once again changed its life.

Unmolested except by the tempers of the terrain and quarrels among themselves, the peoples of Nueva Granada had dwelt remotely. Their connection with the world was through the shipping that plied between Europe and Mexico. It was just that the first news of this western empire should come from Europe to stir the Americans, who had been stirred before by the idea of the Thirteen States, had survived the evils of fanaticism in New England, had demonstrated an ideal of freedom and conceived a republic of gentlemen in whom responsibility for the nonruling classes was implicit. Government, once settled, is withdrawn to the charge of the comparatively few. The slow pressure of the knowledge of the West was inciting people to dwell upon the legend, the rumor, and finally the physical proof brought back by scouts and explorers and traders. It seemed enough to furnish a theme for the American imagination, the turning of a whole national impulse westward. Human reason functioned in making the movement practical and tolerably efficient. But the great migrations in history seem to have in their spirit something transcendent, yet familiar as the compulsion under which trees grow in loamy ground. What is it? Is it a national, or a racial character? The motives, as has been noticed, are sometimes wholly practical; but we have also seen that glory to God was equally important. A poetical splendor informs a tribe or a cult, the wagons are made, the psalms are delivered, and with ceremonial farewells, with consciousness of a stirring adventure in the making, people set out for uncharted lands.

By the time the westward migration took on the force and determination that were to people our Southwest, the American national character had been crystallized: had established its Yankeeness, its Atlantic-states flavor. And never since has it boasted any such neat simplicity, for the grander the nation grew in size, the more varied grew its idealized figure. The pioneer (with Uncle Sam, and later the small-eyed Southern Colonel) stood as one of the few epitomes that the country at large recognized. Certainly in his wildcat excellence, his generosity, his shrewdness, his courage, and his integrity to the thing that pushed him into the West, the pioneer makes a figure whose stature grows the more his achievements are considered.

He, too, but with craftier guile, fought the Indians of the plains. He hunted the antelope, the bear, the buffalo, and the birds for food and clothing; he hunted the snake and the wolf for safety. He trundled his women and children in wagons that were often thrown into fortress formations for battle. He buried his dead on the plains, with his journey half done. He blessed his new child, born into the magnificent loneliness of the country. He kept his guns and provisions in order, he studied the marks of the earth and the portents of the sky for information. He questioned returning traders. He began to see the value of finding a site for a town, and felt good when he sat down to consider, with his fellows, what natural beauties and conveniences a town should possess. If he were asked why he moved West, his answer would perhaps be puzzled, as if no answer were needed. To have his own land, yes, maybe, to discover what kind of country lay out that way, to extend the American prestige —that would be an afterthought as explanation; there would, in short, be no consistent or reasonable answer. It was a thing greater than himself, yet subject to the toil of his body and his spirit across the wide lands. A manifestation of natural law, as mysterious and as acceptable as the impulse that sets cicadas singing with fury and joy in the hot beat of sunlight. Could it be a tribute to the philosophy of hope that men cherish in their religions? Anything remotely like a Promised Land is seductive. Yet the dangers of the new one of the West were so appalling, the disheartening fight with nature and distance and strangeness so challenging, that the Promised Land theme, except for such inspirations as the Mormons', must be put away.

Taken as a whole, the overland movement must remain majestic and magnificent, a moment of history that will live as a triumph of the human spirit. In terms of the lives and deaths of the men and women who carried it through, on the basis of their own characters and ways, their thoughts and their hopes and their fallible humanity, the imperial conquest of the Americans stands as one of the few themes that cover all of America.

The halting but by no means tentative advances of the earliest American pioneers were suddenly overtaken and engulfed by the rush of people who had heard of gold in California. Again this familiar species of zeal intruded, and by its intensity hurried the settling of the western lands. Wagon trains so vast that their tracks became, in effect, roads to the West set out. Travel must be made safe. Armies were detailed to assist in the migration. Forts were built, commerce and communication followed, towns, peopled by a transient and busy population, marked the popular routes of travel. The farther they went, the more valuable showed the trails of their predecessors. Santa Fé, conquered by General Kearney in 1848, was an American provincial capital now, where the survivors of the conquistadores dwelt in a subjection that was theoretical but as real as their own centuries of government over the Indians. Texas, with the glories of a revolution and the foundation of a heroic tradition, and Oklahoma, also on the route, were strange and yet familiar to the farmer who crossed them on the way to the goldfields. Arizona, more Indian than anything else, was menacing, for the tragedies of Death Valley and the other deserts to be crossed were the last great obstacles before the Pacific, and wealth, and American rule under General Kearny's officers.

It was, all along its incredible ox-drawn length, a road of riches. The first fur-traders who lived in the mountains and on the plains like animals, so clever, so native did they seem, made their fortunes every year with their trapping. Knowing the ground, they knew the people; and they stand as admirable images of the early American there. With the coming of the conquest, they aided the military expeditions. In the time of colonization and growth they took on the characters of substantial citizens, yet did not forget the days when a man worth his salt could lick his weight in wildcats, drink whiskey by the gallon, shoot straighter than a die, and dance the Missouri breakdown with something more valuable than mere grace. They deserved to get rich. Commerce took three paths: the old trade with Mexico continued, the new trade with the East grew and commanded new utilities, and the cattle industry became the public concern it has always been since, a concern that has stamped the whole West with its character, has made it, more than any other region of the country, financially independent, and has been, until the rise of the oil industry, the only American generator of folklore in the Southwest.

The railroads followed the course of money and trade, and brought more money, much more money than the land had ever seen before. The Middle Ages and Renaissance of the Indians and the Spaniards were over. Modern life succeeded, with all the false criteria established by a civilization of commerce and trade. So, too, came the luxuries that are dependent upon wealth, luxuries for anyone with the money. Two ideals had been changed in the final conquest of Nueva Granada: the ideal of the aristocratic European who first took the land, and the ideal of the republican American, whose fathers built a nation with enthusiasm for a democratic ideal, and whose sons corrupted that ideal with the huge moneys they made and circulated. Traditions cannot be guided in their making.

OUT OF THE UNION

In the peoples as they exist today, the marks of inevitable compromise can be read. The country has stamped its character on them in one way or another, and they have so affected one another that to describe them now is to indulge in an essay on survivals. The Indians were changed by the Spaniards, who brought them another God and a different brand of fatalism. Then the life that was made up by the Spaniards and Indians together was altered swiftly and thoroughly by the Americans. While each people lived as ruler of the land, its life and ideas, its belief and tradition had gone for centuries unchanged. But with the American arrival, in a vitality that was not only sure to conquer but sure to assimilate the vanquished, change came so fast and in so many departments of life that we can only examine the vestiges today and observe how eloquent they are of upheaval.

The Indian: he repeats in ghostly enactment the tragedy of his Eastern cousins, the spectacle of a race of rulers penned off by a benevolent government and seduced from the integrities of its crafts by the tourist. The Plains tribes of Indians, always more bellicose and restless than the Pueblos, live in reservations where American schools and American clothes unsettle the tribal proprieties in childhood. Through education the Indian's guardian has attempted to give him the benefits of a system of belief and knowledge that is entirely irrelevant to his kind of life. The spectacle is familiar enough: Indian children are placed in government

Indian schools, where they learn orthodox school subjects and military drill and football. When they are old enough to graduate as young men and women, they are turned out, equipped by rote to compete in modern life, and wholly unequipped by temperament, heritage, and desire. One of two courses confronts them: either they may take some menial job in the white man's scheme, a job for which their formal education has provided nothing, or they may return to the pueblo, where the values of a formal education are laughable. But it is the style of the conqueror, and it may take many more years for the birth of the official notion that instead of remodeling the Indian it would be wiser to find out what he is and provide a life for him that is suitable. But that would involve leaving him rather alone, and the zeal of the conqueror is so mixed with the zeal of the missionary that it is hopeless to expect *laissez faire.*

As one of the three dominant themes in our terrain, the Indian offers today hardly a pure view of his kind. In religion, his practices are double. Although he accepted the Christian God of the early priests and built adobe cathedrals, carved and dressed saints for the altars, and partook of Holy Communion, he has never relinquished his own pantheon. The gods of heaven and ground, of sky and rock and weather, still govern his spiritual life. This duality is characteristic of the effect Western ideals have had upon him. He seems able to accept with docility and good sense whatever creed of manners and thought is imposed upon him by his tormentors. Underneath it all, the old long river of his tradition flows the same way from the same wells of lost tribal genesis. In such a course of acceptance, and in the preservation of what is personal to him, the Indian reveals a marvelous dignity, a close relation to something that moves him. Perhaps it is because his conquerors and revisers have no such deep spiritual relevance to the conditions of their lives that they are so eager and so restless in trying out the effects of their scrambled beliefs on everybody that comes along.

Other inevitable corruptions assail the Indian's integrity of race and habit. One is his exploitation by and for the tourists that come in thousands to gaze upon his dwellings, his religious dances, his art, and his person. Indians are selling their handiwork rapidly and easily, and as a consequence are now making their handiwork too rapidly and too easily. Things which in the days of his history the Indian made for use, and made beautifully and significantly, are now made for sale. Something of the spirit of their new purpose has come into the work and destroyed the fine meaning of Indian craftsmanship. The Indian, in his native place, is now a show, for viewing which luxuries are provided and a whole industry developed. How long the life of the Pueblo can continue under such organized scrutiny, it is hard to imagine. Indians are sensitive, and they have by gradual association found it necessary in dealing with the Americans to erect a protective shell of irony around their intercourse. Bitterness seems to be one emotion of which the Indian is innocent. Or perhaps his perfect sense of manners covers up a deep concern for the way his meaning in life is going; or perhaps he doesn't care, so long (the fruits of an American education) as there are plenty of tourists, and the bowls and jars, the necklaces and bracelets, the blankets and drums, are selling rapidly.

In certain localities of Oklahoma Indians have become fabulously wealthy through the discovery of oil upon their lands. Thus a new kind of power has been tasted by the Indian, and his ridiculous ministration of his wealth in many cases has shown how suddenly, without those decades of preparation that are necessary for a change in life, he has been removed from one thing to be plunged into an alien thing.

What, then, is the future for him? Only with complete absorption will his troubles vanish and his history become archaeology. But so far, particularly in New Mexico, there has been remarkably little mingling of races; and it may be that the Pueblo will go on indefinitely in his anomalous capacity of entertainer and oldest resident.

It is unfortunate that the deepest meanings of the Indian must be learned from his most personal, private avowals: his dances of devotion and supplication. The more he is scrutinized, the more he must command the respect of his watchers. As this respect grows, with it should grow the desire to let the Indian retire to the conditions of life that brought him to his high culture and his delicate sense of propriety. Yet, having been discovered as a profitable study, the Indian is doomed to continue his performances. One day his dances, like his craftsmanship, will lose their significance for him. We shall then see a nation at loose ends, without dignity, traitors to everything profoundly pure in its tradition, its citizens trying to be something different from their fathers, and ruefully we shall admit that the cycle of conquest has been completed by the corruption of gold. It is hard to strike a balance between resentment against the conquerors and understanding of the inevitability of their conquest. If there is to be any blame for the gradual counterfeit of Indian life, it must be attached to that spirit of exploration, expansion, discovery, whatever it is, that provided the impulse for the annexation of Nueva Granada; and to blame, to do other than watch with an attempt at understanding, to withhold admiration for this triumph of one kind of humanity over another, is to waste emotion.

The Spaniard: his contribution to posterity was the nomenclature of his discoveries. In the Spanish names of cities, rivers, mountains, and mesas, the Spanish conquest survives. And what liturgical music these names make. What gratified saints find on earth the perpetuation of their glory! The geological piety which seized the explorers on viewing a new range, the confusing zeal with which a newly conquered pueblo would be baptized, these things betray the enthusiasm of the Latin and the natural importance of his religion in his daily acts, an importance so common that the creed may have suffered by a loss of rarity and distinction. Certainly the Spaniard took his agonies of spirit as casually as his descendants today take their daily lives.

The purity of some of the first families still remains intact. This is admirable, and in the face of American incomprehension, unimportant. In Texas and New Mexico there are establishments where the silver in the dining room has been used every day since the first *conde or marqués* and his suite dined at home in his adobe palace; houses where the most profound gallantries are still habitual; where the atavism of an artistocracy is neither surprising nor ridiculous. The pride of name is very strong in such families. But the American is busily unaware of this royalty in his midst. To him, the first families, because of their names, are Mexicans like the rest of the families with Spanish names. It is, it has been for decades, a losing struggle to hold aloft the banners of exclusiveness and pride of race. The American can neither understand such an attitude nor excuse it. Its superiority is disturbing to him. The wistfulness of its decline he hardly notices. It will not last long, that attitude. Its perishing will be the end of an occupation. No one will know when the last flicker of the devout procession of the seventeenth century will struggle and expire. An aged *don*, perhaps, remembering the great herds of his cows which he used to inspect from his silver-buckled saddle; a declining great lady, in her ears the cry of past violins, in her eyes the visions of officers and prelates who would stop under her room on their official trips around the province; a senescent bishop, perhaps, dying in some hospital under the care of American nuns: dying in the one tradition that his fathers have securely implanted; or a young man, with only the purest of the lordly bloods in his veins, taking his part in American life, college, the standards of the cinema, the graces of the country club and its stupefying society, the necessity of owning a Buick sedan: such a young man, it may be, will most tragically enact the doom of his race.

Like the destruction of the Indian integrity, this other destruction is also inevitable. It is always the finer fibers of a culture that weaken and disappear first. The Mexicans, the other part of the surviving empire, dwell with the simplicity and the vigor of peasants, farming, working in the towns, sheepherding, cowpunching. A humorous, fatalistic, and lively people, they contribute all the color to the landscape that a Latin temperament can. Their rogueries, their intrigues, their dances with guitars and brawls, their solemn marriages with white veils and enormous parties of cheering relatives and friends, their dark religious concern in the fraternity of the Penitentes, their genius for a politics that cries aloud with ingenuity and passion and irrelevance, all contribute to the astonishing spectacle of an American citizenry that preserves some antique and southern sprightliness.

Even the thoroughness with which Mexican boys and girls go American is somehow irresistible. If the Indians are a tragic race in the loss of their true style, then the Mexicans (or Spanish-Americans, as the more self-conscious insist on being called)—the Mexicans are irresistibly eager and droll and likable. The glorious corruptions of American slang, when uttered by a Mexican girl in flapper costume, take on a new roguishness, a new and wonderfully inappropriate relaxation. Her boy friend, driving a Ford and playing pool and basketball and keeping regular hours in some job, is no less amusing and charming. What makes them so engaging in spite of their masquerade as hundred-percent Americans is the awareness they seem to have that whatever you do, it can't be as important as all *that*: and this lack of intensity in the daily routine lets them laugh and dance, really dance, not shuffle around with a disguised exhaustion; it lets them make love with originality and delight, it frees their tempers and somebody gets knifed or shot and that's not so good, but hell (they say), it'll come out Aw-Kay.

Such the young people: their mothers still wear the black *rebozo* of the peasant woman, the black shawl that falls from the skull in classic grace. Under the shawl, behind the brown and graven forehead, lie the sharpest suspicions and the profoundest faith in God and his acts. That mouth, which is fingered by those bony little fingers so doubtfully, can open and shrill the most competent of shreweries, it can wither a generation of jazzy Mexican kids, it can whisper the rosary as rapidly as a nun, it can cry little tendernesses to the grandchildren who will be unfamiliar enough to Grandma if she lives long enough to watch them go through public school and become teachers or doctors or lawyers. So long, though, as they don't lose their faith in God, let them do and be anything they want. Let them come to church with her; in the Corpus Christi procession let them notice how nimble she is yet, her little legs swinging the full black of her skirts above the dusty ground. Papá is perhaps a police under-official, with a sliver star and black moustaches, and an air of importance more sinister than a hundred jails. Papá must be approached with stateliness, for the pattern of family life is still patriarchal. The priest is still the most distinguished caller possible, except perhaps his bishop. But that is unheard of, a bishop in our adobe house, clean though it is, and plentiful with crucifixes and exquisitely hideous holy pictures.

In New Mexico, the twin geniuses of religion and government occupy the men of Mexican blood. In the society of the Penitent Brothers there survives a cruel passionate ritual from the Middle Ages. It is an organization composed of men who celebrate the yearly passion of Holy Week with acts of torture and despair, and of ecstasy and salvation. All the week devotions are held and initiates entered. The badge of the order is three long scars of knife-cuts in the back; the climax of the ritual comes in the procession and crucifixion on Good Friday. On Good Friday the dawn comes melancholy over the yellow-lighted mountains. In the remote villages where the church and the government are without practical authority, it is said that a human being is crucified yearly in imitation of Christ. In any case, a cross dragged along a Via Dolorosa. Snow is often underfoot and on the foothills, flashing white around the dark green of the roots of the scrub pine, pale against the tufty brown of the winter earth. Out of the town, moaning and whipping, flinging their cords against their bare backs, singing the triumph of death over life and the exaltation of life after death, they toil across the cold rocks, bleeding and weeping with a terrible joy. Their voices and the suck and whip of their flails echo in the bare hills. The tragedy of Christianity is mimed, participation in the sacrificial drama binds men together. And this solidarity is useful in politics.

There is still a power in the Latin heritage, enough to make it necessary to conduct legislation in New Mexico in both Spanish and English. It suggests the quality of Indian religion, and is one of the confusions that must be endured by the conqueror. Mexicans, Spanish-Americans, whatever their title must be, are excellent politicians. They throw a personal passion into the performance of their functions; they shame their American colleagues, for there is nothing perfunctory, nothing cold-blooded, nothing ganglike about the spoils and divisions and urgencies that inform their politics.

For the rest of their Mexican color—the mantillas, the roses caught in pearly teeth, the guitars at midnight under a balcony, the hiss of passion that is actually possible in a Mexican's mouth—there can be nothing but embarrassment, since the engulfing appetite of the American public has called for and has been given moving pictures in that idiom. It is a sad thing that Hollywood should compose the epitaph for this charming and unpredictable race. But Hollywood is so utterly contemporary that its authority cannot be denied. It is another phenomenon of the American triumph.

The American: a dweller in the strange land of his own mastering, he views the land and its survivals with a certain suspicion, an emotional uncertainty that not only permits him to watch the decay of his predecessors with equanimity, but also permits him to subscribe to the dubious beliefs and impulses which his uncertainty generates. This American is possibly a descendant of the pioneers; he is, just as possibly, a newer immigrant from the East. But in either case, he partakes of a life that is no longer strictly of the ground he is on. Economic development has knit the cattle industry into close dependence upon the vagaries of eastern markets. And the mechanistic regime that establishes the tempo of our national life for us now governs him as thoroughly as the Indian used to be governed by the laws of the weather and the rise and fall of the river.

In Texas, the romance and power of the republican tradition survives in an attitude that is arrogantly independent. There is a regional frame of mind there that assumes an individuality for Texas which only California, among the other states, can remotely challenge. The right to that individuality was earned in battle. It was a progressive step that Texas took for freedom. Since that time, no concerted action has proclaimed Texas as a particularly enlightened empire. It is curious that, as one of the regions most heavily endowed with the lore of the Old West, Texas should at the same time be hindered by the weight of its lore from partaking of the commonplaces of culture and society which characterize most of the other western states. It is true, certainly, that the rarer privileges of intelligence and rich life are possessed by certain families, even by certain cities. But those rarities are possessed by the gifted people everywhere. Texas is so huge, its ancient cattle trails wandered across such varieties of land, its founders were triumphant over so many odds of nature and circumstance, that a simple arrival at the finer life in a mechanized age is hardly to be expected within so short a time.

In any case, Texas is important in its possession of two of the purest backgrounds of folk tradition: the cattle range and the oil industry. These two strains of life, generated by two immense industries, saturate the activity of the Southwest.

The cowboy, the cattle king, the cattle rustler, and their retinues of gamblers, deserters from the army, and other frontier characters, crossed and recrossed all of the states in Nueva Granada. They made legend wherever they went. Their songs are still alive. The conversion of loneliness on wide prairies under starred skies into music and gunplay, lynchings and heroic drunks; the experience of travel across thousands of miles behind a herd of red cattle—these things live for us today in the spirit of that time. As every great business has its antisocial competitors, so the cattle industry had its thieves, who would separate and drive away from the main herd enough cows to make a haul of thousands of dollars. War must follow. Regional civil wars burst into flames, flourished with killings, sensational escapes, heroic jobs of strategy and betrayal and nonchalance. A romantic glamour was attributed to such activities in any part of the world that heard of them. English younger sons came over to join the scramble. The national imagination was stirred by the vitality of the goings-on in the West. Who would have thought that the settlers would produce such gunplay and scandal!

In all of the states in the Southwest this private martial spirit had its day. The western sheriff became a symbol for shrewd justice. The desperado, born of the profits to be reaped from illicit cattle dealing, from gambling in the frontier towns that dripped with gold from trading and newly discovered mines, and from pillage of traveling coaches and trains—the desperado was judged worthy of the tersest, the longest-jawed sheriff that could be sent against him with six-guns in his Prince Albert coat and an image of his pioneer mother and the meaning of righteousness in his heart. For the entertainment of desperado and cowboy and sheriff alike, a race of glorious females with wide hips, small waists, and tireless dancing abilities appeared in the saloons and bordellos. Such women were currently regarded as valuable for the grace of their feminine touch in the rude cow camps and shack cities of the West. Their hearts were known to be of solid gold; a denial of the maxim could easily result in an immediate rejoinder from a swiftly handled gun. True, a brunette with pale eyes and slanted nostrils could confirm the rumor of her half-breeding by a piece of treachery involving a bartender and a monte dealer and the sheriff's best gal. But in her exposure, no onus, it was felt, could attach itself to the charming girls who remained agreeable companions, superb dancers, and perfectly respectable whores.

The conventions of such a society were established as normal for those men who found their lives in the West. It became necessary, in viewing them, to suspend the judgments of older cultures and societies. Life conditions must always be met with compromise. The westerner who followed the pioneer in possession of the land and its offerings had a different kind of hazard to confront from that of the American trail-maker. It was the necessity of bringing with him some sort of social propriety that would seem natural to the life he was living. The solution of individual martial law, goodhumored prostitutes, and a canon of loyalty to his word that the westerner protected with the most hair-triggered scrappiness, was immediate and practical. It had neither grace nor charm; but nothing had those qualities, for they are qualities which come with luxury, and luxury comes decades after the frontiersmen perform their tasks.

But the older patterns of society gradually overtook the frontiersman. Perhaps he married his favorite blonde from the Golden Wildcat Saloon; he built, at immense trouble and expense, a red brick house with white wooden turrets and scroll-saw embellishments; he uneasily subscribed to the foundation of a church; his cartidge belt was hung up among the skins of the animals he had brought down for food in the old days; and the temper of life in the nineteenth century governed a new territory.

Accelerated commerce and the new communication by telegraph replaced the long wagon trains and overland mail riders. The slow, the enormous knitting of American national life into a series of related regions got under way. Though local lores still ruled, the localities were no longer independent of the rest of the nation in all particulars. Just as the pioneers conquered the Indian and Spanish civilization they found, so the rest of America conquered the pioneers. What we have from their time is ghostly survivals in legend, in song, and in the persons of a few lingering old men and women whose memories resound dimly with the ancient glories, the tragedies and hardships and heroisms of the day when life was tentative and intense.

It is a long jump from the individualism of the settler to the other pride of today, when the aim of every town and city is to be as like the metropolises of the East as possible, and the desire of every politician and businessman is to fit into the pattern of progressive America, for which society and business and emotional life are standardized by the newspapers and the movies. But the old men and women, with their pride of memory that sets them apart like museum pieces which can talk, watch the newer life flow across their lands and cannot partake of it. Change is the very death of desire to live in the tempers of old people. It would be easier to die, and less desirable, if nothing changed after the time of one's power and importance. It confuses them, these fragile embodiments of a passed time, to feel that before one's memories, even, can be greeted with respect, the very vocabulary of those memories must first be explained.

An old man, tremendously fat, slapping his ten-gallon hat upon his head with angry indifference, takes his way downtown in midmorning to feel the sunlight on his rounded back, and to contribute legend and tobacco juice to the daily gathering at the corner of Main Street and Second, where he would have scorned to linger a few years ago. But now it is his privilege and power to recount the events that happened on that corner one day very much like this one, only a trifle cloudy in the east, when word came in that Bonney was free of the jail at Lincoln, had disappeared after killing two men, someone's horse was stolen too. Just as if I was standing here now, they rode up from Lincoln, I was right here when they told it. . . . The traffic lights change. Cars resume their rush and turn. The fat old man lets his eyes go pink in the shadow of his large brim. He rolls his tobacco in his cheek with a mighty and fluid scorn. He heaves his lips and spits far beyond the gutter. The eloquence of his whole opinion and experience makes a brown trajectory to the pavement. In one of the cars, somebody looks out and says, "What a disgusting old man!"

Others are not disgusting, either; fewer each year, but while they last the Old-Timer spirit is still aloft. Its references to the past are pallid, thin; our ears are disappointed. But the memories which so valiantly support these old lives are all but incommunicable, except by the fire of the eye of the teller; in that glisten, we can surmise the blood and life and fire of the things we read about, and the things they try to tell us. When they have all died, taking their halting stories and their fiery memorable eyes with them, the lives they created and the land they created will at last meet indissolubly. Their survivors will bury them with appropriate platitudes. "Another Old-Timer gone." The immediate importance of the Old-Timer will vanish. It will be forgotten for a few decades, and then the strength of his legend, the yellowed pages of his observation will have a new flowering, as legend always puts forth new vitality when the passage of time has erased its prosaic familiarity.

In the meantime: the transplanted roots of general American idealism and culture take hold in the kingdom of Nueva Granada. Only two differences from the East are visible: the one is in the quality of the land—a difference that waives humanity. The other is a suggestion of greater social freedom than the East allows itself. There are definite relaxations from the stricter standards of a more urban life. The taste of the mass is considerably lower. The temper of life is more really democratic, more unanimously impulsive, and hence more dangerous and savage if it is disturbed, as in lynchings and criminal bigotries. There is, also, a refreshing willingness to try anything new. There survive hints of the Old-Timer's shrewdness and of his generosity, which are wholly unwedded as qualities in the more individualistic East. There is a spaciousness about the country which invites a spacious friendliness from people. Most westerners become claustrophobes in the East, in a country engirt by hills, or in a city choked away from sunlight and sky by its buildings. The men of the West are still rude in many ways, and their women are as a result doubly pretentious and hopeful with their social activities. A good deal of boasting goes on, civic boasting and private boasting. The latter sometimes retains some of the grandiose humor of the Old-Timer; the former is a confession of provincialism, and a proof of the uneasiness that underlies the newer life.

But it is precisely in the nature of that newer life, in its derivative evolution, in its relation to the three great traditions of race that nourish it, that the new regional consciousness should operate. Appreciation of its true and splendid provincialism must resist the standardization of its life and even its history that the Southwest faces, and encourages by its attempt to assume a flat character, to be one with the rest of simple-minded America, to laugh happily at the universal joke at the expense of dignity and respectful self-consciousness.

For it is the radio that focusses the national character now, and the newspaper, and the movies. The values which these agencies bring to the people and (worse yet) particularly to the young people of every region of the country are so easy to digest, so handily put up for absentminded consumption by even the most incurious soul, that whatever racial strains of integrity and hardness and fight the regions may have had are in danger of atrophying through disuse. Even the sterile tradition of the Puritan gave him something to gnaw on. But we feed our future countrymen on pap. The appetite for pap grows quickly satiated; but having been given nothing but mush to work on, the system becomes incapable of handling more than mush. And so the stultifying process goes on. There will soon be no need for regional self-consciousness if the nationwide entertainment and education in taste continue without stringent revision. With the rest of the world, America and its departments face a fatal softening and enervation through the mechanistic values and devices that govern them. It is well, in watching the present unroll before our eyes, to partake of the wholly human significance of the past; to recognize those qualities of heroism and courage and will that brought earlier peoples to new lands and new lives; to watch, with understanding, the decline of race that is natural, and to savor the tragic emotion which is reserved for human beings alone in the midst of natural decay. And it is desirable to love the land, to study its beauties, and to rely upon its comforts of grandeur and natural resource.

THE LAND

For it is the land which is still supreme in Nueva Granada. From its rusty earth must grow the grasses for the range on which the red cows rove, when winter withdraws before the southern breath of spring, when the young rains come sweeping across the plains from the Gulf, up over the yellow fields of Oklahoma into the scrubby pine hills and leonine mountains of New Mexico, and westward to the deserts of Arizona where the scarlet and the white flowers, monster-glorious, shout and blossom under the sun. It is the cattle, feeding on the nourished ground, that still establish the economics of the region, if no longer the legendary character of it. And any people that must depend so directly on the rain to bring food is still subservient to the land and its tempers and its conditions. The Southwest still exists upon realities, instead of symbols of realities like urban systems of commerce and finance and machines. It exists upon realities because the land is so tremendous, so bare of human life in so many million acres, because there are so many plains rising sharply to mountainhood, so much communion between sky and earth with great slow-sailing clouds and stars that watch the night like near eyes; because to go from one place to another it is necessary so very often to drive in cars along lonely roads with nothing in sight but the gently lifting and falling horizons of low hills; because the conditions of natural life raise no clamor like that sustained daily by tiring nerves in other regions; because, no matter what the manner of people, they must be moved by the beauty of Texas plains and Oklahoma wheat fields and New Mexico mountains and Arizona deserts alike; and because, though the survivals are only travesties to be noticed amidst the developments of our time, the color of past splendors of race and deed is mixed with the land by the agency of our imaginations; and we pay it tribute, as it nourishes us.

Dragons

DAVID SEARCY

Dragons are animals that do not pretend;
They sit in trees and smile
While white knights are resting and saying their prayers.

And when armored men rush like fire upon their chargers,
I hear the dragons at night from my bed;

They stand in my garden and sound like crickets.

Upon the Sweeping Flood

JOYCE CAROL OATES

NOT LONG AGO in Eden County, in the remote marsh and swamplands to the south, a man named Walter Stuart was stopped in the rain by a sheriff's deputy along a country road. Stuart was in a hurry to get home to his family—his wife and two daughters—after having endured a week at his father's old farm, arranging for his father's funeral, surrounded by aging relatives who had sucked at him for the strength of his youth. He was a stern, quiet man of thirty-nine, beginning to lose some of the muscular hardness that had always baffled others, masking as it did Stuart's remoteness, his refinement, his faith in discipline and order which seemed to have belonged, even in his youth, to a person already grown safely old. He was a district vice-president for one of the gypsum mining plants, a man to whom financial success and success in love had come naturally, without fuss. When only a child he had shifted his faith with little difficulty from the unreliable God of his family's tradition to the things and emotions of this world, which he admired in his thoughtful, rather conservative way, and this faith had given him access, as if by magic, to a communion with persons vastly different from himself—with someone like the sheriff's deputy, for instance, who approached him that day in the hard, cold rain. "Is something wrong?" Stuart said. He rolled down the window and had nearly opened the door when the deputy, an old man with gray eyebrows and a slack, sunburned face, began shouting against the wind, "Just the weather, mister. You going far along here? How far are you going?"

"Two hundred miles," Stuart said. "What about the weather? Is it a hurricane?"

"A hurricane—yes—a hurricane!" the man said, bending to shout at Stuart's face. "You better go back to town and stay put. They're evacuating up there. We're not letting anyone through."

A long line of cars and pickup trucks, tarnished and gloomy in the rain, passed them on the other side of the road. "How bad is it?" said Stuart. "Do you need help?"

"Back at town, maybe, they need help," the man said. "They're putting up folks at the schoolhouse and the churches, and different families —The eye was spost to come by here, but last word we got it's veered further south. Just the same, though—"

"Yes, it's good to evacuate them," Stuart said. At the back window of an automobile passing them two children's faces peered out at the rain, white and blurred. "The last hurricane here—"

"Ah, God, leave off of that!" the old man said, so harshly that Stuart felt, inexplicably, hurt. "You better turn around, now, and get on back to town. You got money they can put you up somewheres good—not with these folks coming along here."

This was said without contempt, but Stuart flinched at its assumptions. "I'm going in to see if anybody needs help," he said. He had the car going again before the deputy could even protest. "I know what I'm doing! I know what I'm doing!" Stuart said.

The car lunged forward into the rain, drowning out the deputy's outraged shouts. The slashing of rain against Stuart's face excited him. Faces staring out of oncoming cars were pale and startled, and Stuart felt rising in him a strange compulsion to grin, to laugh madly at their alarm. . . . He passed cars for some time. Houses looked deserted, yards bare. Things had the look of haste about them, even trees—in haste to rid themselves of their leaves, to be stripped bare. Grass was twisted and wild. A ditch by the road was overflowing and at spots the churning, muddy water stretched across the red clay road. Stuart drove splashing through it. After a while his enthusiasm slowed, his foot eased up on the gas pedal. He had not passed any cars or trucks for some time.

The sky had darkened and the storm had increased. Stuart thought of turning back when he saw, a short distance ahead, someone standing in the road. A car approached from the opposite direction. Stuart slowed, bearing to the right. He came upon a farm—a small, run-down one with just a few barns and a small pasture in which a horse stood drooping in the rain. Behind the roofs of the buildings a shifting edge of foliage from the trees beyond curled in the wind, now dark, now silver. In a neat harsh line against the bottom of the buildings the wind had driven up dust and red clay. Rain streamed off roofs, plunged into fat, tilted rainbarrels, and exploded back out of them. As Stuart watched another figure appeared,

30   THE SOUTHWEST REVIEW READER

running out of the house. Both persons—they looked like children—jumped about in the road, waving their arms. A spray of leaves was driven against them and against the muddy windshield of the car that approached and passed them. They turned: a girl and a boy, waving their fists in rage, their faces white and distorted. As the car sped past Stuart water and mud splashed up in a vicious wave.

When Stuart stopped and opened the door the girl was already there, shouting, "Going the wrong way! Wrong way!" Her face was coarse, pimply about her forehead and chin. The boy pounded up behind her, straining for air. "Where the hell are you going, mister?" the girl cried. "The storm's coming from this way. Did you see that bastard, going right by us? Did you see him? If I see him when I get to town—" A wall of rain struck. The girl lunged forward and tried to push her way into the car; Stuart had to hold her back. "Where are your folks?" he shouted. "Let me in!" cried the girl savagely. "We're getting out of here!" "Your folks," said Stuart. He had to cup his mouth to make her hear. "Your folks in there!" "There ain't anybody there—Gah*dam* you!" she said, twisting about to slap her brother, who had been pushing at her from behind. She whirled upon Stuart again. "You letting us in, mister? You letting us in?" she screamed, raising her hands as if to claw him. But Stuart's size must have calmed her, for she shouted hoarsely and mechanically: "There ain't nobody in there. Our pa's been gone the last two days. LAST TWO DAYS. Gone into town BY HIMSELF. Gone drunk somewhere. He ain't here. He left us here. LEFT US HERE!" Again she rushed at Stuart, and he leaned forward against the steering wheel to let her get in back. The boy was about to follow when something caught his eye back at the farm. "Get in," said Stuart. "Get in. Please. Get in." "My horse there," the boy muttered. "You little bastard! You get in here!" his sister screamed.

But once the boy got in, once the door was closed, Stuart knew that it was too late. Rain struck the car in solid walls and the road, when he could see it, had turned to mud. "Let's go! Let's go!" cried the girl, pounding on the back of the seat. "Turn it around! Go up on our drive and turn it around!" The engine and the wind roared together. "Turn it! Get it going!" cried the girl. There was a scuffle and someone fell against Stuart. "It ain't no good," the boy said. "Let me out." He lunged for the door and Stuart grabbed him. "I'm going back to the house!" the boy cried, appealing to Stuart with his frightened eyes, and his sister, giving up suddenly, pushed him violently forward. "It's no use," Stuart said. "Gahdam fool," the girl screamed, "gahdam fool!"

The water was ankle deep as they ran to the house. The girl splashed ahead of Stuart, running with her head up and her eyes wide open in spite of the flying scud. When Stuart shouted to the boy his voice was slammed back at him as if he were being mocked. "Where are you going? Go to the house! Go to the house!" The boy had turned and was running toward the pasture. His sister took no notice but ran to the house. "Come back, kid!" Stuart cried. Wind tore at him, pushing him back. "What are you—"

The horse was undersized, skinny and brown. It ran to the boy as if it wanted to run him down but the boy, stooping through the fence, avoided the frightened hooves and grabbed the rope that dangled from the horse's halter. "That's it! That's it!" Stuart shouted as if the boy could hear. At the gate the boy stopped and looked around wildly, up to the sky—he might have been looking for someone who had just called him; then he shook the gate madly. Stuart reached the gate and opened it, pushing it back against the boy, who now turned to gape at him. "What? What are you doing here?" he said.

The thought crossed Stuart's mind that the child was insane. "Bring the horse through!" he said. "We don't have much time."

"What are you doing here?" the boy shouted. The horse's eyes rolled, its mane lifted and haloed about its head. Suddenly it lunged through the gate and jerked the boy off the ground. The boy ran in the air, his legs kicking. "Hang on and bring him around!" Stuart shouted. "Let me take hold!" He grabbed the boy instead of the rope. They stumbled together against the horse. It had stopped now and was looking intently at something just to the right of Stuart's head. The boy pulled himself along the rope, hand over hand, and Stuart held onto him by the strap of his overalls. "He's scairt of you!" the boy said. "He's scairt of you!" Stuart reached over and took hold of the rope above the boy's fingers and tugged gently at it. His face was about a foot away from the horse's. "Watch out for him," said the boy. The horse reared and broke free, throwing Stuart back against the boy. "Hey, hey!" screamed the boy, as if mad. The horse turned in midair as if whirled about by the wind, and Stuart looked up through his fingers to see its hooves and a vicious flicking of its tail, and the face of the boy being yanked past him and away with incredible speed. The boy fell heavily on his side in the mud, arms outstreatched above him, hands still gripping the rope with wooden fists. But he scrambled to his feet at once and ran alongside the horse. He flung one arm up around its neck as Stuart shouted, "Let him go! Forget about him!" Horse and boy pivoted together back toward the fence, slashing wildly at the earth, feet and hooves together. The ground erupted beneath them. But the boy landed upright, still holding the rope, still with his arm about the horse's neck. "Let me help," Stuart said. "No," said the boy, "he's my horse, he knows me—" "Have you got him good?" Stuart shouted. "We got—we got each other here," the boy cried, his eyes shut tight.

Stuart went to the barn to open the door. While he struggled with it the boy led the horse forward. When the door was open far enough Stuart threw himself against it and slammed it around to the side of the barn. A cloud of hay and scud filled the air. Stuart outstretched his arms, as if pleading with the boy to hurry, and he murmured, "Come on. Please. Come on." The boy did not hear him, or even glance at him: his own lips were moving as he caressed the horse's neck and head. The horse's muddy hoof had just begun to grope about the step before the door when something like an explosion came against the back of Stuart's head, slammed his back, and sent him sprawling out at the horse.

"Damn you! Damn you!" the boy screamed. Stuart saw nothing except rain. Then something struck him, his shoulders and hand, and his fingers were driven down into the mud. Something slammed beside him in the mud and he seized it—the horse's foreleg—and tried to pull himself up, insanely, lurching to his knees. The horse threw him backward. It seemed to emerge out of the air before and above him, coming into sight as though out of a cloud. The boy he did not see at all—only the hooves—and then the boy appeared, inexplicably, under the horse, peering intently at Stuart, his face struck completely blank. "Damn you!" Stuart heard, "He's my horse! My horse! I hope he kills you!" Stuart crawled back in the water, crab fashion, watching the horse form and dissolve, hearing its vicious tattoo against the barn. The door, swinging madly back and forth, parodied the horse's rage, seemed to challenge its frenzy; then the door was all Stuart heard, and he got to his feet, gasping, to see that the horse was out of sight.

The boy ran bent against the wind, out toward nowhere, and Stuart ran after him. "Come in the house, kid! Come on! Forget about it, kid!" He grabbed the boy's arm. The boy struck at him with his elbow. "He was my horse!" he cried.

In the kitchen of the house they pushed furniture against the door. Stuart had to stand between the boy and the girl to keep them from fighting. "Gahdam sniffling fool!" said the girl. "So your gahdam horse run off for the night!" The boy crouched down on the floor, crying steadily. He was about thirteen: small for his age, with bony wrists and face. "We're all going to be blownt to hell, let alone your horse," the girl said. She sat with one big thigh and leg outstretched on the table, watching Stuart. He thought her perhaps eighteen. "Glad you came down to get us?" she said. "Where are you from, mister?" Stuart's revulsion surprised him; he had not supposed there was room in his stunned mind for emotion of this sort. If the girl noticed it she gave no sign, but only grinned at him. "I was—I was on my way home," he said. "My wife and daughters—" It occurred to him that he had forgotten about them entirely. He had not thought of them until now and, even now, no image came to his mind: no woman's face, no little girls' faces. Could he have imagined their lives, their love for him? For an instant he doubted everything. "Wife and daughters," said the girl, as if wondering whether to believe him. "Are they in this storm too?" "No—no," Stuart said. To get away from her he went to the window. He could no longer see the road. Something struck the house and he flinched away. "Them trees!" chortled the girl. "I knew it! Pa always said how he ought to cut them down, so close to the house like they are! I knew it! I knew it! And the old bastard off safe now where they can't get him!"

"Trees?" said Stuart slowly.

"Them trees! Old oak trees!" said the girl.

The boy, struck with fear, stopped crying suddenly. He crawled on the floor to a woodbox beside the big old iron stove and got in, patting the disorderly pile of wood as if he were blind. The girl ran to him and pushed him. "What are you doing?" Stuart cried in anguish. The girl took no notice of him. "What am I doing?" he said aloud. "What the hell am I doing here?" It seemed to him that the end would come in a minute or two, that the howling outside could get no louder, that the howling inside his mind could get no more intense, no more accusing. A goddam fool! A goddam fool! he thought. The deputy's face came to mind, and Stuart pictured himself groveling before the man, clutching at his knees, asking forgiveness and for time to be turned back. . . . Then he saw himself back at the old farm, the farm of his childhood, listening to tales of his father's agonizing sickness, the old peoples' heads craning around, seeing how he took it, their eyes charged with horror and delight. . . . "My wife and daughters," Stuart muttered.

The wind made a hollow, drumlike sound. It seemed to be tolling. The boy, crouching back in the woodbox, shouted: "I ain't scairt! I ain't scairt!" The girl gave a shriek. "Our chicken coop, I'll be gahdammed!" she cried. Try as he could Stuart could see nothing out the window. "Come away from the window," Stuart said, pulling the girl's arm. She whirled upon him. "Watch yourself, mister," she said, "you want to go out to your gahdam bastardly worthless car?" Her body was strong and big in her men's clothing; her shoulders looked muscular beneath the filthy shirt. Cords in her young neck stood out. Her hair had been cut short and was now wet, plastered about her blemished face. She grinned at Stuart as if she was about to poke him in the stomach, for fun. "I ain't scairt of what God can do!" the boy cried behind them.

When the water began to bubble up through the floorboards they decided to climb to the attic. "There's an ax!" Stuart exclaimed, but the boy got on his hands and knees and crawled to the corner where the ax was propped before Stuart could reach it. The boy cradled it in his arms. "What do you want with that?" Stuart said, and for an instant his heart was pierced with fear. "Let me take it. I'll take it." He grabbed it out of the boy's dazed fingers.

The attic was about half as large as the kitchen and the roof jutted down sharply on either side. Tree limbs rubbed and slammed against the roof on all sides. The three of them crouched on the middle beam, Stuart with the ax tight in his embrace, the boy pushing against him as if for warmth, and the girl kneeling with her thighs straining her overalls. She watched the little paneless window at one end of the attic without much emotion or interest, like a large, wet turkey. The house trembled beneath them. "I'm going to the window," Stuart said, and was oddly relieved when the girl did not sneer at him. He crawled forward along the dirty beam, dragging the ax along with him, and lay full length on the floor about a yard from the window. There was not much to see. At times the rain relaxed, and objects beneath in the water took shape: tree stumps, parts of buildings, junk whirling about in the water. The thumping on the roof was so loud at that end that he had to crawl backward to the middle again. "I ain't scairt, nothing God can do!" the boy cried. "Listen to the sniveling baby," said the girl, "he thinks God pays him any mind! Hah!" Stuart crouched beside them, waiting for the boy to press against him again. "As if God gives a good damn about him," the girl said. Stuart looked at her. In the near dark her face did not seem so coarse; the set of her eyes was almost attractive. "You don't think God cares about you?" Stuart said slowly. "No, not specially," the girl said, shrugging her shoulders. "The hell with it. You seen the last one of these?" She tugged at Stuart's arm. "Mister? It was something to see. Me an' Jackie was little then—him just a baby. We drove a far ways north to get out of it. When we come back the roads was so thick with sightseers from the cities! They took all the dead ones floating in the water and put them in one place, part of a swamp they cleared out. The families and things—they were mostly fruit-pickers—had to come by on rafts and rowboats to look and see could they find the ones they knew. That was there for a day. The bodies would turn round and round in the wash from the boats. Then the faces all got alike and they wouldn't let anyone come anymore and put oil on them and set them afire. We stood on top of the car and watched all that day. I wasn't but nine then."

When the house began to shake, some time later, Stuart cried aloud: "This is it!" He stumbled to his feet, waving the ax. He turned around and around as if he were in a daze. "You going to chop somethin with that?" the boy said, pulling at him. "Hey, no, that ain't yours to—it ain't yours to chop—" They struggled for the ax. The boy sobbed, "It ain't yours! It ain't yours!" and Stuart's rage at his own helplessness, at the folly of his being here, for an instant almost made him strike the boy with the ax. But the girl slapped the boy furiously. "Get away from him! I swear Ill kill you!" she screamed.

Something exploded beneath them. "That's the windows," the girl muttered, clinging to Stuart, "and how am I to clean it again! The old bastard will want it clean, and mud over everything!" Stuart pushed her away so that he could swing the ax. Pieces of soft, rotted wood exploded back onto his face. The boy screamed insanely as the boards gave way to a deluge of wind and water, and even Stuart wondered if he had made a mistake. The three of them fell beneath the onslaught and Stuart lost the ax, felt the handle slam against his leg. "You! You!" Stuart cried, pulling at the girl—for an instant, blinded by pain, he could not think who he was, what he was doing, whether he had any life beyond this moment. The big-faced, husky girl made no effort to hide her fear and cried, "Wait, wait!" But he dragged her to the hole and tried to force her out. "My brother—" she grasped. She seized his wrists and tried to

36

get away. "Get out there! There isn't any time!" Stuart muttered. The house seemed about to collapse at any moment. He was pushing her through the hole, against the shattered wood, when she suddenly flinched back against him and he saw that her cheek was cut and she was choking. He snatched her hands away from her mouth as if he wanted to see something secret: blood welled out between her lips. She coughed and spat blood onto him. "You're all right," he said, oddly pleased, "now get out there and I'll get the kid. I'll take care of him." This time she managed to crawl through the hole, with Stuart pushing her from behind; when he turned to seize the boy the boy clung to his neck sobbing something about God. "God loves you!" Stuart yelled. "Loves the least of you! The least of you!" The girl pulled her brother up in her great arms and Stuart was free to climb through himself.

It was actually quite a while—perhaps an hour—before the battering of the trees and the wind pushed the house in. The roof fell slowly, and the section to which they clung was washed free. "We're going somewhere's!" shouted the girl. "Look at the house! That gahdam old shanty seen the last storm!"

The boy lay with his legs pushed in under Stuart's and had not spoken for some time. When the girl cried, "Look at that!" he tried to burrow in farther. Stuart wiped his eyes to see the wall of darkness dissolve. The rain took on another look—a smooth, piercing, metallic glint, like nails driving against their faces and bodies. There was no horizon. They could see nothing except the rushing water and a thickening mist that must have been rain, miles and miles of rain, slammed by the wind into one great wall that moved remorselessly upon them. "Hang on," Stuart said, gripping the girl. "Hang on to me."

Waves washed over the roof, pushing objects at them with soft, muted thuds—pieces of fence, boards, branches heavy with foliage. Stuart tried to ward them off with his feet. Water swirled around them, sucking at them, sucking the roof, until they were pushed against one of the farm buildings. Something crashed against the roof—another section of the house—and splintered, flying up against the girl. She was thrown backward, away from Stuart, who lunged after her. They fell into the water while the boy screamed. The girl's arms threshed wildly against Stuart. The water was cold and its aliveness, its sinister energy, surprised him more than the thought that he would drown—that he would never endure the night. Struggling with the girl he forced her back to the roof, pushed her up. Bare, twisted nails raked his hands. "Gahdam you, Jackie, you give a hand!" the girl said as Stuart crawled back up. He lay, exhausted, flat on his stomach and let the water and debris slush over him.

His mind was calm beneath the surface buzzing. He liked to think that his mind was a clear, sane circle of quiet carefully preserved inside the chaos of the storm—that the three of them were safe within the sanctity of this circle; this was how man always conquered nature, how he subdued things greater than himself. But whenever he spoke to the girl it was in short grunts, in her own idiom: "This ain't so bad!" or "It'll let up pretty soon!" Now the girl held him in her arms as if he were a child, and he did not have the strength to pull away. Of his own free will he had given himself to this storm, or to the strange desire to save someone in it—but now he felt grateful for the girl, even for her brother, for they had saved him as much as he had saved them. Stuart thought of his wife at home, walking through the rooms, waiting for him; he thought of his daughters in their twin beds, two glasses of water on their bureau. . . . But these people knew nothing of him: in his experience now he did not belong to them. Perhaps he had misunderstood his role, his life? Perhaps he had blundered out of his way, drawn into the wrong life, surrendered to the wrong role. What had blinded him to the possibility of many lives, many masks, many arms which might so embrace him? A word not heard one day, a gesture misinterpreted, a leveling of someone's eyes in a certain unmistakable manner, which he had mistaken just the same! The consequences of such errors might trail on insanely into the future, across miles of land, across worlds. He only now sensed the incompleteness of his former life. . . . "Look! Look!" the girl cried, jostling him out of his stupor. "Take a look at that, mister!"

He raised himself on one elbow. A streak of light broke out of the dark. Lanterns, he thought, a rescue party already. . . . But the rain dissolved the light; then it reappeared with a beauty that startled him. "What is it?" the boy screamed. "How come it's here?" They watched it filter through the rain, rays knifing through and showing, now, how buildings and trees crouched close about them. "It's the sun, the sun going down," the girl said. "The sun!" said Stuart, who had thought it was night. "The sun!" They stared at it until it disappeared.

The waves calmed sometime before dawn. By then the roof had lost its peak and water ran unchecked over it, in generous waves and then in thin waves, alternately, as the roof bobbed up and down. The three huddled together with their backs to the wind. Water came now in slow drifts. "It's just got to spread itself out far enough so's it will be even," said the girl, "then it'll go down." She spoke without sounding tired, only a little disgusted—as if things weren't working fast enough to suit her. "Soon as it goes down we'll start toward town and see if there ain't somebody coming out to get us, in a boat," she said, chattily and comfortably, into Stuart's ear. Her manner astonished Stuart, who had been thinking all night of the humiliation and pain he had suffered. "Bet the old bastard will be glad to see us," she said, "even if he did go off like that. Well, he never knew a storm was coming. Me and him get along pretty well— he ain't so bad." She wiped her face; it was filthy with dirt and blood. "He'll buy you a drink, mister, for saving us how you did. That was something to have happen—a man just driving up to get us!" And she poked Stuart in the ribs.

The wind warmed as the sun rose. Rain turned to mist and back to rain again, still falling heavily, and now objects were clear about them. The roof had been shoved against the corner of the barn and a mound of dirt, and eddied there without much trouble. Right about them, in a kind of halo, a thick blanket of vegetation and filth bobbed. The fence had disappeared and the house had collapsed and been driven against a ridge of land. The barn itself had fallen in, but the stone support looked untouched, and it was against this they had been shoved. Stuart thought he could see his car—or something over there where the road used to be.

"I bet it ain't deep. Hell," said the girl, sticking her foot into the water. The boy leaned over the edge and scooped up some of the filth in his hands. "Lookit all the spiders," he said. He wiped his face slowly. "Leave them gahdam spiders alone," said the girl. "You want me to shove them down your throat?" She slid to the edge and lowered her legs. "Yah, I touched bottom. It ain't bad." But then she began coughing and drew herself back. Her coughing made Stuart cough: his chest and throat were ravaged, shaken. He lay exhausted when the fit left him and realized, suddenly, that they were all sick—that something had happened to them. They had to get off the roof. Now, with the sun up, things did not look so bad: there was a ridge of trees a short distance away on a long, red clay hill. "We'll go over there," Stuart said. "Do you think you can make it?"

The boy played in the filth, without looking up, but the girl gnawed at her lip to show she was thinking. "I spose so," she said. "But him—I don't know about him."

"Your brother? What's wrong?"

"Turn around. Hey, stupid. Turn around." She prodded the boy, who jerked around, terrified, to stare at Stuart. His thin bony face gave way to a drooping mouth. "Gone loony, it looks like," the girl said with a touch of regret. "Oh, he had times like this before. It might go away."

Stuart was transfixed by the boy's stare. The realization of what had happened struck him like a blow, sickening his stomach. "We'll get him over there," he said, making his words sound good. "We can wait there for someone to come. Someone in a boat. He'll be better there."

"I spose so," said the girl vaguely.

Stuart carried the boy while the girl splashed eagerly ahead. The water was sometimes up to his thighs. "Hold on another minute," he pleaded. The boy stared out at the water as if he thought he was being taken somewhere to be drowned. "Put your arms around my neck. Hold on," Stuart said. He shut his eyes and every time he looked up the girl was still a few yards ahead and the hill looked no closer. The boy breathed hollowly, coughing into Stuart's face. His own face and neck were covered with small red bites. Ahead the girl walked with her shoulders lunged forward as if to hurry her there, her great thighs straining against the water, more than a match for it. As Stuart watched her something was on the side of his face—in his ear—and with a scream he slapped at it, nearly dropping the boy. The girl whirled around. Stuart slapped at his face and must have knocked it off—probably a spider. The boy, upset by Stuart's outcry, began sucking in air faster and faster as if he were dying. "I'm all right, I'm all right," Stuart whispered, "just hold on another minute . . . ."

When he finally got to the hill the girl helped pull him up. He set the boy down with a grunt, trying to put the boy's legs under him so he could stand. But the boy sank to the ground and turned over and vomited into the water; his body shook as if he were having convulsions. Again the thought that the night had poisoned them, their own breaths had sucked germs into their bodies, struck Stuart with an irresistible force. "Let him lay down and rest," the girl said, pulling tentatively at the back of her brother's belt, as if she were thinking of dragging him farther up the slope. "We sure do thank you, mister," she said.

Stuart climbed to the crest of the hill. His heart pounded madly, blood pounding in his ears. What was going to happen? Was anything going to happen? How disappointing it looked, ridges of land showing through the water, and the healthy sunlight pushing back the mist. Who would believe him when he told of the night, of the times when death seemed certain . . . ? Anger welled up in him already, as he imagined the tolerant faces of his friends, his children's faces ready to turn to other amusements, other oddities. His wife would believe him; she would shudder, holding him, burying her small face in his neck. But what could she understand of his experience, having had no part in it? —Stuart cried out; he had nearly stepped on a tangle of snakes. Were they alive? He backed away in terror. The snakes gleamed wetly in the morning light, heads together as if conspiring. Four—five of them—they too had swum for this land, they too had survived the night, they had as much reason to be proud of themselves as Stuart.

He gagged and turned away. Down by the water line the boy lay flat on his stomach and the girl squatted nearby, wringing out her denim jacket. The water behind them caught the sunlight and gleamed mightily, putting them into silhouette. The girl's arms moved slowly, hard with muscle. The boy lay coughing gently. Watching them Stuart was beset by a strange desire: he wanted to run at them, demand their gratitude, their love. Why should they not love him, when he had saved their lives? When he had lost what he was just the day before, turned now into a different person, a stranger even to himself? Stuart stooped and picked up a rock. A broad hot hand seemed to press against his chest. He threw the rock into the water and said,"Hey!"

The girl glanced around but the boy did not move. Stuart sat down on the soggy ground and waited. After a while the girl looked away; she spread the jacket out to dry. Great banked clouds rose into the sky, re-flected in the water—jagged and bent in the waves. Stuart waited as the sun took over the sky. Mist at the horizon glowed, thinned, gave way to solid shapes. Light did not strike cleanly across the land, but was marred by ridges of trees and parts of buildings, and around a corner at any time Stuart expected to see a rescuing party—in a rowboat or something.

"Hey, mister!" He woke; he must have been dozing. The girl had called him. "Hey! Whyn't you come down here? There's all them snakes up there."

Stuart scrambled to his feet. When he stumbled downhill, embar-rassed and frightened, the girl said chattily, "The sons of bitches are crawling all over here. He chast some away." The boy was on his feet and looking around with an important air. His coming alive startled Stuart—indeed, the coming alive of the day, of the world, evoked alarm in him. All things came back to what they were. The girl's alert eyes, the firm set of her mouth, had not changed—the sunlight had not changed, or the land, really; only Stuart had been changed. He wondered at it . . . and the girl must have seen something in his face that he himself did not yet know about, for her eyes narrowed, her throat gulped a big swallow, her arms moved slowly up to show her raw elbows. "We'll get rid of them," Stuart said, breaking the silence. "Him and me. We'll do it."

The boy was delighted. "I got a stick," he said, waving a thin whip-like branch. "There's some over here."

"We'll get them," Stuart said. But when he started to walk a rock slipped loose and he fell back into the mud. He laughed aloud. The girl, squatting a few feet away, watched him silently. Stuart got to his feet, still laughing. "You know much about it, kid?" he said, cupping his hand on the boy's head.

"About what?" said the boy.

"Killing snakes," said Stuart.

"I spose—I spose you just kill them."

The boy hurried alongside Stuart. "I need a stick," Stuart said; they got him one from the water, about the size of an ax. "Go by that brush," Stuart said, "there might be some there."

The boy attacked the bush in a frenzy. He nearly fell into it. His enthusiasm somehow pleased Stuart, but there were no snakes in the brush. "Go down that way," Stuart ordered. He glanced back at the girl: she watched them. Stuart and the boy went on with their sticks held in midair. "God put them here to keep us awake," the boy said brightly, "see we don't forget about Him." Mud sucked at their feet. "Last year we couldn't fire the woods on account of it so dry. This year can't either on account of the water. We got to get the snakes like this."

Stuart hurried as if he had somewhere to go. The boy, matching his steps, went faster and faster, panting, waving his stick angrily in the air. The boy complained about snakes and, listening to him, fascinated by him, in that instant Stuart saw everything. He saw the conventional dawn that had mocked the night, had mocked his desire to help people in trouble; he saw, beyond that, his father's home emptied now even of ghosts. He realized that the God of these people had indeed arranged things, had breathed the order of chaos into forms, animated them, had animated even Stuart himself forty years ago. The knowledge of this fact struck him about the same way as the nest of snakes had struck him—an image leaping right to the eye, pouncing upon the mind, joining itself with the perceiver. "Hey, hey!" cried the boy, who had found a snake: the snake crawled noisily and not very quickly up the slope, a brown-speckled snake. The boy ran clumsily after it. Stuart was astonished at the boy's stupidity, at his inability to see, now, that the snake had vanished. Still he ran along the slope, waving his stick, shouting, "I'll get you! I'll get you!" This must have been the sign Stuart was waiting for. When the boy turned Stuart was right behind him. "It got away up there," the boy said. "We got to get it." When Stuart lifted his stick the boy fell back a step but went on in mechanical excitement, "It's up there, gotten hid in the weeds. It ain't me," he said, "it ain't me that—" Stuart's blow struck the boy on the side of the head, and the rotted limb shattered into soft wet pieces. The boy stumbled down toward the water. He was coughing when Stuart took hold of him and began shaking him madly, and he did nothing but cough, violently and with all his concentration, even when Stuart bent to grab a rock and brought it down on his head. Stuart let him fall into the water. He could hear him breathing and he could see, about the boy's lips, tiny flecks or bubbles of blood appearing and disappearing with his breath.

When the boy's eyes opened Stuart fell upon him. They struggled savagely in the water. Again the boy went limp; Stuart stood, panting, and waited. Nothing happened for a minute or so. But then he saw something—the boy's fingers moving up through the water, soaring to the surface! "Will you quit it!" Stuart screamed. He was about to throw himself upon the boy again when the thought of the boy's life, bubbling out between his lips, moving his fingers, filled him with such outraged disgust that he backed away. He threw the rock out into the water and ran back, stumbling, to where the girl stood.

She had nothing to say: her jaw was hard, her mouth a narrow line, her thick nose oddly white against her dirty face. Only her eyes moved, and these were black, lustrous, at once demanding and terrified. She held a board in one hand. Stuart did not have time to think, but, as he lunged toward her, he could already see himself grappling with her in the mud, forcing her down, tearing her ugly clothing from her body— "Lookit!" she cried, the way a person might speak to a horse, cautious and coaxing, and pointed behind him. Stuart turned to see a white boat moving toward them, a half mile or so away. Immediately his hands dropped, his mouth opened in awe. The girl still pointed, breathing carefully, and Stuart, his mind shattered by the broken sunshine upon the water, turned to the boat, raised his hands, cried out, "Save me! Save me!" He had waded out a short distance into the water by the time the men arrived.

The Wheel

WILLIAM BURFORD

Free! the world before him, he
Made his way to the Wild West arcade,
Saw his old faces, cried out his names—
"Jesse"—"Dan'l Boone"—echoes,
Dying, in a hall of games.

And rode, at last, to hell and back
The turning, eternal ferris wheel,
Over his history, the caravans reeling
Overland to the wagonwheeling sea,
In the circle of his dreaming.

Found, and led back again, he
Told the strange tale of his day free:
"Out of the deep and over the wall
Enormous the wheel come crawlin';
And it caught me—do you see and nought

Believe?—mote on the scroll of the law."

Legend

HANIEL LONG

She told the old women, "I have no people.
 I belong to the deep and the sky.
I lie down in darkness; I have no people.
 You make me cry.
I see that my kinsmen are pierced by the arrow,
Burnt by the fire, blackened by sorrow.
Some people get sick and do not get better;
Some countries get sick and do not get better.
 They will die, tomorrow."

The old women beat her and drove her out.
 She burned down her house that day
And went to a plateau with snow-caps about
 Where the sun is gay.
There are sacred lakes in that country for swimming,
And she swims in them all, half real, half dreaming.
She likes them, and lingers; she learns their lessons.
The aspens about, and the vines that weave them
 Weave her in their gleaming.

She will never go back. She knows of a crater
 Where warm springs bubble and flow,
And lingers naked in shining vapor
 And washes in snow.
Blue spruce and pine woo again and again,
They merge in her dreams with flesh and blood men
And give her their cones. And she grows younger,
And winters pass, and she stays longer,
 Cleansing her bosom.

The young men woo her with ancient singing,
    A faint faint echo of His.
They make their music of sun-fingers springing
    Where the dawn is,
Or of prairie and valley in lands yellow-lighted,
Of rainbows unseen, cascades unsighted.
Yet their voices shake, they look away,
For they know that life turns ashen-gray
    In a country blighted.

They sing, but she sees that their feet are bleeding
    And their eyes have the look of doom.
Yet they try the old old trail, leading
    To quiet, to bloom.
Those young men in whom she knew Him,
Him the Ancestor—in whom she could view Him!
Their eyes are lakes when the sun is shining,
Their bodies cliffs and cliff-flowers combining,
    And they teach her to love Him.

She will never go back. She is changing to legend,
    For those young men who can hear.
Quietly one by one to that region
    They come, with their Fear.
Water has shown her her destiny spun
Of the Eros of brother, lover, and son;
And she knows how to save them, hunting, riding,
The young men who need her, vertical, gliding,
    In whom He is living.

The Great Frontier and Modern Literature

WALTER PRESCOTT WEBB

IT HAS always seemed to me that literature represents the fragrance of culture, the expression through highly talented persons of the genius of a society. This genius is expressed in other forms, in art, in music, and in architecture; but literary expression differs from the others in that it can be available to the many instead of the few, and moreover it can be understood by any literate person without commentary or explanation by a special priesthood. It is self-explanatory. Literature, after the invention of printing, became the most democratic of all the arts, and in a way it comprehends within itself all the others. There is not another art I can think of that would be worthy of the name without its literary accompaniment, and yet literature could exist pretty much in its present form without music, painting, sculpture, or any other art form.

In a large sense literature may be defined as an accented and often idealized recording of human experiences. It is not a photograph, not a reproduction, but more of a sketch or painting with the lights and shadows used skillfully for dramatic effect. It may ignore history's exactitude in pursuit of salients of truth, but it can rarely, if ever, escape completely that which it ignores, for history is the medium in which literature operates. History furnishes literature a frame, a background, and substance with which to work. The main difference between the two is that history is earthbound by its heavy cargo of facts, whereas literature travels light and can soar to the gates of heaven or hell on the wings of imaginaton.

Imagination! That is the thing which concerns us, for it is the essence. The application of imagination to the doings of human beings gives literature its distinctive quality and its separate place in the categories of human endeavor. The art in literature—that which distinguishes it from its prosaic sister—depends on the skill, taste, and beauty with which the imagined is engrafted on what is known by the reader, grafting done in such a manner that the result is an image of what might have been, what may be, and what could be tomorrow. "And," says Professor John Livingston Lowes in *The Road to Xanadu*, "the imagination has always leaped to seize, from the vivid and chaotic welter of fresh impressions which crowd the pages of the adventures, matter which it may transmute into elements of whatever fabric it is shaping." A special characteristic of literature—one shared by no other art—is that it can project itself backward or forward in time and outward in geography, and this ability to project beyond experience is made possible only by imagination.

It is important to note, however, that imagination must always have a base to take off from and a place to land when it returns. It is easily airborne, almost to infinity, but it cannot remain aloft forever; it must begin with facts and must keep in touch with them in order to maintain a sense of reality. Therefore, literature may be thought of as having a factual core of some sort with an extension which at the periphery borders on the unreal, i.e., the unknown. The core is historical; the periphery imagined. The realm of literature may be represented graphically by a series of concentric circles, the central one of which is factual, represented by a solid circle, while the outer ones may be thought of as an expansion of the central one through the imagination. The outer circles are in a sense the imagined enlargement of the central core which is known to be true.

Imagination would seem therefore to be the impatient and flustered forerunner of truth, seeking to anticipate all other means of attaining it. It must be off to the future before the manuscripts of history are written, a sort of John the Baptist crying in a recordless wilderness. It outruns the scientist, who proceeds but slowly and often without enough imagination for his own good or ours. Imagination misses the mark quite often, but even so it has anticipated many profound truths long before the proofs of them could be furnished. Under control, it exercises the human mind, sharpens the wits, and whets the appetite for the reality underlying what it guesses at. Moreover, it has furnished mankind a deal of fun and made the earth a more pleasant abode. It is the stuff that literature is made of.

The figure of concentric circles, with a solid core of fact and truth, may prove useful in an effort to explain why the Golden Age of literature, of imagination, coincided with a time when men had some knowledge, but not too much, of the Great Frontier. Let us assume, as the scientists would say—and what is an assumption but an imagination?—that the outside circle in the figure represents the outer limits of knowledge; and however scant that knowledge may be, it marks the outer limits to which imagination may safely go. The black central spot represents what is definitely known, what has already been proved and placed out of bounds as a major field for imagination to operate in. Obviously, the enormous area lying within the outer circle, but not including the central core of the known, is the realm for investigation and the free playground for unrestrained imaginings. The investigation results in the discovery of more truth, and thereby enlarges the black dot, causing it to encroach on the total area. This process of enlarging the known area has gone on relentlessly since 1500, and as it has proceeded the realm left to the imagination has been correspondingly reduced. If knowledge should ever become coterminous with imagination, then imagination as we have known it and literature also would be drowned in a sea of facts and realism. There would be no romance, nothing to be romantic about. There would also be nothing to investigate. It is devoutly to be hoped that the scientists will not deprive us of something very precious and themselves of a job.

Geography offers the clearest illustration of the idea set forth above, though many other examples could be found. A series of contemporary maps spaced at intervals of fifty years from 1450 to 1850 would tell the story of the enlargement of the black dot of geographical knowledge, and a corresponding reduction of the area on this earth for geographic guesswork and literary imagination. In this case it may be said that so far as map-making is concerned the earth now holds few and insignificant secrets. After Magellan's voyage the main landmarks of the world were known. The knowledge thereafter was just sufficient to free the imagination, but not abundant enough to restrain it. The map-makers proceeded to do their worst, inhabiting the Great Frontier with fantastic creatures never known on land or sea. But even so, what these early map-makers did was not so bad as what the map-makers of the earlier period had done when all the world outside the three continents was a matter of pure fantasy.

Nothing, I think [says the versatile Lowes], is harder to translate into terms of our own blasé experience than the pregnant fact that the little pre-

Columbian world was literally islanded in the unknown—an unknown, none the less, across which came drifting signs and rumors of some kindred knowable beyond. . . . No documents in the world are more eloquent than the laconic legends of the early maps.

It may be a coincidence, but a curious one, that modern imaginative literature reached its apex in the modern world in those centuries when the white space in the circle representing the slightly known was greater in proportion to the black space, representing the well known, than it has ever been in the history of mankind. There was in the sixteenth and seventeenth centuries a preponderance of new material of all sorts from geology to astronomy which the world had discovered but had not yet investigated, analyzed, classified, or understood. Therefore, there was an equally vast area over which imagination could range in search of material and inspiration. Animated by an insatiable curiosity, supplied with enough facts to make a safe beginning, inspired by an abundance of new data, and rewarded with enough success to sustain interest, men of imagination cut their moorings, shook off the formalism of the classical style, and charted new paths leading forward into the Great Frontier. There is hardly a writer after 1550 who was not affected directly or indirectly; many prior to that date were influenced. Taken all together they formed a towhead of genius such as the world has not seen since.

There is another coincidence worth noting about this Golden Age. Above we have looked at imaginative literature as a whole, as something of the Metropolis, as a unit without regard to nations. When we break it up into the subdivisions of the growing nationalism, and speak of Portuguese, Spanish, English, and French literature, we find that in general each nation's Golden Age coincides more or less with that nation's supremacy in frontier activity. Perhaps supremacy is too strong a word, so let us say that the Golden Age was contemporary with intense frontier ferment. It seems to be that as the frontier boom got under way in any country, the literary genius of that nation was liberated to become an important part of a triumphal procession.

Portugal was the first to tap the secrets of the frontier world; her mariners sought the eastern water route, found the Cape of Good Hope and the way to India. In celebration of this event, Luís de Camoëns wrote the great epic of Portuguese literature. This is *The Lusiads*, which was written largely in the distant lands and published in 1572. It tells the story of Vasco de Gama's voyage to India, but weaves into the story the adventures of other explorers and much of the history of the tiny Iberian land. *The Lusiads* not only represents the apex of Portuguese literature, but stands in a class by itself as a literary celebration of the exploits of explorers, and has been called the epic of commerce.

By the lucky discovery of the Western Hemisphere among other reasons, Spain soon surpassed Portugal as a frontier power; her Golden Age of literature came a little later, from 1530 to 1680. Within this period fall the literary names of Juan de la Cruz, Cervantes, Lope de Vega, and Calderón. Twenty-one universities were founded in Spain in the sixteenth century and five in the seventeenth. By 1532 Victoria had laid the foundation of international law, and just a generation later Suarez formulated its abstract principles. It cannot be said that the literary men of Spain paid much attention to the New World, although Lope de Vega devoted one drama to *The New World of Columbus*. No epic comparable to *The Lusiads* appeared in Spain or any other country. This does not mean, however, that the writers were not influenced and inspired by the general ferment—not to mention the prosperity—which the frontier had created.

The Dutch were engaged in the twofold task of freeing themselves from Spanish dominion and fighting their way to India to participate in the new wealth overseas. The formation of the Dutch East India Company in 1602 marks the rise of the Dutch, who in 1623 settled New York. Grotius was led to compose his masterpiece on international law because he was assigned to defend one Heemskirk, who had captured a Portuguese galleon in the Far East in 1603. The seventeenth is called the Golden Century of Dutch literature, and the four most notable figures— Jacob Cats, Pieter Hooft, Joost van den Vondel, and Constantijn Huygens—died between 1660 and 1687. None of these men seems to have been much concerned with the New World, but they were much concerned with worldly things. The main point about this towhead of literary talent is that it occurred in the same century in which the Dutch were reaping great profits from the distant lands.

England's period of greatness was the Elizabethan Age, culminating in Shakespeare. This Golden Age is the period when the English sea dogs and pirates were probing the Spanish Main and bringing their booty to London. The English did not yet possess the frontier, but they had made its acquaintance and were receiving tremendous stimulus to the imagination from the rich prizes found there and the hazardous daring involved in securing them. John Maynard Keynes points out that the boom, which he attributes to profit inflation induced by the sudden influx of American treasure, lasted in Spain from 1520 to 1590, in England from 1550 to 1650, and in France from 1530 to 1700. He comments on the fact that Shakespeare lived from 1564 to 1616 "when any level-headed person in England disposed to make money could hardly help doing so." He observes the relationship between national good times and literary genius:

I offer it as a thesis for examination by those who like rash generalisations, that by far the larger proportion of the world's greatest writers and artists have flourished in the atmosphere of buoyancy, exhilaration and freedom from economic cares felt by the governing class, which is engendered by profit inflations.

Keynes, with his eyes fixed on money and its influence, could well overlook the intangible effects which the conditions favorable to men who would make money might also have on men who make imagination. If literature resulting from imagination is dependent on national wealth, profit, inflation, and boom conditions, then Shakespeare and the Shakespearean Age should have served only as a threshold to a greater literature, for England grew constantly richer until the end of the nineteenth century. Actually England was not so rich in the last quarter of the sixteenth century, but she was in that state of nervous ecstasy which comes with the hint of great things ahead. In the case of Spain, Holland, and England, the Golden Age of literature came in the beginning stages of prosperity rather than after its full realization.

Whether the Golden Age was induced by wealth or by the presence of a little-known frontier is for us not the primary question. Our concern is with the impact of the frontier on the human imagination as expressed in literature. Imagination, as the common denominator of all literature worthy of the name, gives us something to take hold of, a unifying element in a chaotic sea of form and content. At least we can ask ourselves what subject matter imagination was applied to in a given period. Having got that far, we can find that subject matter which was frontier in character and isolate it, put it in a pile as it were and see what it looks like; we can set it over against what is left, and if our patience and erudition are sufficient we may eventually evaluate the literature inspired by the frontier and compare it with that on other subjects.

Though we wander off from a discussion of imagination into talk about literature, we are compelled to return to imagination as the unique quality, the unifying element of the whole subject. Centering our attention on the frontier, we ask this question: What did the human imagination do with a New World? What record of this imaginative activity has been left us in literary form? We might reverse the first question and ask, What did the frontier do to the human imagination? Was the effect on literature as great as it was on life? If so, then R. B. Cunninghame-Graham has attempted to describe it.

There has been but one real conquest worthy of the name—that of the New World. The human race in all its annals holds no record like it. Uncharted seas, unnavigated gulfs; new constellations, the unfathomable black pit of the Magellan clouds; the Cross hung in the sky; the very needle varying from the pole; islands innumerable and an unknown world rising from out the sea; all unsuspected races living in a flora never seen by Europeans, made it an achievement unique in all the history of mankind.

Perhaps the best way to answer these questions is to suggest subjects from the frontier around which the imagination of literary men played as lightning plays on the dark crest of the distant mountain. From the list must be omitted historical records such as the books of travelers and reports of voyages, though these furnished necessary substance for the literary productions. About the following subjects there can be no dispute:

1. Primitive man and nature
2. Eldorados
3. Utopias
4. Civilized man in isolation
5. Man in conflict with nature

Around these five subjects the poets and prose writers spun the gossamer tissues of a modern literature. As treated by literary men each subject overlaps one or more of the others. Another point is that the subjects are worldly in the extreme, with hardly a hint of religion in the lot. God may be called upon in extreme emergencies, but neither gods nor devils play an important role. Neither Dante nor Milton would have been very comfortable in the situations or the societies dealt with. In the third place, it is implied in each subject that the action takes place between the Metropolis and the Frontier. Primitive man is of the frontier and is presented as he appears to the metropolitan observer. Eldorado was never sought within the Metropolis, but always in the distant lands, and always by misguided individuals from the Metropolis. The point is illustrated in Poe's "Eldorado."

> Gaily bedight,
>   A gallant knight,
> In sunshine and in shadow,
>   Had journeyed long,
>   Singing a song,
> In search of Eldorado.
>
> But he grew old—
>   This knight so bold—
> And o'er his heart a shadow
> Fell, as he found
>   No spot of ground
> That looked like Eldorado.

The first and most important utopias, those ideal societies usually composed of primitive people who lived pure lives in contrast to the corrupt society of Europe, were always located far from Europe to be observed by the narrator through metropolitan eyes. This is true of More's *Utopia*, Bacon's *New Atlantis*, Chateaubriand's *Paul et Virginie*, or Hardy's *The Admirable Crichton*; the point of view is metropolitan, and in most cases the vantage point is not of the observer's choosing. Nor is the case different in those conflicts with nature recorded by the Ancient Mariner. That he was pretty far off base is evident when he says, "We were the first that ever burst into that silent sea." Shipwreck and storm, tempest and mutiny are nasty incidents near home, but when touched by the genius of Shakespeare, Stevenson, or Melville, they are also enchanted by distance from the Metropolis.

When the human imagination concerned itself in a literary way with the above subjects, it was involved—or likely to be—with two important elements, adventure and distance. The adventure was always that of the metropolitan in getting to some distant place, getting along after he got there, and finally in getting away so that he could come back to the Metropolis to tell his tale and reap the acclaim of his envious stay-at-home acquaintances. There is probably no record of an observer of utopia, however delightful its society might be, or of a Robinson Crusoe or an Ancient Mariner, or of any other, who did not hurry back to the printing presses rather than throw in his fortunes and stay where his adventures were found. Of the Ancient Mariner, Lowes says: "But even the ancient Mariner returned in the end to the kirk and the hill and the lighthouse top. . . ."

One would suspect too that when the literary traveler returned, his mind was centered more on the lighthouse top than on the kirk or the hill. At heart the modern writer has been full of egotism, an imaginative extrovert bursting with superiority and importance. He had escaped from God and the devil and become the most important thing in his universe, a talented agent whose business it was to prove, through his hero, that the world was a good place to spend a lifetime; it was a place where excitement and interest existed in full measure. He was a little above the Metropolis because he had been to the Great Frontier; and he was so much better than the frontier because he came from the Metropolis. This delightful circle of self-aggrandizement often enabled the author to play over his own head and perform feats of imagination difficult for those who live in less exuberant days to understand.

As we look back on this body of literature formed around primitive man and nature, Eldorados, utopias, and civilized men caught in nature's traps, we feel the need of a convenient literary term which will encompass the various subjects and convey a notion of their essential quality as a class. We have a rare combination of elements, all tending toward something unusual. Egoism, distance, adventure, an inadequate knowledge of all the facts, a complete ignorance of what may lie ahead and a momentary disregard of the past, all these things form a mixture out of which the tales that emerge cannot escape being—romantic. If we may return to the figure of the circle with its central core of fact, we may again see in the white space outside the core the enormous area in which imagination and fancy could freely play. That white area represents the Great Frontier, distant, slightly known, but not yet explored or half understood. There lay the realm of adventure, there the impossible feats could be performed, there anything could happen. There, on the periphery of the known, almost beyond it, lay the land of romance. When the ship set out to an unknown shore, the question was asked with awe: "Where lies the land to which the ship would go?" And as it drew away from the familiar harbor, dipped lower on the horizon, and finally disappeared, it was to those left behind the symbol of all that is meant by the word *romantic*. It made no difference to those on shore what happened to or on the ship, it was romance. The ship might be becalmed or wrecked by storm; the sailor's teeth might drop out from scurvy and his body be scourged by fever and lice—that to the stay-at-home was romance. To the shorebound, that ship, in its departure, its return, and all between, was a vehicle of romance.

There may be a better term than romantic to describe the tales which represented life on the Great Frontier, but there is no other term commonly understood that carries the desired connotations quite so well. Professor Gilbert Chinard has written a cycle of books and a number of articles dealing with exoticism and its influence on France and French literature. In general what he does is to show the influence of things foreign, curious, outlandish on French culture. Exotic plants, animals, and people were brought into France from the sixteenth century on, just as they were brought into all other European countries. Under the head of exoticism Professor Chinard deals with these subjects that are romantic in their effect. Still, exoticism will not serve as a substitute for the romantic in this study of the frontier. It will not serve because exoticism is metropolitan in essence. The exotic is not exotic until it is rooted out of its natural habitat, as of the frontier, and set down in another land and another environment where its strangeness can be admired in exotic rapture. "Nothing was so splendid and exotic," said Evelyn, "as the ambassador." Indeed! Exotic to whom? In modern times exoticism would seem to have national limits, and what is exotic to one nation could well be, as in the case of the ambassador, native to another. The romantic is not thus limited, for it overrides national boundaries and is well-nigh universal.

The romantic character of the literature of the frontier resulted, not from the import of the exotic into the Metropolis, but in the export of the metropolitan imagination into the frontier where it was in reality an exotic. We Americans have never seen ourselves through Indian eyes, though we have had some hints of how we appeared to them. For example, George Catlin, the artist, once took a band of Indians to Europe, and the Indians thought the Europeans were a very strange people. They led dogs about by strings, they drank from strange bottles which went *Chick-a-bob-boo* when the corks were pulled. Noting the many different religious denominations, Fast Dancer observed that the white man had several ladders all too short to reach heaven, whereas the Indians had one long one which reached up to the happy hunting grounds. Indians thought it very strange for a fine people like the English to be ruled over by a young squaw such as Victoria was at the time. The substitution of squaw for queen still shocks our sensibilities, but no more than the substitution of a feminine ruler for a masculine one shocked the Indians. Their descriptions of Europe and their mimicry of its people must have struck the Indians who remained in the forest of America as sheer romance.

Even though exoticism cannot be accepted as a term for the impact of the frontier on the metropolitan imagination as represented in literature, it has its uses, and in the skillful hands of Professor Chinard it has taken on tremendous meaning for those who would understand the interaction between an old world and a new one:

> Over three centuries of French literature we have studied the influence exercised by the recitals of voyages to America upon the history of ideas. We have tried to determine what had been the attitude of the French with respect to the new lands; in what ways their mentality and their sensibility had been affected by the revelations of the great discoveries; how finally one can see appear at rare intervals . . . a promise of artistic expression, a literary or sentimental theme. In this long review we have had to employ the word exoticism in default of a more satisfactory term to designate that which is a variety of exoticism but not exoticism entirely.

It is when Professor Chinard undertakes to analyze the meaning of the term he has adopted that he immediately comes up against our concept of the frontier. The difference between him and us is that he looks out on the frontier as the source of the exotic imported into France, whereas we take our position on the frontier and observe the reverse phenomenon, namely, the sweep of the metropolitan imagination across the wide circle of the strange lands, so that metropolitan folk can get some idea of what those lands are like. But again let Professor Chinard speak for himself in his *L'Exotisme Américain dans L'Oeuvre de Chateaubriand*:

> At the very foundation of exoticism there is indeed found an eternal desire to escape from one's own time, from the civilization that surrounds one, to change one's environment. . . . In the epochs when the discontent produced by intense civilization has coincided with important geographical discoveries, a new sentiment has appeared: a desire to escape from present

conditions, not by taking refuge in the past, but in changing climate. If, under other skies, men who are not familiar with our laws, nor our religion, live more happily, more freely, more easily than ourselves, . . . why not sail toward the Fortunate Isles? The dreamers, the poets, after having absorbed the recitals of discoveries of new lands, have then voyaged in spirit to the corners of the earth, giving free rein to their imaginations and painting to themselves this recovered Paradise, the conquest of which . . . they left to others more audacious. . . .

The author observes, as we have above, that those whose imagination has been touched rarely remain in the land found so perfect, and if perchance they do remain there, they bring with them "all the inquietudes, all the passions poorly extinguished, all the vague desires of their former existence." Of the Europeans he says, "They have asked of the new lands more than they could give; incapable of rejuvenating a soul three thousand years old, they have felt pass by them in the solitudes of the forest and on the wind of the savannah a happiness impossible to fix."

Finally, let us look at the five subjects, derived from the Great Frontier, around which the metropolitan imagination played with magic literary effect. Literary concern with primitive man and nature expressed itself in what is sometimes known as primitivism, and resulted in the creation of the natural man of Rousseau and others, in the noble savage concept which permeated not only literature but philosophy and political science as well. The study of nature became a cult, and led directly into romanticism as distinguished from the classical forms of literature which emerged from the Renaissance attention to the Greek and Roman forms, and distinguished also from the medieval literature which was concerned with things out of this world. It is not easy to select literary prose masterpieces to illustrate this primitive category, but it is impossible to examine the fabric of general literature of the seventeenth and eighteenth centuries without discovering increased attention to nature, a glorification of the primitive, and the romantic if unreal image of the noble savage in the great tapestry. The utopias are pregnant with primeval nature, and through the pages enough noble savages move to show by contrast the ignobility and meanness of civilized man. Even the sophisticated Byron thought there was a pleasure in the pathless wood and a wild beauty on the lonely shore, and this despite the fact that he was careful never to spoil either by his urbane intrusion. Byron was an inveterate romantic, ranging backward in time and outward in space to find things to remind him of his own sentimental sorrow.

The Eldorados seemed to exert more influence on explorers and fortune hunters than on literary men. After all, literature cannot make a hero of gold or any inanimate object. But, like primitivism, gold forms an ingredient which literary craftsmen used liberally to flavor and color what otherwise might have been a dull dish. It is not difficult to keep a tale going and make activity seem worthwhile if the promise of gold stands outlined a short way ahead on the horizon. It was the thing that caused Tom Sawyer and Huck Finn to dig a little deeper, on the theory advanced by Tom that the treasure was often found in the last few licks with the pick and shovel, made after all hope had been abandoned. Robert Louis Stevenson knew the value of gold as a literary prop, and used it effectively to keep the adventure going in *Treasure Island* and in other stories.

As we come to the utopias, we seem to be on firm and sure ground so far as the frontier influence is concerned. The first utopia, the principal ones, and the most famous ones—those which established the vogue— are on the frontier, both in physical location and in substance. It is against the backdrop of the forest in an environment remote from the Metropolis, among simple and uncorrupted people, that these ideal societies had their imaginary existence. Those of the modern period form a cluster caught in the river of time where the currents of the New World and the Old swirled together to fire the imagination of literary and political observers.

The question might be raised as to whether the utopias belong in the field of literature or that of political philosophy. Often they were fictional tracts, cut loose from reality, with political and social intent. They are literature in the sense that they are fictional, romantic in the sense that they are unreal and farfetched, and some of them were political in effect. For example, it is said that the farmers of the American democratic government were greatly influenced by James Harrington's *Oceana*, and certainly the various idealistic experiments in utopia which were popular in the first half of the nineteenth century drew their inspiration from the books. The climax was reached in impracticability when three poets, Coleridge, Southey, and Lovell, decided to marry sisters and all remove to America to found a Pantisocracy. Fortunately for poetry, and probably for the sisters, the scheme never got far beyond the altar.

Looked at in the long perspective, the utopias offer evidence of the existence of a point of view, a philosophical concept, that is in a sense modern. All of them assume that progress can be made, that man can mend his own net without divine assistance, that human perfection is attainable and worth striving for. The new abundance of wealth had enabled men to make real progress in economic affairs. Science and criticism had eaten away the pillars of superstition and unreasoning faith, cut the moorings and set men adrift to shift for themselves in a sea of disbelief. If man could make progress in economics and finance, perfect a fortune, why could he not also by taking thought improve his government and perfect society? If man could by his own wit conquer the material world, why could he not be able to control and direct himself and his fellows? A little thought would have shown him the magnitude of the last task in comparison with the first one. The material world which he was conquering was inanimate and did not talk back or argue or have other plans of its own. Man's attack on it was motivated by selfishness and the prospect of personal gain, i.e., progress. But his proposal to change human society, to make it ideal, was based on selflessness, a willingness to sacrifice, an abnegation, and at a time when self-seeking was never more rewarding. The time for asceticism is when there is not much to be had anyway, and whatever may be said of the utopias, they were a call to asceticism to people who were approaching the groaning board with huge appetites. Hence utopias were impractical, romantic, and wholly out of joint with their times, and with human nature at all times.

The classic of the form of literature dealing with civilized man in isolation is *Robinson Crusoe*, the scene of which was laid by Defoe on an island off the western coast of South America. Defoe based his story on the narratives of Captain William Dampier, who wrote three books dealing with his voyages, the first in 1697 and the third in 1709. It was on the second voyage that Alexander Selkirk was abandoned on the island of Juan Fernandez in September, 1704; he was picked up by Dampier on a third voyage commanded by Captain Woodes Rogers in 1709. Defoe was acquainted with Dampier and drew liberally on his writings in his *Robinson Crusoe* story.

We come finally to that category of frontier-inspired literature which deals with man in conflict with nature. A great section of this literature is of the sea, which has to play some part in metropolitan experience in the new lands because the sea was the only highway by which the metropolitans could reach their frontier destination. "Only with the eighteenth century," says Bonner, does the sea occupy a place in English literature at all comparable with its place in English life." It is further observed that though English prose turned to the sea in the early eighteenth century, the poets did not get around to it until almost a century later. To the Europeans after 1500 the seas were as much frontier as the new continents, and mightily did they affect the men of imagination.

Every writer mentions the fact that Shakespeare's *The Tempest* is the story of storm and shipwreck in the Atlantic. "Before Coleridge and the Romantic poets, scarcely anyone . . . wrote poetry filled with the beauty and mystery of the sea." "The Rime of the Ancient Mariner," published in 1798, represents the poetic imagination of the man of the Metropolis sweeping the frontier seas as does no other work, prose or poetry. Also there is no other character in literature who is caught so starkly in the viselike grip of nature as was the Ancient Mariner. It would be impossible to say anything original about this piece of literary art because Lowes has said it all in *The Road to Xanadu*. Coleridge was steeped in travel literature, knew what the ancients thought about geography, and probably borrowed his albatross from Shelvocke's *Voyage*. There is hardly a line in "The Rime of the Ancient Mariner" that does not reflect the most painstaking research on the part of the poet, proof of which is found in his notebooks, and in the exhaustive study by Lowes. The Ancient Mariner is caught in about all the traps that Neptune can lay for puny man and the fragile ship on which he dared to sweep the seas, following in the wake of Magellan and Drake, through torrid calm and frozen waste. The remarkable achievement of "The Ancient Mariner" is that Coleridge compressed into 144 stanzas the human aspiration to know, the misapprehensions of the past, the daring to investigate at all hazards, and the ability to track the facts. Such an achievement can be attained only through the application of an all-inclusive imagination to a vast body of digested facts wrought into a simple work of art whose meaning and significance are commensurate with the reader's knowledge. The story is so simple that it is easily understood by a child who is held by its graphic imagery, and yet it is so profound that all its implications cannot be discovered by a mind less erudite than that of the mature scholar. As "The Ancient Mariner" is represented and illuminated by

Lowes, it would seem that the poet overtook the travelers and geographers and told their story in essence with that economy of words and fullness of spirit which only the poet commands. After dealing with the weird speculation and guesswork of the early map-makers, and the fumbling and often tragic voyagers whose exploration finally brought forth the accurate map of the world, Lowes inquires:

What has all this to do with "The Rime of the Ancient Mariner"? Well, here was a route from sea to sea, to which repeated use had given the familiarity of an established type. Ship after ship sailed south into the Atlantic, past the great skull-shaped westward rondure of Africa, across the Line, and down around the jutting shoulder of Brazil toward the Horn. They were driven . . . past the tempestuous headland into fields of floating ice. Once round the cape, they ran before the trade winds toward the Line again, to lie becalmed for days or weeks, under a heaven that was burning brass above them, in a tranced and breathless sea. Beyond which sea . . . we need not follow them. But that vast, sweeping curve, cutting the Equator, with its apex toward the pole, and bending up again from the white terrors of the austral ice to the long nightmare of equatorial calms—that mighty loop thrown round a continent from flaming heat to pitiless cold and back to heat again —not merely translates into living fact the fabulous barriers of the antique maps, but is also the graphic symbol of the track of a host of ships, the absorbing tales of which by the end of the eighteenth century, had been set down in books.

Of Coleridge's log of his ship, which he set down in prose as the route of the Ancient Mariner, Lowes says:

The basic structure of the voyage regarded as a voyage is as austerely true to fact as an Admiralty report. Yet that stark outline . . . is itself a compendium of the premonitory dreams, and the imaginative vision, and the intrepid daring of two-score generations. And now on this frame, as upon a loom, the imagination was to weave another, and this time a magic pattern.

I feel sure that Lowes would have no objection to my seizing on his figure of the loom and the magic pattern, and extending it beyond "The Rime of the Ancient Mariner" to an entire class of literature of which the Ancient Mariner is representative. Any reader of *The Road to Xanadu* will see that the author's primary purpose is "a study in the ways of the imagination" and "an attempt to get at the workings of the faculty itself." That is exactly what we are trying here to get at—a glimmering of the relationship between the Great Frontier and human imagination as represented in modern literature. The borrowed loom and magic pattern are therefore more useful in presenting a vision of a gigantic literary action carried out on a stupendous scale. One side of the loom is the Metropolis, the other the Great Frontier, and as the shuttle of the imagination flew back and forth between the well known and the less well known it produced a fabric of literature which combined in its magic patterns the elements, the colors, shades, and tones of two worlds, one old and the other new.

In this view of literature as a tapestry woven in its frame of the Old World on one side and the New World on the other—a tapestry three centuries in the weaving—there is something epic. It tells the story of how the two worlds got acquainted. This getting acquainted was made up of many episodes, much tragedy, some comedy, all combined in a drama magnificent in its proportions. In the course of that drama we see the fusion, the slow mixture and blending of the elements of the old metropolitan culture with the strange new materials of the frontier world. It may be true that the Metropolis conquered the frontier, but it remains to be seen whether the frontier did not dictate the terms of its own surrender. The two are becoming one, and though contrasts still exist, they are due more to habit, tradition, and inertia than to lack of common knowledge. The period of fusion is about over, the loom is about full, the tapestry of an epoch is almost finished, and in the late weaving it is all but impossible to separate the elements derived from the Great Frontier from those out of the Metropolis.

Let us look at the tapestry and see if we can recognize the episodes of the drama unfolded by literary men and other artists. There Camoëns celebrates in *The Lusiads* Da Gama's voyages to the East and the greatness of Portugal. He sings the feat of men who conquered the fear of the surrounding seas. Shakespeare's *The Tempest* rages around a new island of the Atlantic, and beyond in distant America the Utopians of More live as people should while those of Bacon's *New Atlantis* carry on their ideal life in a region equally remote. In the Pacific off the South American coast Robinson Crusoe tames his goats and shows his superiority in a most egotistical manner over Friday, while across the way and in a lower latitude all sorts of adventures take place around Treasure Island. The Ancient Mariner makes his way in the frozen Antarctic:

The ice was here, the ice was there,
The ice was all around:
It cracked and growled, and roared and howled,
Like noises in a swound!

And later that same ship stood becalmed in a still and rotting sea:

Day after day, day after day,
We stuck, nor breath nor motion;
As idle as a painted ship
Upon a painted ocean.

This is the center of the tapestry, but on the western margin Cooper's Leatherstocking moves in his simple way among a group of unreal and highly romantic red men and white women, while Mark Twain deals in more robust and honest fashion with the doings of Tom Sawyer and Huck Finn along the mighty river, and Walt Whitman and Herman Melville sing their faith in the new society. In the realm of art George Catlin is romanticizing the American Indian, along with Alfred Jacob Miller and Charles Bodmer, while at a later time Frederic Remington and Charlie Russell are filling the western art galleries—which were saloons—and the eastern magazines with representations of a half-imagined and half-real cowboy life. Nor must we omit John James Audubon sitting at his easel in the forests to record in lifelike manner the birds of America in their native haunts as no one else has ever done. Theirs are only a few of the many subthemes worked out by the men of imagination, magic patterns which make details of the great canvas. Since we are dealing primarily with literature, we must leave to one side the historical pageant, the real characters who were finding adventure, quick fortunes, and sudden death among the more enduring characters of the human imagination. But it is important to bear in mind that among the deathless aristocracy of literature moved real men, pirates knocking over treasure ships, conquistadores searching for Eldorados, Indian fighters, rivermen, freebooters, cowboys, and cattle kings: models and source books, as it were, for the artists and writers who were making the record in print and on canvas.

As we look at the nearly completed tapestry we cannot fail to see that it belongs to a bygone age, to an era now ending. There is no room in the present world for such as this stuff our modern literature was made of. The imagination cannot play any more with the mystery and uncertainty of a half-known world, for there is no such thing. The map is finished, the roads are surveyed, and all the paths to that kind of adventure are plainly marked. Da Gama would have a score of safe ports to call, and no hope of his voyage's bringing glory to his country. Robinson Crusoe would be picked up by an airplane before he could make a pirogue or tame a goat. The Eldorados are sought by geophysicists and men with Geiger counters. The noble savage would be exposed in the next Sunday supplement by a sociologist or anthropologist who had seen him and measured his head both ways. The Ancient Mariner would be thrown out of the court of credibility if he claimed to be the first that ever burst into any sea. Cooper's Indians are drinking Coca Cola on the reservation; Tom Sawyer would be lucky to escape a camp for under-privileged children; Russell and Remington would be painting horses that would frighten one—pictures that no saloonkeeper would tolerate; Audubon would be teaching ornithology to a few disinterested students and hoping for a grant from a foundation; and Walt Whitman would probably turn his savage genius on the frustrations of the democratic vista.

All this does not mean that the human imagination will not still operate, that literature will not continue to be produced. It does mean that the imagination must make its way henceforth amidst a different set of conditions, that it must operate *among* men and not beyond them, that it must deal with what is well known rather than with what is only vaguely known. No more can the imagination sweep out from the Metropolis into the frontier and spin its fantastic tales of adventure and conquest. Man again has been turned back on himself to find his romance and adventure. If we may judge by current manifestations, literature is no longer concerned with man caught between an old world that is curious and a new one that is excitingly strange. It becomes more and more subjective, and seems to be concerned mainly with whether man is all sex or all psychology.

The end of an age is always touched with sadness for those who lived it and those who love it. It is usually attended with much knowledge, some wisdom, and a sort of jaded sophistication. Neither knowledge nor wisdom brings happiness; more often they bring disillusionment. It would be very interesting to speculate on what the human imagination is going to do with a frontierless world where it must seek its inspiration in uniformity rather than in variety, in sameness rather than in contrast, in safety rather than in danger, in probing the harmless nuances of the known rather than the thundering uncertainties of unknown seas and continents. The dreamers, the poets, and the philosophers are after all but instruments which make vocal and articulate the hopes and aspirations of a people. The people themselves are going to miss the frontier more than words can express. For four centuries they heard its call, listened to its promise, and bet their lives and fortunes on its outcome. It calls no more, and regardless of how they bend their ears for its faint whisper they cannot hear the suggestion of a promise. The literary men have already caught up their frustration and are making it the subject of their art. As yet no masterpiece has resulted, but there are fragments of writing which hint at what the human imagination may be able to do with the closed frontier.

John Steinbeck wrote a story entitled "The Leader of the People." It is about a small boy, Jody Tiflin, who lived on a western ranch with his father, Carl, and his mother. But in this story that family are only props for Jody's grandfather, his mother's father, who is coming for a visit. Carl Tiflin, an unimaginative and practical man, does not like Grandfather, who bores him by telling the same story, of how he led the people across the plains, how they fought Indians and overcame all the difficulties. Always the same story. Carl cannot stand the prospect of hearing it again.

"Well, how many times do I have to listen to the story of the iron plates, and the thirty-five horses? That time's done. Why can't he forget it, now it's done? . . . He came across the plains. All right! Now it's finished. Nobody wants to hear about it over and over."

Grandfather overheard Carl say all this, and of course he was deeply hurt, but not as one would expect him to be.

"I don't mind what you said, but it might be true, and I would mind that," remarked Grandfather gently. Carl, feeling sorry for having been honest, left and Grandfather later justified himself to Jody.

"It wasn't Indians that were important, nor adventures, nor even getting out here. It was a whole bunch of people made into one big crawling beast. . . . It was westering and westering. Every man wanted something for himself, but the big beast that was all of them wanted only westering. I was the leader. . . . The thing had to have a head. . . .

"When we saw the mountains at last, we cried—all of us. But it wasn't getting here that mattered, it was movement and westering.

"We carried life out here and set it down the way those ants carry eggs. And I was the leader. The westering was as big as God, and the slow steps that made the movement piled up until the continent was crossed.

"Then we came down to the sea, and it was done."

"Maybe I could lead the people some day," Jody said.

The old man smiled. "There's no place to go. There's the ocean to stop you. There's a line of old men along the shore hating the ocean because it stopped them."

"In boats, I might, sir."

"No place to go, Jody. Every place is taken. But that's not the worst— no, not the worst. Westering has died out of the people. Westering isn't a hunger any more. It's all done."

And as we linger in contemplation of the great tapestry of modern literature which has left us symbols of what the human imagination did with a New World, we know that it was a special kind of experience, that it is done, and our last impression as we turn away is that to many of us it was as big as God.

Ben Lilly

ROBERT TRAMMELL

Ben Lilly
      Bear Hunter
who could flat foot it out of a four foot barrel
and did for Teddy Roosevelt
                          President of the United States
wore three layers of clothes
weighed 170
would think nothing of running a bear 10 miles
and then
         killing him with a knife
was found naked cleaning himself in the North Carolina snow
wore mule shoes on his boots
and was last seen an old man tracking a mule in a circle

Exploration of Inner Space

BILL D. SCHUL

FOR A NUMBER OF CENTURIES the scientific method and its insistence on hard data which could be physically demonstrated was to a large degree the antithesis of religious truths. But today—through a revolution as important as the Copernican Revolution which launched science's climb to status—it is the scientist who is making breakthroughs into the spiritual realms and confirming the religious and mystical traditions.

In making the above statement, Dr. Elmer Green, Director of the Menninger Foundation's Psychophysiological Laboratory in Topeka, Kansas, was referring to the work to which he and a growing number of other scientists are devoting their time and energies in the belief that it carries the highest priority for the benefit of mankind.

In the spring of 1971, a highly selective corps of these scientists participated in a project which was defined by several of them as being in every way as epochal as man's construction of a science of the galaxies.

The project was the Interdisciplinary Conference on the Voluntary Control of Internal States of Consciousness. It was called by the world-renowned Menninger Foundation, which, in addition to its work in providing postdoctoral training in psychiatry, clinical psychology, and psychoanalysis, and the varied research, training, and consultative activities of its Department of Preventive Psychiatry, carries on research in psychology, psychiatry, sociology, neurology, and brainwaves. Attendance was limited to ninety highly qualified mathematicians, physicists, theologians, psychiatrists, psychologists, and educators, who came from Denmark, Canada, Germany, France, Ireland, Japan, India, and England, as well as this country. It is doubtful whether a more important assemblage of learned men has gathered in many years.

The invitations read in part: "We have reached a point in history at which the exploration of internal states has become not only a legitimate but also high-priority business of science."

The title of the conference, however, does not adequately describe an agenda which had the express purpose of exploring the entire labyrinth of existing and potential human consciousness. There is significance here of no small dimension: an expression of sufficient belief on the part of accredited scientists for them to determine that the investigation of states of awareness which range beyond the limitations of the body mechanisms, nervous system, and brain not only was warranted but could be sufficiently demonstrated by scientific methods.

Religious devotees, theologians, philosophers, and mystics of all ages have always contended that the physical body of man is a vehicle for the spiritual nature and that man's consciousness is neither limited to nor dependent upon this physical vehicle and its organs. The scientist, also, of course, could and sometimes did believe this, depending upon his religious convictions. And, yet, higher states of consciousness, unless personally experienced by the subject, had to be accepted on faith, for there were no means of scientific measurement.

The Conference on the Voluntary Control of Internal States of Consciousness was the first of its kind. It did not, however, initiate the research represented in the program contents. Most of the conference participants had been involved for many years in the work which brought them together at the conference. The belief that separated them from other scientists and had become the nucleus of their research was that man was not only a physical, emotional, and mental being, but also a transpersonal, or spiritual being with much greater possibilities and potentialities than are generally thought to exist. To be able to demonstrate this hypothesis on scientific grounds was a matter which these respected investigators held to be profound implications for the human race. For the most part, however, their work has been overlooked by a public attracted to the more visible results of the space age.

Ever since the first Russian satellite invaded the heavens, the scientists working toward the investigation of outer space have gained the heroic image in the public's eye and have attracted the attention of the press. Not always certain in what way touching base with the moon would affect their personal lives, the public, nonetheless, were convinced they had indirectly through television witnessed the most historic event since the discovery of America, if not in the whole history of mankind.

But while some of our scientists were laboring with the urgency of conquering the unknowns in extended space, others have been equally committed to investigating the uncharted regions of man himself. And while some have expressed the hypothesis that mankind's survival on this planet depends on his success in reaching other globes, another camp of scientific intellectuals has been dedicated to the belief that earth's inhabitants will not survive unless they can understand themselves. The members of this group assess their task as the examination of that which perceives the product of any exploration—the human consciousness. A certain relevancy emerges from their philosophical tenet that what is of greater importance than that which is observed is that which observes it.

Those so committed could at least take comfort in the ancient adage, "Man, know thyself." In following this instruction, the scientists of inner space have become encamped with the theologians and philosophers while keeping their professional credentials in order by pursuing their goals within the most rigid scientific procedures. Prior to fairly recent technological advancements, the scientists had no tools with which to engage the issues proposed by the philosopher: "What is man?" "How does he perceive?" "What is the purpose of life?" or even, "What is life?" Any measure of subjective states was limited to the subject himself, and the serious scientist could only devote himself to the study of objective data.

But the technology which produced a landing on the moon also developed instruments intricate and precise enough to measure not only the objective world outside of man but also the subjective states within. Instead of discovering data to support the old mechanistic theory of man, the explorers of inner space found that their electroencephlographs, sensitive transducers, high-gain amplifiers, and infrared films unfolded vistas of man's nature alluded to through the centuries by the mystics and metaphysicians.

The results of these investigations may well eclipse public focus on explorations of outer space, when the implications are fully recognized. Most of the examinations in the brainwave and psychophysiological laboratories have been reported in scientific journals which have escaped the attention of the public. Yet, the message—though proclaimed in scientific nomenclature—is quite clear: man's states of awareness are not dependent upon nor limited to his physical body.

Speaking of the need to broaden current psychological theories of man in order to incorporate recent discoveries of man's transcendental or transpersonal states, Dr. Green, who was a member of the conference planning committee, stated at the annual meeting of the Association for Humanistic Psychology in Miami Beach:

In a single phrase it can be said that transpersonal refers to a concern with values, ultimate values, those qualitative factors in living, in philosophy, and in psychology, which have been out of style because until recently there was no experimental consensus concerning the reality and validity of transpersonal levels of being. The former private reverse of the mystics and occultists is now, however, in the public domain.

Dr. Willis W. Harman, director of one of the two U.S. Educational Policy Research Centers, stated in a paper entitled "The New Copernican Revolution":

Much evidence suggests that a group of questions relating to the commonality and interpretation of man's subjective experiences, especially of the "transcendental," and hence to the bases of human values, are shifting from the realm of the "philosophical" to the "empirical." If so, the consequences may be even more far-reaching than those which emerged from the Copernican, Darwinian, and Freudian revolutions.

Dr. Harman was awarded the Ph.D. in engineering and was involved in systems analysis before broadening his interests during the mid-1960s to include analysis of social systems. He served as the first director of Stanford University's Department of Engineering-Economic Systems before joining the U.S Office of Education to explore "alternative futures" for education and for society. His search for "the issues behind the issues" in education led him to comparisons of alternative philosophies and belief systems. It is from this perspective that Dr. Harman stated that the Interdisciplinary Conference on the Voluntary Control of Internal States "represents an unprecedented assemblage of scientists working with altered states of consciousness through such techniques as autohypnosis and group hypnosis, aural feedback of alphawave signals, and psychedelic drugs."

In his "Copernican" paper, presented prior to the conference, Dr. Harman proposed the following:

As future historians look back on our times what will they conclude to have been the most significant event of the present decade in terms of its impact on the future? The riots in the cities? The Vietnam War? The Great

Society programs? The hippie movement? Student protest? Technological and scientific advances? Man to the moon?

None of these, I would make bold to guess. Nor any of the events or trend discontinuities which the in-vogue forecasters are picking out with their current methodologies. I will suggest below that it will be something quite different from any of these, an event perhaps well symbolized by an obscure scientific conference to be held in Council Grove, Kansas.

The by-invitation-only conference was held at White Memorial Church Camp at Council Grove Reservoir on April 12-16, 1971. Sixty miles from Topeka and isolated from traffic, telephones, and the usual social interruptions synchronous with most professional gatherings, the participants spent their days and much of their nights in quiet pursuit of the nature of consciousness and the spiritual qualities of man.

The participants were requested to indicate on their invitation replies their interests as to the following subjects: objective and subjective data in altered states of consciousness research; humanistic education; religion; non-allopathic healing; parapsychology; psychosynthesis; illicit drug use; transpersonal psychology; biofeedback; dreams; sensory awareness and sensory deprivation; psychotherapy; psychophysiological correlates; structural integration; and creativity.

According to Dr. Stanley Krippner, conference chairman and director of the Dream Laboratory at Maimonides Medical Center in Brooklyn, New York, the specific task of the conference was to share information and research on the following:

1. What is reality?

2. What is the reality of individually experienced events not shared in common with others?

3. Do altered states of consciousness lead us toward or away from reality?

4. How can scientific research help find the answers to these questions?

5. Of what practical use are altered states of consciousness and the voluntary control of internal states?

6. Are there types of learning which can be enhanced during altered states of consciousness?

7. What kind of learning is involved in voluntary control of internal states?

The discussions of these matters were held during general sessions in the church camp's large dining hall and during small group workshops in the five cottages which housed the participants during their stay. Unscheduled gatherings on the lawns and along the nearby shores of the lake occurred throughout the days and evenings as colleagues exchanged information or borrowed a few minutes from an active agenda for quiet meditation.

During one of the scheduled evening sessions Dr. Charles Tart, author of several papers and books on altered states of consciousness and associate professor of psychology at the University of California at Davis, presented a talk on "The Reality of Non-Ordinary Reality," in which he appealed to the scientists for more serious and systematic study of experiences but which are not commonly shared but which can be answered, measured, and documented. "Our immense success in the development of the physical sciences," Dr. Tart said,

has not been particularly successful in formulating better philosophies of life, or increasing our real knowledge of ourselves. The science we have developed to date is not a very human science. It tells us how to do things, but gives us no scientific insights into the questions of what to do, what not to do, or why to do things. . . . Much of the current crisis in our culture today can be traced to a breakdown in the functioning of our old religious systems, and the inadequacy of a scientific view of life to replace them with something more functional. . . . A basic question then is whether we will continue to let altered states of consciousness exert their profound power over human life as scattered, chaotic bits of knowledge, subject to great misunderstanding, or whether we will attempt to expand our conception of science and develop state-specific sciences which could vastly improve our ability to function in, understand, and learn from such altered states of consciousness.

A plea for more research in the study of consciousness was made by a parapsychologist, Charles Honorton, a researcher with the Dream Laboratory at Maimonides Medical Center, who stated that it would be necessary for the medical laboratories to become more deeply involved in the exploration of inner space if greater knowledge was to be gained in the understanding of human behavior and motivation.

"We need a new strategy for studying states of consciousness," he told the group. "Biofeedback has offered a means of consistently measuring mental state apart from behavior. We should use, however, as many means or methods as are available to us."

Honorton described his work in testing subjects for extranormal responses while they were being measured for alpha-theta brainwave patterns. "Although our research is far from complete at this point," he said, "the results indicate a correlation between those subjects who produce a high percentage of alpha and theta brainwaves and those with extrasensory perceptions."

Arthur Hastings, assistant professor of Public Address and Small Group Communication at Stanford University, in a talk entitled "State-Dependent Learning," pointed out:

We must bear in mind that the state of mind that is investigating an altered state of consciousness may also be an altered state of consciousness. The question becomes, then, what is a non-altered state of consciousness and perhaps in the final analysis there are not altered states but only a singular vision that becomes extended if we can keep it from becoming polluted. . . . In any study of reality, it must be remembered that not all people perceive life nor objects as we do, and I think we must also bear in mind that language structure is not necessarily a reality structure. Sometimes in order to move closer to reality we need to divest ourselves of the way we carry out the reasoning process.

Other presentations were made by Dr. Green, who described the work of the Menninger Foundation's Psychophysiological Laboratory in the measurement and study of brainwaves and voluntary control of internal states of consciousness; Dr. Roland Fisher, who described his work in experimental psychology and pharmacology at Ohio State University; Grenville Moat, director of Bucks County Seminar House, Erwinna, Pennsylvania, who told of undergoing a month's training at a mystical school in Chile; Dr. Stanislav Grof, director of psychiatric research at Maryland Psychiatric Research Center, who discussed a recent trip to India to attend an international conference on the scientific study of man's spiritual states; and Dr. Eleanor Criswell, professor of psychology at Sonoma State College, Robert Park, California, who discussed her work in brainwave research.

But to a large extent personal experiences of altered and expanded states of consciousness eclipsed academia as the scientists found themselves gravitating toward those persons who could testify to and sufficiently demonstrate their abilities to function within transcendental states of awareness.

One of these was Shirley Harrison, a well-known psychic-sensitive and president of the Research Foundation for Parapsychological Study in West Buxton, Maine. Mrs. Harrison's personal experiences with altered states of consciousness have gained for her the recognition of having unusual powers of extranormal perception. She spoke on "Paranormal Phenomena and the Voluntary Control of Altered Conscious States," and discussed the nature of paranormal powers in the light of recent research in the area.

Dr. Krippner, who introduced the speaker, explained that Mrs. Harrison has over a period of years compiled a long record of authenticated medical diagnoses. He related how Mrs. Harrison had correctly diagnosed his own illness which had eluded the medical profession. "As a result of her correct diagnosis, steps were taken which resulted in a quick and complete cure," Dr. Krippner stated.

Robert Monroe, a Charlottesville, Virginia, businessman, captured the attention of the scientists in relating his twelve years of experiencing states of conscious awareness while allegedly separated from his physical body. Monroe stated that he had kept an extensive diary of more than nine hundred experiences of consciousness apart from his body during which time he was able to travel considerable distances and report observations which later were documented. "It is difficult to describe my state while being out of my body," he said. "I am aware and I can think, feel, and move, but without the normal physical limitations."

Monroe has been the subject of a number of scientific studies on awareness beyond the physical plane. He is author of *Journeys Out of the Body*, published in October, 1971, by Doubleday, with an introduction by Dr. Tart.

The altered conscious state described by Monroe has a high enough rate of incidence reported to be labeled by parapsychologists as "out-of-the-body experiences." It has been extensively researched by several of the scientists who were in attendance at the Council Grove conference, including Dr. Tart, Dr. Krippner, and Charles Honorton, who supported Monroe's comments as being consistent with the information received from their research.

Rolling Thunder, chief medicine man of the Shoshone Indian nation, played an active role throughout the conference, giving a talk to the assembly, participating in group discussions, doing individual counseling, giving a healing ceremony for a participant with an injured leg—a highly successful healing verified by several physicians attending the conference—and, on the final day of the conference, presenting an Indian sunrise service.

"This is the first time since the great acquisition of our lands that the Indian has been willing to share his teachings with the white man," Rolling Thunder said. It is interesting to note that the medicine man's comments were made at Council Grove, the site of the last great treaty between the Indian and the white man.

Rolling Thunder related how the Indian nations had kept their teachings alive through the centuries. He told the scientists:

The great teachings are highly protected secrets and are taught to only a few who demonstrate their ability to use this knowledge for the benefit of others. We have not shared this body of knowledge with the white man, for he was not ready to listen; but the time has come when we must do so, for the need is great. Perhaps even survival itself depends on it.

Rolling Thunder, who spent six years of intensive study in becoming a medicine man, explained that he could not reveal the nature of the teachings in their entirety, as this would be reserved for those selected for training. He did, however, give the group sufficient information concerning the different degrees of initiation in the Indian medicine schools so that several participants commented that they were amazed at the similarity between these teachings and those of the mystery schools in other parts of the world.

Current plans for a 1972 conference have been envisioned by the Conference Planning committee as an effort to bring coherence and synthesis to current and future explorations and experimentation in states of consciousness. The purpose of the conferences has been defined as follows:

To develop an experimental and theoretical basis for a possible science of consciousness, in which existential development and academic attainment are interrelated. This basic purpose underlays the inclusion of the ancient systems for the development of voluntary control of internal awareness.

In an appraisal of these goals, Dr. Green stated, "If the needs of some millions of people are effective—those who in the last ten years have suddenly become aware of an inner domain—then a new branch of psychological science will necessarily evolve."

This idea was reflected in the thinking of Dr. James Fadiman of Stanford University, who in writing about the conference in the *News-*

letter of the American Association for Humanistic Psychology, stated, "I am sure there will be a science of altered states of consciousness."

Assuming that the evidence substantiating man's transcendental states continues to grow, then the Council Grove conference and the new scientific interest in the study of man's subjective states have the most profound implications for the future. They say most emphatically that we have limited man and underestimated his potentialities, and we have misunderstood the intuitive wisdom which reveals that one of the most important characteristics of any society is its vision of itself and its future. They imply that the most profound revolution of education would not be the cybernation of knowledge transmission, but the inclusion of an exalted image of what man can be and the development of an improved self-image in each child. Further, the implications are that the solution to the alienation and broad disaffection in our society is not to be found only in vast social programs, but will emerge through general adoption of a new spiritual image of mankind and man's relationship to man. They indicate that the most pervasive illness of our country is loss of the guiding vision, and the cure resides in a nobler image of man and of a society in which his growth finds better nourishment. And there is reassurance that an image of fully realized man and of a new social order need not be constructed of the gossamer of wishful thinking, but that a sound foundation can be established from the research findings of the most daring explorers of the nature of man and his universe—the explorers of inner space.

Pollution   ROBERT BURLINGAME

They pulled in the wagon full of flowers
the street lifted up its long thin nose—
this perfume, is it all right, is it all right?

Antaeus

BORDEN DEAL

THIS WAS during the wartime, when lots of people were coming North for jobs in factories and war industries, when people moved around a lot more than they do now and sometimes kids were thrown into new groups and new lives that were completely different from anything they had ever known before. I remember this one kid, T.J. his name was, from somewhere down South, whose family moved into our building during that time. They'd come North with everything they owned piled into the back seat of an old-model sedan that you wouldn't expect could make the trip, with T.J. and his three younger sisters riding shakily on top of the load of junk.

Our building was just like all the others there, with families crowded into a few rooms, and I guess there were twenty-five or thirty kids about my age in that one building. Of course, there were a few of us who formed a gang and ran together all the time after school, and I was the one who brought T.J. in and started the whole thing.

The building right next door to us was a factory where they made walking dolls. It was a low building with a flat, tarred roof that had a parapet all around it about head high and we'd found out a long time before that no one, not even the watchman, paid any attention to the roof because it was higher than any of the other buildings around. So my gang used the roof as a headquarters. We could get up there by crossing over to the fire escape from our own roof on a plank and then going on up. It was a secret place for us, where nobody else could go without our permission.

I remember the day I first took T.J. up there to meet the gang. He was a stocky, robust kid with a shock of white hair, nothing sissy about him except his voice—he talked in this slow, gentle voice like you never heard before. He talked different from any of us and you noticed it right away. But I liked him anyway, so I told him to come on up.

We climbed up over the parapet and dropped down on the roof. The rest of the gang were already there.

"Hi," I said. I jerked my thumb at T.J. "He just moved into the building yesterday."

He just stood there, not scared or anything, just looking, like the first time that you see somebody or something you're not sure you're going to like.

"Hi," Blackie said. "Where are you from?"

"Marion County," T.J. said.

We laughed. "Marion County?" I said. "Where's that?"

He looked at me for a moment like I was a stranger, too. "It's in Alabama," he said, like I ought to know where it was.

"What's your name?" Charley said.

"T.J.," he said, looking back at him. He had pale blue eyes that looked washed-out but he looked directly at Charley, waiting for his reaction. He'll be all right, I thought. No sissy in him . . . except that voice. Who ever talked like that?

"T.J.," Blackie said. "That's just initials. What's your real name? Nobody in the world has just initials."

"I do," he said. "And they're T.J. That's all the name I got."

His voice was resolute with the knowledge of his rightness, and for a moment no one had anything to say. T.J. looked around at the rooftop and down at the black tar under his feet. "Down yonder where I come from," he said, "we played out in the woods. Don't you-all have no woods around here?"

"Naw," Blackie said. "There's the park a few blocks over, but it's full of kids and cops and old women. You can't do a thing."

T.J. kept looking at the tar under his feet. "You mean you ain't got no fields to raise nothing in? . . . no watermelons or nothing?"

"Naw," I said scornfully. "What do you want to grow something for? The folks can buy everything they need at the store."

He looked at me again with that strange, unknowing look. "In Marion County," he said, "I had my own acre of cotton and my own acre of corn. It was mine to plant and make ever' year."

He sounded like it was something to be proud of, and in some obscure way it made the rest of us angry. "Jesus!" Blackie said. "Who'd want to have their own acre of cotton and corn? That's just work. What can you do with an acre of cotton and corn?"

T.J. looked at him. "Well, you get part of the bale offen your acre," he said seriously. "And I fed my acre of corn to my calf."

We didn't really know what he was talking about, so we were more puzzled than angry; otherwise, I guess, we'd have chased him off the roof and wouldn't let him be a part of our gang. But he was strange and different and we were all attracted by his stolid sense of rightness and belonging, maybe by the strange softness of his voice contrasting our own tones of speech into harshness.

He moved his foot against the black tar. "We could make our own field right here," he said softly, thoughtfully. "Come spring we could raise us what we want to . . . watermelons and garden truck and no telling what all."

"You'd have to be a good farmer to make these tar roofs grow any watermelons," I said. We all laughed.

But T.J. looked serious. "We could haul us some dirt up here," he said. "And spread it out even and water it and before you know it we'd have us a crop in here." He looked at us intently. "Wouldn't that be fun?"

"They wouldn't let us," Blackie said quickly.

"I thought you said this was you-all's roof," T.J. said to me. "That you-all could do anything you wanted to up here."

"They've never bothered us," I said. I felt the idea beginning to catch fire in me. It was a big idea and it took a while for it to sink in but the more I thought about it the better I liked it. "Say," I said to the gang. "He might have something there. Just make us a regular roof garden, with flowers and grass and trees and everything. And all ours, too," I said. "We wouldn't let anybody up here except the ones we wanted to."

"It'd take a while to grow trees," T.J. said quickly, but we weren't paying any attention to him. They were all talking about it suddenly, all excited with the idea after I'd put it in a way they could catch hold of it. Only rich people had roof gardens, we knew, and the idea of our own private domain excited them.

"We could bring it up in sacks and boxes," Blackie said. "We'd have to do it while the folks weren't paying any attention to us, for we'd have to come up to the roof of our building and then cross over with it."

"Where could we get the dirt?" somebody said worriedly.

"Out of those vacant lots over close to school," Blackie said. "Nobody'd notice if we scraped it up."

I slapped T.J. on the shoulder. "Man, you had a wonderful idea," I said, and everybody grinned at him, remembering that he had started it. "Our own private roof garden."

He grinned back. "It'll be ourn," he said. "All ourn." Then he looked thoughtful again. "Maybe I can lay my hands on some cottonseed, too. You think we could raise us some cotton?"

We'd started big projects before at one time or another, like any gang of kids, but they'd always petered out for lack of organization and direction. But this one didn't . . . somehow or other T.J. kept it going all through the winter months. He kept talking about the watermelons and the cotton we'd raise, come spring, and when even that wouldn't work he'd switch around to my idea of flowers and grass and trees, though he was always honest enough to add that it'd take a while to get any trees started. He always had it on his mind and he'd mention it in school, getting them lined up to carry dirt that afternoon, saying in a casual way that he reckoned a few more weeks ought to see the job through.

Our little area of private earth grew slowly. T.J. was smart enough to start in one corner of the building, heaping up the carried earth two or three feet thick, so that we had an immediate result to look at, to contemplate with awe. Some of the evenings T.J. alone was carrying earth up to the building, the rest of the gang distracted by other enterprises or interests, but T.J. kept plugging along on his own and eventually we'd all come back to him again and then our own little acre would grow more rapidly.

He was careful about the kind of dirt he'd let us carry up there and more than once he dumped a sandy load over the parapet into the areaway below because it wasn't good enough. He found out the kinds of earth in all the vacant lots for blocks around. He'd pick it up and feel it and smell it, frozen though it was sometimes, and then he'd say it was good growing soil or it wasn't worth anything and we'd have to go on somewhere else.

Thinking about it now, I don't see how he kept us at it. It was hard work, lugging paper sacks and boxes of dirt all the way up the stairs of our own building, keeping out of the way of grownups so they wouldn't catch on to what we were doing. They probably wouldn't have cared, for they didn't pay much attention to us, but we wanted to keep it secret anyway. Then we had to go through the trapdoor to our roof, teeter over a plank to the fire escape, then climb two or three stories to the parapet and drop down onto the roof. All that for a small pile of earth that sometimes didn't seem worth the effort. But T.J. kept the vision bright within us, his words shrewd and calculated toward the fulfillment of his dream; and he worked harder than any of us. He seemed driven toward a goal that we couldn't see, a particular point in time that would be definitely marked by signs and wonders that only he could see.

The laborious earth just lay there during the cold months, inert and lifeless, the clods lumpy and cold under our feet when we walked over it. But one day it rained and afterward there was a softness in the air and the earth was live and giving again with moisture and warmth. That evening T.J. smelled the air, his nostrils dilating with the odor of the earth under his feet.

"It's spring," he said, and there was a gladness rising in his voice that filled us all with the same feeling. "It's mighty late for it, but it's spring. I'd just about decided it wasn't never gonna get here at all."

We were all sniffing at the air, too, trying to smell it the way that T.J. did, and I can still remember the sweet odor of the earth under our feet. It was the first time in my life that spring and spring earth had meant anything to me. I looked at T.J. then, knowing in a faint way the hunger within him through the toilsome winter months, knowing the dream that lay behind his plan. He was a new Antaeus, preparing his own bed of strength.

"Planting time," he said. "We'll have to find us some seed."

"What do we do?" Blackie said. "How do we do it?"

"First we'll have to break up the clods," T.J. said. "That won't be hard to do. Then we plant the seed and after a while they come up. Then you got you a crop." He frowned. "But you ain't got it raised yet. You got to tend it and hoe it and take care of it and all the time it's growing and growing, while you're awake and while you're asleep. Then you lay it by when it's growed and let it ripen and then you got you a crop."

"There's those wholesale seed houses over on Sixth," I said. "We could probably swipe some grass seed over there."

T.J. looked at the earth. "You-all seem mighty set on raising some grass," he said. "I ain't never put no effort into that. I spent all my life trying not to raise grass."

"But it's pretty," Blackie said. "We could play on it and take sunbaths on it. Like having our own lawn. Lots of people got lawns."

"Well," T.J. said. He looked at the rest of us, hesitant for the first time. He kept on looking at us for a moment. "I did have it in mind to raise some corn and vegetables. But we'll plant grass."

He was smart. He knew where to give in. And I don't suppose it made any difference to him, really. He just wanted to grow something, even if it was grass.

"Of course," he said, "I do think we ought to plant a row of watermelons. They'd be mighty nice to eat while we was a-laying on that grass."

We all laughed. "All right," I said. "We'll plant us a row of watermelons."

Things went very quickly then. Perhaps half the roof was covered with the earth, the half that wasn't broken by ventilators, and we swiped pocketfuls of grass seed from the open bins in the wholesale seed house, mingling among the buyers on Saturdays and during the school lunch hour. T.J. showed us how to prepare the earth, breaking up the clods and smoothing it and sowing the grass seed. It looked rich and black now with moisture, receiving of the seed, and it seemed that the grass sprang up overnight, pale green in the early spring.

We couldn't keep from looking at it, unable to believe that we had created this delicate growth. We looked at T.J. with understanding now, knowing the fulfillment of the plan he had carried alone within his mind. We had worked without full understanding of the task, but he had known all the time.

We found that we couldn't walk or play on the delicate blades, as we had expected to, but we didn't mind. It was enough just to look at it, to realize that it was the work of our own hands, and each evening the whole gang was there, trying to measure the growth that had been achieved that day.

One time a foot was placed on the plot of ground . . . one time only, Blackie stepping onto it with sudden bravado. Then he looked at the crushed blades and there was shame in his face. He did not do it again. This was his grass, too, and not to be desecrated. No one said anything, for it was not necessary.

T.J. had reserved a small section for watermelons and he was still trying to find some seed for it. The wholesale house didn't have any watermelon seed and we didn't know where we could lay our hands on them.

T.J. shaped the earth into mounds, ready to receive them, three mounds lying in a straight line along the edge of the grass plot.

We had just about decided that we'd have to buy the seed if we were to get them. It was a violation of our principles, but we were anxious to get the watermelons started. Somewhere or other, T.J. got his hands on a seed catalogue and brought it one evening to our roof garden.

"We can order them now," he said, showing us the catalogue. "Look!"

We all crowded around, looking at the fat, green watermelons pictured in full color on the pages. Some of them were split open, showing the red, tempting meat, making our mouths water.

"Now we got to scrape up some seed money," T.J. said, looking at us. "I got a quarter. How much you-all got?"

We made up a couple of dollars between us and T.J. nodded his head. "That'll be more than enough. Now we got to decide what kind to get. I think them Kleckley Sweets. What do you-all think?"

He was going into esoteric matters beyond our reach. We hadn't even known there were different kinds of melons. So we just nodded our heads and agreed that Yes, we thought the Kleckley Sweets too.

"I'll order them tonight," T.J. said. "We ought to have them in a few days."

"What are you boys doing up here?" an adult voice said from behind us.

It startled us, for no one had ever come up here before, in all the time we had been using the roof of the factory. We jerked around and saw three men standing near the trapdoor at the other end of the roof. They weren't policemen, or night watchmen, but three men in plump business suits, looking at us. They walked toward us.

"What are you boys doing up here?" the one in the middle said again.

We stood still, guilt heavy among us, levied by the tone of voice, and looked at the three strangers.

The men stared at the grass flourishing behind us. "What's this?" the man said. "How did this get up here?"

"Sure is growing good, ain't it?" T.J. said conversationally. "We planted it."

The men kept looking at the grass as if they didn't believe it. It was a thick carpet over the earth now, a patch of deep greenness startling in the sterile industrial surroundings.

"Yes sir," T.J. said proudly. "We toted that earth up here and planted that grass." He fluttered the seed catalogue. "And we're just fixing to plant us some watermelon."

The man looked at him then, his eyes strange and faraway. "What do you mean, putting this on the roof of my building?" he said. "Do you want to go to jail?"

T.J. looked shaken. The rest of us were silent, frightened by the authority of his voice. We had grown up aware of adult authority, of policemen and night watchmen and teachers, and this man sounded like all the others. But it was a new thing to T.J.

"Well, you wan't using the roof," T.J. said. He paused a moment and added shrewdly, "So we just thought to pretty it up a little bit."

"And sag it so I'd have to rebuild it," the man said sharply. He started turning away, saying to another man beside him, "See that all that junk is shoveled off by tomorrow."

"Yes sir," the man said.

T.J. started forward. "You can't do that," he said. "We toted it up here and it's our earth. We planted it and raised it and toted it up here."

The man stared at him coldly. "But it's my building," he said. "It's to be shoveled off tomorrow."

"It's our earth," T.J. said desperately. "You ain't got no right!"

The men walked on without listening and descended clumsily through the trapdoor. T.J. stood looking after them, his body tense with anger, until they had disappeared. They wouldn't even argue with him, wouldn't let him defend his earth-rights.

He turned to us. "We won't let 'em do it," he said fiercely. "We'll stay up here all day tomorrow and the day after that and we won't let 'em do it."

We just looked at him. We knew that there was no stopping it. He saw it in our faces and his face wavered for a moment before he gripped it into determination.

"They ain't got no right," he said. "It's our earth. It's our land. Can't nobody touch a man's own land."

We kept on looking at him, listening to the words but knowing that it was no use. The adult world had descended on us even in our richest dream and we knew there was no calculating the adult world, no fighting it, no winning against it.

We started moving slowly toward the parapet and the fire escape, avoiding a last look at the green beauty of the earth that T.J. had planted for us . . . had planted deeply in our minds as well as in our experience. We filed slowly over the edge and down the steps to the plank, T.J. coming last, and all of us could feel the weight of his grief behind us.

"Wait a minute," he said suddenly, his voice harsh with the effort of calling. We stopped and turned, held by the tone of his voice, and looked up at him standing above us on the fire escape.

"We can't stop them?" he said, looking down at us, his face strange in the dusky light. "There ain't no way to stop 'em?"

"No," Blackie said with finality. "They own the building."

We stood still for a moment, looking up at T.J., caught into inaction by the decision working in his face. He stared back at us and his face was pale and mean in the poor light, with a bald nakedness in his skin like cripples have sometimes.

"They ain't gonna touch my earth," he said fiercely. "They ain't gonna lay a hand on it! Come on."

He turned around and started up the fire escape again, almost running against the effort of climbing. We followed more slowly, not knowing what he intended. By the time we reach him, he had seized a board and thrust it into the soil, scooping it up and flinging it over the parapet into the areaway below. He straightened and looked at us.

"They can't touch it," he said. "I won't let 'em lay a dirty hand on it!"

We saw it then. He stooped to his labor again and we followed, the gusts of his anger moving in frenzied labor among us as we scattered along the edge of the earth, scooping it and throwing it over the parapet, destroying with anger the growth we had nurtured with such tender care. The soil carried so laboriously upward to the light and the sun cascaded swiftly into the dark areaway, the green blades of grass crumpled and twisted in the falling.

It took less time than you would think . . . the task of destruction is infinitely easier than that of creation. We stopped at the end, leaving only a scattering of loose soil, and when it was finally over a stillness stood among the group and over the factory building. We looked down at the bare sterility of black tar, felt the harsh texture of it under the soles of our shoes, and the anger had gone out of us, leaving only a sore aching in our minds like overstretched muscles.

T.J. stood for a moment, his breathing slowing from anger and effort, caught into the same contemplation of destruction as all of us. He stooped slowly, finally, and picked up a lonely blade of grass left trampled under our feet and put it between his teeth, tasting it, sucking the greenness out of it into his mouth. Then he started walking toward the fire escape, moving before any of us were ready to move, and disappeared over the edge.

We followed him but he was already halfway down to the ground, going on past the board where we crossed over, climbing down into the areaway. We saw the last section swing down with his weight and then he stood on the concrete below us, looking at the small pile of anonymous earth scattered by our throwing. Then he walked across the place where we could see him and disappeared toward the street without glancing back, without looking up to see us watching him.

They did not find him for two weeks. Then the Nashville police caught him just outside the Nashville freight yards. He was walking along the railroad track; still heading south, still heading home.

As for us, who had no remembered home to call us . . . none of us ever again climbed the escapeway to the roof.

Mountain

WITTER BYNNER

"Go back to earth again, you live too soon,
Your changes are too violent, too small.
Why do you not, like me, remain immune
And yet with differences continual
Which differ only in their range of beauty?
Are you aware, you little villagers?
What are these words of yours—deity, duty,
Devotion, daring, death? When evening stirs,
Your words are lost like water in a brook
That runs along my side and then is gone.
Record your dead contentions in a book,
Then test your words against my living stone.
Go down to death and crawl to me in sand—
Lay down your varying voice, your hostile hand."

BORDEN DEAL   87

The Giraffe

CHARLES EDWARD EATON

Not one more animal, someone said, not one more—
And I agreed, having put a padlock on my private zoo,
When there was the delicate, left-out giraffe peering through
    the door.

I had to give in, I had to yield, I had to laugh—
One cannot leave out anything, one simply cannot:
If you do, you'll find the shingles of your house, in lieu
    of leaves, attracting the giraffe.

This demoiselle with a neck so long it sways
Lets her hobbled body crumple forward as it moves,
Too thin at the same time that her style is cramped by stays.

Go up to the second story, look the elongated darling in the face,
Tell her life is short and art is very, very long,
And, lacking elevator shoes to love her, you have, alas, not acted
    altogether in good grace.

It is good for art and even better for the soul
To climb up where the left-out have to look
And wear forever their tender, alienated faces on a pole.

No doubt the door cannot always be kept open, just in hope, just
    by chance,
Yet nothing but good can come of a quick, redemptive trip upstairs
For the high and lonely view of those who must conduct on stilts
    their version of romance.

The Writer and His Region

J. FRANK DOBIE

"They were made for singing and nae for printing," an old woman of the Highlands said to Sir Walter Scott when he presented her with a copy of his border ballads. This piece was made for speaking to the Texas Institute of Letters at its annual dinner in Dallas, November 11, 1949. Some parts of it were not written out. In finishing it, at the request of the editor of the SOUTHWEST REVIEW, *for publication, I have omitted a few side remarks and filled in several observations.*

GOOD WRITING about any region is good only to the extent that it has universal appeal. Texans are the only "race of people" known to anthropologists who do not depend upon breeding for propagation. Like princes and lords, they can be made by "breath," plus a big white hat—which comparatively few Texans wear. A beef stew by a cook in San Antonio, Texas, may have a different flavor from that of a beef stew cooked in Pittsburgh, Pennsylvania, but the essential substances of potatoes and onions, with some suggestion of beef, are about the same, and geography has no effect on their digestibility.

A writer—a regional writer, if that term means anything—will whenever he matures exercise the critical faculty. I mean in the Matthew Arnold sense of appraisal rather than of praise, or, for that matter, of absolute condemnation. Understanding and sympathy are not eulogy. Mere glorification is on the same intellectual level as silver tongues and jukebox music.

In using that word *intellectual*, one lays himself liable to the accusation of having forsaken democracy. For all that, "fundamental brainwork" is behind every respect-worthy piece of writing, whether it be a lightsome lyric that seems as careless as a redbird's flit or a formal epic, an impressionistic essay or a great novel that measures the depth of human destiny. Nonintellectual literature is as nonexistent as education without mental discipline. Billboards along the highways of Texas advertise certain towns and cities as "cultural centers." No chamber of commerce, of course, would consider advertising an intellectual center—not because it does not exist. The culture of a nineteenth-century finishing school for young ladies was divorced from intellect, but a true culture, beyond the sociological use of the word, is always informed by intellect. The American populace has been taught to believe that the more intellectual a professor is, the less common sense he has; nevertheless, if American democracy is preserved it will be preserved by thought and not by physics.

Editors of all but a few magazines of the country and publishers of most of the daily newspapers cry out for brightness and vitality and at the same time shut out critical ideas. They want intellect, but want it petrified. Happily, the publishers of books have not yet reached that form of delusion. In an article entitled "What Ideas Are Safe?" in the *Saturday Review of Literature* for November 5, 1949, Henry Steele Commager says:

If we establish a standard of safe thinking, we will end up with no thinking at all. . . . We cannot . . . have thought half slave and half free. . . . A nation which, in the name of loyalty or of patriotism or of any sincere and high-sounding ideal, discourages criticism and dissent, and puts a premium on acquiescence and conformity, is headed for disaster.

Unless a writer feels free, things will not come to him, he cannot burgeon on any subject whatsoever.

One hundred and fifty years ago Davy Crockett's Autobiography was published. It is one of the primary social documents of America. It is as much Davy Crockett, whether going ahead after bears in a Tennessee canebrake or going ahead after General Andrew Jackson in Congress, as the equally plain but also urbane Autobiography of Franklin is Benjamin Franklin. It is undiluted regionalism. It is provincial not only in subject but in point of view.

No provincial mind of this day could possibly write an autobiography or any other kind of book co-ordinate in value with Crockett's "classic in homespun." In his time, Crockett could exercise intelligence and still retain his provincial point of view. Provincialism was in the air over his land. In these changed times, something in the ambient air prevents any active intelligence from being unconscious of lands, people, struggles far beyond any province.

Not long after the Civil War, in Harris County, Texas, my father heard a bayou-billy yell out:

Whoopee! Raised in a canebrake and suckled by a she-bear!
The click of a sixshooter is music to my ear!
The further up the creek you go, the worse they git,
And I come from the head of it! Whoopee!

If it were now possible to find some section of country so far up above the forks of the creek that the owls mate there with the chickens, and if this section could send to Congress one of its provincials untainted by the outside world, he would, if at all intelligent, soon after arriving on Capitol Hill become aware of interdependencies between his remote province and the rest of the world.

Biographies of regional characters, stories turning on local customs, novels based on an isolated society, books of history and fiction going back to provincial simplicity will go on being written and published. But I do not believe it possible that a good one will henceforth come from a mind that is regional in outlook, a mind that does not in outlook transcend the region on which it is focused. This is not to imply that the processes of evolution have brought all parts of the world into such interrelationships that a writer cannot depict the manners and morals of a community up Owl Hoot Creek without enmeshing it with the complexities of Lake Success. Awareness of other times and other wheres, not insistence on that awareness, is the requisite. James M. Barrie said that he could not write a play until he got his people off on a kind of island, but had he not known about the mainland he could never have delighted us with the islanders—islanders, after all, for the night only. Patriotism of the right kind is still a fine thing; but, despite all gulfs, canyons, and curtains that separate nations, those nations and their provinces are all increasingly interrelated.

No sharp line of time or space, like that separating one century from another or the territory of one nation from that of another, can delimit the boundaries of any region to which any regionalist lays claim. Mastership, for instance, of certain locutions peculiar to the Southwest will take their user to the Aztecs, to Spain, and to the border of ballads and Sir Walter Scott's romances. I found that I could not comprehend the coyote as animal hero of Pueblo and Plains Indians apart from the Reynard of Aesop and Chaucer.

In a noble opinion respecting censorship and freedom of the press, handed down on March 18, 1949, Judge Curtis Bok of Pennsylvania said:

It is no longer possible that free speech be guaranteed Federally and denied locally; under modern methods of instantaneous communication such a discrepancy makes no sense. . . . What is said in Pennsylvania may clarify an issue in California, and what is suppressed in California may leave us the worse in Pennsylvania. Unless a restriction on free speech be of national validity, it can no longer have any local validity whatever.

Among the qualities that any good regional writer has in common with other good writers of all places and times is intellectual integrity. Having it does not obligate him to speak out on all issues or, indeed, on any issue. He alone is to judge whether he will continue to sport with Amaryllis in the shade or forsake here to write his own Areopagitica. Intellectual integrity expresses itself in the tune as well as in argument, in choice of words—words honest and precise—as well as in ideas, in fidelity to human nature and the flowers of the fields as well as to principles, in facts reported more than in deductions proposed. Though a writer write on something as innocuous as the white snails that crawl up broomweed stalks and that roadrunners are wont to carry to certain rocks to crack and eat, his intellectual integrity, if he has it, will infuse the subject.

Nothing is too trivial for art, but good art treats nothing in a trivial way. Nothing is too provincial for the regional writer, but he cannot be provincial-minded toward it. Being provincial-minded may make him a typical provincial; it will prevent him from being a representative or skillful interpreter. Horace Greeley said that when the rules of the English language got in his way, they did not stand a chance. We may be sure that if by violating the rules of syntax Horace Greeley sometimes added forcefulness to his editorials, he violated them deliberately and not in ignorance. Luminosity is not stumbled into. The richly savored and deliciously unlettered speech of Thomas Hardy's rustics—the very cream of rusticity—was the creation of a master architect who had looked out over the ranges of fated mankind and looked also into hell. Thomas Hardy's ashes were placed in Westminster Abbey, but his heart, in accordance with a provision of his will, was buried in the churchyard of his own village.

I have never tried to define regionalism. Its blanket has been put over a great deal of worthless writing. Robert Frost has approached a satisfying conception. "The land is always in my bones," he said—the land of rock fences. But, "I am not a regionalist. I am a realmist. I write about realms of democracy and realms of the spirit." Those realms include The Woodpile, The Grindstone, Blueberries, Birches, and many other features of the land North of Boston.

To an extent, any writer anywhere must make his own world, no matter whether in fiction or nonfiction, prose or poetry. He must make something out of his subject. What he makes depends upon his creative power, integrated with a sense of form. The popular restriction of creative writing to fiction and verse is illogical. Carl Sandburg's life of Lincoln is immeasurably more creative in form and substance than his fanciful *Potato Face*. Intense exercise of this creative power sets, in a way, the writer apart from the life he is trying to sublimate. Becoming a Philistine will not enable a man to interpret Philistinism, though Philistines who own big presses think so. Sinclair Lewis knew Babbitt as Babbitt could never know either himself or Sinclair Lewis.

There is no higher form of art and, therefore, no higher form of patriotism than translating the features of the patria into forms of dignity, beauty, and nobility. I would not trade Roy Bedichek's chapters on the mockingbird for all the essays and orations that the Fourth of July has occasioned during the past one hundred and seventy-five years.

In an essay on "The Spirit of the Place," D. H. Lawrence—whom I do not consider a very wise soul but who sometimes penetrated truth—said: "Men are free when they are in a living homeland, not when they are straying and breaking away." What is the spirit, the tempo, the rhythm of this plot of earth to which we belong and as writers endeavor to express? Often it seems that the essential spirit has been run over and killed. But nature is as inexorable, as passionless, and as patient in revenge as she is in fidelity to "the heart that loves her." In the long run, she cannot be betrayed by man; in the long run, man can betray only himself by not harmonizing with her.

Wise Mary Austin, who was a true prophet of the Land of Little Rain, held that "no man has ever really entered into the heart of any country until he has adopted or made up myths about its familiar objects"; until, that is, he has achieved a sympathetic understanding, based on both knowledge and feeling, of the land's features, animate as well as inanimate. As an interpreter of the spirit of the Southwest, John

Joseph Mathews of the Osages and the blackjacks belongs in the small company that Mary Austin heads. The sage of his *Sundown* says, talking to his own people:

You are Indian. You are part of this earth here like trees, like rabbit, like birds. Our people built their lodges here. That which came out of ground into their feet and over their bodies into their hands, they put into making of their lodges. They made songs out of that which came out of ground into their bodies. Those lodges were good and beautiful. Those songs were good and beautiful. . . . White man came out of ground across the sea. His thoughts are good across the sea. His houses are beautiful across the sea, I believe. His houses are ugly here because they did not come out of this earth.

Probably few Americans, as we call ourselves, will ever belong to the land as intimately as some of the American Indians belonged, will ever let the rhythms of the earth—Mary Austin's phrase—so seep into their natures. Yet not all the houses are as ugly as they were. The more modern architecture becomes, the more do dwellings seem to "come out of this earth." The other kind of architecture and the way of life represented by that other kind of architecture put population into fast-running cars and faster-flying airplanes. Man, however, has no prospect of a machine that will fly him away from himself. Though he were to become so entirely a product of machinery that he could subsist on Coca-Cola and protein tablets, they still come from the earth that he came from and is bound to. Actually, hardly an individual wants to escape the earth, but regard the mass of us: We spend our prime energies building cities and then spend what's left trying to escape the progress we have made. Many a time while paying four or five dollars for a two-dollar noisy hotel room I have wished that by doubling the price I could be transported to a blanket on mesquite grass somewhere where the crickets chirp. Happiness is a state of being in harmony with one's environment.

During World War I Frederick Russell Burnham, as he tells in *Scouting on Two Continents*, was searching for manganese in the mountains of California. He grubstaked various old prospectors to search. One day one of them on a high mountain amid desert desolation, after sitting a long while in silence as he was wont to sit, leaned toward Burnham and said: "The mountains are all whispering to me. If I could only understand."

Writers will always be listening for the rhythms of their living places. Whatever the rhythm of our part of the earth is, not one of us will catch it unless we can sometimes sit in "wise passiveness" and hear "tidings of invisible things."

The tidings we are after are both visible and invisible, both audible and inaudible. It is not easy to get the right words, but getting them calls for less acuteness than getting the essential rhythm. One may read *Deserts on the March* and study mountains of documents on erosion, restoration of grasses, and plant ecology and thereby become a useful technician, but the rhythm of the grasses and of the soil that grows them cannot be documented.

Much noise has made it retreat. The mass productions of press, radio, and film have made the West a place of roaring guns, men with tense grim tones, and action—action always. You have to go out into remoteness to find the rhythms that belong.

Sam Galloway, O. Henry's "Last of the Troubadours," never "sat up when he could lie down and never stood when he could sit." He was a great hand to linger. For the cowman in Andy Adams's novel there was always "ample time." Frederic Remington painted many pictures of Western action, but he never painted an action picture that catches the Spirit of the Place as does a little-known one of his called "The Blue Bird." It shows an Indian who has been walking in the forest standing with hands raised in a kind of prayer of thankfulness at sight of the first bluebird of spring.

For me at least, the buzzard expresses better the tempo of the land than any airplane trying to run him down. One time, as an old Negro tale tells, a buzzard was sailing slow, around and around, in great circles high in the air.

A hawk arrowing by him paused to say, "What are you waiting round for, Brother Buzzard?"

"I'm awaiting the will of God," the buzzard replied, and he sailed on slow and majestical.

After a while the hawk shot by again. "Come with me," he said. "Let's get going and catch some meat."

"No, I thank you," the buzzard said. "I await the will of God." He sailed on as easy as a cottonwood leaf floating on glass-smooth water.

A third time the hawk shot into the buzzard's circle. "Old Slow Thing," he said, "I'm going to show you how to get meat. See that mockingbird perched way down yonder on that sharp stob of the dead tree?"

"I see," said the buzzard. "In the sand right under the mockingbird a thousandlegs is curled up."

"Now, Brother Buzzard, watch me." And the hawk bulleted straight for the mockingbird.

But somehow he missed his aim. Just as he was at the target, the mockingbird flew and the hawk rammed his breast against the stob of the dead tree. He fell to the ground dead. The buzzard, still unhurried, began to shorten the circle of his flight. Slowly, slowly, he spiraled groundward. He had awaited the will of God.

Two kinds of people of this world have each with their kind deep kinships, no matter what language they speak or in what latitude they live: people with cultivated minds and people of the soil. An old Indian of Tutepec in Oaxaca had the rhythm that belongs to all places where shade is gracious. Down there in Oaxaca every man's house has a *ramada* (a shed), and every *ramada* is hung with hammocks. I had come to know this old Indian and one afternoon as I approached his house he arose from his hammock to welcome me. He motioned me to the hammock beside his, and as we reclined in harmony, he said, "Señor, isn't God good! He gives us the nights to sleep in and the days to rest in."

Tempo, like anything else, can be overstressed. The writer of a region can never know enough about it. He has to know how far "a fur piece" is and how long "after a while" may be. He has to know how deep the shadow on the rock lies and sometimes what "maybe so" denies. He has to know so much that as he writes he will be constantly obliged to exercise that most difficult of arts—the "art of omission."

Only sympathy, acting through knowledge, can unlock for him some of the knowable, though invisible, realities. Two skillful writers are now writing the history of a certain oil company. This company has taken a great deal of oil from the old Tom O'Connor ranch on the Texas coast. Oil is a tremendous fact in the economy of the world. A kind of oil culture dominates Texas with more force than cattle ever dominated it. It is mighty. It is a mighty subject for writing, but only the devil would want to pipe it into the green pastures of heaven. After all the oil has been pumped from beneath the surface of O'Connor land, the grasses will still be green there and wave in the Gulf breeze as they waved thousands of years before Cabeza de Vaca walked across them. The history of the oil company will contain many facts. It can hardly be expected to suggest the sympathy for the land that Tom O'Connor had.

He had deeds to scores of sections of lands and he owned ten thousand cattle on the prairies and in the brush, and now Old Tom O'Connor could no longer ride across the sea of grass and watch his cattle thrive. One day he told his boss, Pat Lambert, to take all hands out early the next morning and bring in the biggest herd they could gather. To Pat Lambert, early morning always meant by four o'clock. After he and his hands had ridden out a ways, they stopped to wait for daylight. They rode hard and they rode far, and about an hour before sundown they drove a vast herd of mixed cattle to the holding and cutting grounds not far from the O'Connor ranch house. Bulls were challenging, cows were bawling, steers and stags were bellowing, calves were bleating. Heifers, yearlings, old moss-horned steers, all ages of cattle of both sexes, were milling about, their blended voices rising above the dust from their hooves.

While some of the hands held the herd and others changed horses, Pat Lambert went into the room where Tom O'Connor lay on his bed.

"We made a big drag, Mr. Tom," he said.

"I hear them," Tom O'Connor replied. His voice was thin.

"What do you want me to do with them, Mr. Tom?"

"Nothing. Just hold them there. I'm dying, Pat, and I want to go out with natural music in my ears."

Christy

WILLIAM GOYEN

WHAT WAS THIS MAN with a long hound-face and a glistening silver eye? His image is teardrops of bird's blood speckled on his denimed thigh, a waist girdled by a wreath of small dead birds. And about his image there resounds an echo of frenchharp music and of clashing beaks of horn.

Christy was big and had dark wrong blood and a glistening beard, the bones in his russet Indian cheeks were thick and arched high and they curved round the deep eye-cavities where two great silver eyes shaped like bird's eggs were set in deep, half-closed lids furred round by grilled lashes that laced together and locked over his eyes.

He was a hunting man; and hunted; and his mother Granny Ganchion was a shaggy old falcon that had caught him like a surrendered bird and held him close to her, home; as though he had been hunted in his own hunting, the hunter hunted; and captured: by trap or talon; or treed; or set or pointed at and stalked in his own secret woods and brought home, driven toward stall and what forage, at nightfall, to her, the hunter's huntress. He had one friend before me, he said, and that was his mother (O cries into a deaf world!) who could not hear him, only read off his lips his agony that lay so fair and lovely, trembling on his full wiener-colored lips. He had just talked so long into deafness that he came to judge the whole world deaf, and so he no longer said anything much (could or would he be heard?)—it was what he didn't say that said what he said (I think I know now what he didn't say). He became a man of gestures: shrugging his humped shoulders under his workshirt like a big bag carried there; waving his long arms with raveled strips of fingers, long-nailed and hanging down at the end of his arms like the raveling of arms (the isinglass nails shaped like oval shells were bent over sharp and tough like rooster's spurs); throwing his great dark head from side to side or tossing it up and down in horse movements; and, in his despairs, heaving up in the air the whole huge bouyant winged upper portion of his body, arms and torso, like enormous agitating wings of a huge and sinewed man-angel.

Christy made everything seem like an evil secret—the songs he sang to his guitar: "Write me a letter, send it by mail; send it in care of Birmingham Jail . . . ," and he would be in jail singing this song because he had done something wrong in the woods or with the Mexicans. He had a circumcisional-like scar, pink and folded, on his brown neck over which he would gently rub his fingers and tell me how it was a knifecut because of a woman. When Christy yodeled, flashing his silver eye, "You get a line, I'll get a pole; we'll go fishin in a crawdad hole, Ba-abe . . . " he was telling me long long stories of woods-meetings. He would go off hunting, leaving me behind and wondering ("One day when you're old enough I'll take you hunting with me, we'll go hunting, Boy") and then come back to us as though he had been in some sorrow in the woods, with bird's blood on him and a bouquet of small wilted doves hanging from his waist over his thigh, or a wreath of shot creatures: small birds with rainbowed necks, a squirrel with a broken mouth of agony. Then he would come to me and speak, for he had found words, "Listen Boy, listen; come out to the woodshed with me quick and let me show you somethin, come with me quick; by Gum I've got somethin . . ." What would he show me if I went?

They said around Charity that he was a niggerlover; they said he was a KuKlux; they said he was adopted by Granny Ganchion and was a no-good Peepin Tom whose parents were probably foreigners or Jews or thieves in the Pen; and some of this was true and he was bad. But after he dived down into the river and found Otey his wife and brought her up to the shore, drowned, he was a changed, good man.

Christy played a frenchharp out in the woodshed caught in his cuddling, trembling raveled hands, blowing and sucking sounds and calls like birds and moaning voices of animals, or making wind sounds, train sounds, chiming sounds, tinkling and tinny trumpet sounds; and I remember hearing these in my bed like a mystic music played from the moon that rocked like an azure boat in our sky framed by my window. Everything Christy never said was whispered, lipped, blown into his frenchharp; and his pale lips curled like some obscene membrane; or like the workings of fishes' mouths that might be saying something under water.

He had had a little wife named Otey and they had lived some time together in a shack up the road beyond the House; then they both went home again, she to her folks at Clodeen and he back to Granny Ganchion. Otey had big daisy eyes, yellow with lashes like sun rays radiating from the hazel centers; and a sunlight shone from them. But her hands were long and frail and purplish, shaped like frogfeet, with tiny white bones white under the skin. O her frail frogfeet hands holding a bouquet of Cups and Saucers brought from the fields to Granny Ganchion (who always sneezed immediately). (Granny would say Christy what's the matter with Otey, she's as white as a pile of chalk; she's just tarred, Mama, Christy would say. She's such a sunk-in little thing, all bowed over. I don't see how she's worth much at her chores, that Otey's sick, Christy, her skin's real crepy.)

They would come down the sandy road, Christy deep in his silence, Otey's bare feet glad in the cool yellow sand of the old wagon road, coming bent over, and good, down the road to the house. Christy would say Otey we got to go and be with Mama, Mama's lonesome. Then they would come on down to us and Christy and Granny'd just sit, not saying a word much, Granny uttering her *uck uck* sounds because of her goitre, that sounded like an old setting hen safe with her eggs.

Sometimes if they didn't come, Granny would say why don't Christy come down to see me; why don't none of my children ever come to see me. And then she would send me up the road after Christy. I would find him setting on their little porch, huge and quiet, and Otey no place to be found. Then Christy would call into the trees for her, sounding her name through all the woods; and finally she would come very softly and bent over from the trees, holding some wood she had gathered. "We got to go down to the house, Otey," he'd say. "Mama wants us." I know that while he sat on the little porch of his shack in the woods, voices called to him come home come home, and that the doves moaned this and the owls hooted it, come home come home; and that I must have seemed to him like another bird when I came to him from the house calling they want you home.

There was a long time of waiting when I knew I was being prepared for something. And then, finally, it was the time Christy had whispered about. We rose early and went away into the woods in a blue, wet world to hunt together. The sky was streaked like broken agate, as if the huge bowl were porcelain or agate and had cracked; and it seemed there were

100

no clouds anywhere in the world. Christy and I were sleepwalkers going away from a house of breath and dream. The sound of a chopping ax echoed in the acoustics of the agate heavens. I was so afraid; we were going, it seemed, toward some terrible mission in the woods. The sad, dirty face of Clegg's house looked at us as we passed it.

A fragile melodious Oriental language blew in on the wind like the odor of a flower and we saw the string of smoke from a gypsy camp somewhere in the woods. The sliding of our feet in the road flushed a flutter of wings from the bush. The fields were alive with things rushing and running; winged and legged things were going where they would, no engine or human to stop them. Out in the fields under the thick brush and in the grass and green were myriad unseen small things that were running or resting from running. Under the trees as we went we swept back the webs and broke them as we went. What was this terrifying rising of something in me, like a rising of fluid? Some wild and mourning thing was calling and claiming me. It was autumn and the time of the killing of hogs; there were wild squeals in the distance. Dandelions whirled like worlds of light . . . hickory nuts were falling.

We climbed a little hill and he stood for a moment on the hill, all his life breaking with loneliness and memory inside him, looking down on the country of Charity behind and the river ahead like the wolf in the picture in Aunty's room. As we came down the hill on the river's side we were walking down the slopes of the strangest, yellowest world to a wide field that seemed the color of a pheasant's wing. And then a bird appeared. Instantaneously Christy shot it dead. He picked it up and went on.

And then we came into the bottomlands where the palmettos were turning yellow. At the river, which seemed to have just waked and was clucking in its cradle, we saw the leaves falling into the river. Now not a living creature ran or rustled. There was only the occasional comma of dropped cones punctuating the long flowing syntax of the river's sentence. Then the river bent and we followed it, and there the river was drugged in the early morning and creeping so slowly that where many leaves had fallen and gathered the river seemed a river of leaves.

Once we saw, in the sand, the prints of knees left by someone who had kneeled and drunk from the river; and then I saw Christy get down on his hands and knees and drink like a beast from the river, and I saw the signs his body left there.

We walked along under the ragged trees and pieces of them were forever falling falling about us as we went; as though the world was raveling into pieces and falling upon us as we went, Christy ahead, silent and huge under his hunting cap, his isinglass nails shining, and I behind, afraid and enchanted. No fishes were making the noise that sounds like a rock dropping in the water; only a watermoccasin, once, was skiffing along soundlessly with his brown head erect like the head of an arrow. We were going through the ruin and falling away of dreams, Christy and I . . .

And then a purring, gurgling sound came as if it were the river; but it was Christy's frenchharp.

We passed a muscadine vine with grapes that had some silvery frenchharp music's breath blown on them. There was the sound of the hopping of birds on leaves.

And then Christy suddenly shot at a turtle that looked like a rock, and got him.

He shot again and a dove fell, followed by the falling blessing of feathers. He looked at me, asking me to pick up the fallen dove. I picked it up, ruined. We went on.

We were going after all marvelous things; silently; he going ahead blowing and sucking his frenchharp; I behind, timid, and terrified and marching in an enchantment by the music in the woods. For a time he was leading me like a piper to the River; and for a time I was following in a kind of glory, and eager, and surrendered, and wanting to follow— just as he was, in his own dumb sorcery and splendor, leading me, victor, proud, like a captive. But the uncaptured, unhypnotized part of me was afraid and reluctant, wanting to run home (where was home to run to, toward where?); for I knew he was leading me to a terrible dialogue in the deepest woods. All his hunting, all his shooting and gathering up of shot birds was a preparation—like a meditation in which there is a collection of words, for prayer or protestation or farewell or betrayal—in which he would tell me some terrible secret. In it he would finally, after making me wait until I was almost mad with desire for words from him, tell me all the Evil that there could be and be had, in the world; and I would have no one to tell it to, to contain it, just as he had had no one, only the hunt and this boy. But until the moment of speech in the deepest shadowed woods where it seemed we would be in a cistern, let down alone together for this terrible revelation of secrets, Christy's silence was the ringing starry soundlessness of night in the woods, of deafness got

102

from his mother. (I carried his Evil News for years within me until now I tell it: steal Joy he told me, rob it out of the world, find it! suffer for it but steal Joy like a thief of despair.) Now the River flowed like his own wordless speech.

We looked across the River toward the ahead . . . long flat brown land . . . and we wanted separately and silently to start across the field away toward something ahead. He said to me fly away from here . . . I give you these bird's wings to fly away with from here where we are all just the sawed off ends of old tubafours rottin on a sawdust heap; fly up and away, across the River past Riverside and on away. And what brings you down will be what gave you wings to fly up and away, will be what needs to use you to speak with; be bird, be word. (Yet as we went come home come ho-o-me the voices called. The doves moaned this and the owls hooted it, come home come ho-o-me . . .)

But when I would run home, what would there be for me to do? Only set by Mama while she rocked and hear her go uck uck in her throat and watch the goitre sliding up and down under her lank skin, rising and falling. But in the woods I had my life . . . and in some other places.

Toward the River—across! The birds! What went by? Wings! O wing me over! Come over come over let Christy come over! Hell -o! Hell-ooo! Listen to the echo O-O-O! suffering from the other side. But Boy we'll send you over. Let me shoot you like a shining cartridge over the river and into the fields of the world.

But now let us go . . . we are going after it, what we never had. If it lies across the River, I cannot cross the River. O Bird! Wing me over the River! This young brightness following me will one day cross the River for all of us, we will send him over. I will tell him to go, by killing the next bird I will tell him to . . . there's the wing of a dove, sounds like a flying frenchharp . . . got it by Gum, look at the falling wings, look look at the falling wings! Let Boy run to get it like any birddog. Hey young sad birddog, Hey Birddog!

To wash out my mind of all these remembrances—who can I tell, to get rid of them to? Boy will listen, he is just nothing but a little quiet listener, I'll tell him, tell him with words when the moment comes. It will be in the Thicket and he will be waitin for it, he is always waitin to hear. Children are the ones to tell things to, they are the only keepers of secrets in the world. I'll tell Boy. (Hey Birddog!)

WILLIAM GOYEN

I remember an Owal. I remember a blue Owal in a grotto by the bend of this river. I saw him at twilight as we were headin home from our huntin trip, Walter Warren, Ollie Cheatham and myself; first I *felt* somethin in there, then I looked and it was the blue Owal. I never told anyone, but I knew there was an Owal in there. I've remembered that Owal for years, for fifteen years that Owal has been in the grotto of my memory, settin there blue and still. What does anything settin like that mean? What does Mama mean, sittin there in that house? in that cellar? There's a meanin, there's a meanin!

Onetime we stood on a hill and looked down at the crawling river below. There were animals down there, I don't know what kind, couldn't make em out, but I could *feel* animals down there. There was a huge moon about to bust in the sky. Suddenly lookin down there, with the moon heavy over me and the animals movin around below, I felt somethin that had been like this before, way back somewhere, the way you do, you know, the same kind of feelin—it was in Derider Loosiana when we was all there and kids, and Pappa was travelin for the rayroad; and one night in my room I was waked up by the *feelin* of the sky pressin down on me, as though it was hot and soft and pressin down on me, and of somethin movin, some life of some kind rustlin around me, and I went to the winda and looked out to see this big lopsided moon about to bust in the sky and across in the next house I saw a bare arm reach out from a bed and slowly pull down the shade. As the shade was comin down I saw legs wound around in a kind of fightin; and then the light went out. I squatted there and couldn't hear nothin, couldn't see nothin, but I knew there was some commotion of life goin on in there in that blinded room, I could *feel* it. (There's a meanin! there's a meanin!) And then I knew there was a fight goin on in the world—for things I dreamt of but never thought you could get but so wanted, so wanted. And then O I wanted to holler out because I was so clost to bustin like the moon, because I was so lonesome and so lonesome.

O Otey why did what happened have to happen? I married you too young. She lived in a house way back in some trees and was just a funny kind of bowed over girl (from carrying brothers and sisters on her hip) that hardly ever came out of the trees into town, with a lot of the yellowest cornsilky hair and a loose dress with no belt. Why didn't they tell her that when we married I would want to touch her? She screamed and ran from me that wedding night out the door and down the rayroad tracks and slipped on the ties and fell and cut over her eye that left a scar like a shriveled apricot. She was a rabbit in the house after I brought her back panting and damp from running, and bloody, and then I was dyin dyin to touch her and could have almost killed her in my hands she was so limp and little and white; but I said all right little Otey, I'll wait for you, I'll wait until you grow up big enough to be my wife. I was workin at the sawmill then, straw-bossin the niggers with the mules that pulled the logs from the kiln to the plane, through the black sawdust in the mud, surrounded by the tearin sound of the cuttin of the logs, like goods bein ripped all day long. I'd go home at dinner and she'd have good butterbeans and peppersauce and cornbread for me like I like and we'd eat and O Lord I'd want to touch her but I wouldn't. Then they sent me out to the Thicket with a crew to cut new timber and we stayed there for a whole month and I would not touch any niggers or any of the Indian squaws that lived on the reservation around there; and when I came back Otey was gone. She had run home; and I let her stay. I went home, back home and Mama said here is where you belong, come on back to this house with all of us. I never told that I had never touched her—and no one ever knew. But I'll tell Boy, this little listener will listen, I'll tell him when the time comes.

And all that winter I made a little ship inside a turpentine bottle.

And then one day Sam Riddle came to say three girls swimmin in the river by White Rock had fallen in a deep hole and they had got two out but the third was drowned and would I come help dive for the body. I went with them and got to the river and they said to me one of them is Otey Bell. I took off my clothes and dove in where they said she had sunk and went down down to China it seemed, prayin to touch Otey there, and in time; and Lord God I touched her. Then I opened my eyes quick and saw a sight I'll see in dreams until I die: Otey was sittin bent over like her head was on her knees in some sorrow, and nekkid, and I grabbed her hair, her beautiful cornsilky hair and crushed it in my hand for a second; and then I caught her hands with my hands and we were joined, just by our fingertips, so lightly, and came up slowly slowly. It was so long coming up, like a lifetime of Otey and me being together in darkness, alone and not saying a word—but the bubbles of our breath were bathing us, we were wrapped in the bubbles of our breath, and they were our words speaking for us—and I prayed Lord Lord don't let me lose Otey, don't let her get away this time, because she had surrendered to me at last, she was mine, my wife now; and came up with me so quietly without fighting, and I was nekkid with her. Bubbles of her last breath rose and sprayed my loins and clung to the hairs on me like diamonds breathed out by her and we must have looked beautiful to fishes in our underwater marriage, glittering with diamonds of breath and rising nekkid and touching ever so lightly at our fingertips together, joined and flowing into each other, up to the shore. As we rose up together all our life that we never had together happened in me—Otey cooking and singing in our warm winter kitchen and me chopping wood in the mornings. As we floated up through watery vines and ferns and slippery roots through scales and petals of sunlit water, layers breaking over us as we broke through them like thin leaves of silver, I remembered that a hand does let down to you if you get lonesome and lost enough, that a big broken bird-bloodied hand does reach down to you, wet and alone and so lonesome; and that you are washed clean by the touch of this hand. And as we came something suddenly burst inside me and this was for Otey, a love for Otey, drowned but rescued Otey. I did get to the top with her and then those on the banks saw what it was and Jim Moody yelled Christy's found her and jumped in to help but I was nearly passed out and thought they were trying to take Otey away from me, and this time it seemed she wanted to stay with me, even nekkid, and I fought them off like a wildcat. Then Jim Moody hit me hard up against the head and that was all I remembered till I woke up lyin out on the bank with the feeling of Otey's fingertips on my fingertips. And I looked over to see the three boys rollin poor Otey over a log to try to get the river-water out of her lungs; but Otey was drownded dead.

When I was young because I was big and bighanded they used me like a plowox—but I had in me the beautiful thing that could happen to me. Something is over us, flies over us, always over us, and we must bring it down for ourselves; something is under down under and we must bring it up for ourselves and for everybody.

I was mean and wrong and unused until my one great moment that lasted all my lifetime, it seemed, going down to find Otey—now I know what going down to find anything means: go *down*, Boy, after what is folded over like a child of sorrow, egg in its womb, and is all your life and love never had for your own, never owned but always waiting to embrace and hold warm to you, and *bring it up*, pulling it up with all the strength you've got in you to pull up anything with, holding it just by your fingernails (that I bit them, once!), bring it up through all the darkness of the world, through all the circles of Hell, to the top and deliver it, though gone, though unbreathing and dead, retrieved and brought home to you where it has always belonged, to the rescuers of the perished on the shore. For below the level where we are nothing but nekkid murmurings and whisperings over the world, only breath breathing dialogues in bubbles: remembering and yearning, grieving and desiring, we are the life that lasts in us and has its meaning in us all; we touch there where we have never touched before, in the world where we can touch and join and enter into one another forever.

We had come into the deepest gloom of woods, vaulted by enormous pinetrees, called the Thicket, and I knew it was time. I had a large garland of birds Christy had shot and I had run to gather up like flowers in a wild enchantment . . . how long had we been hunting? We were standing by a pool of the river. I looked at my quivering image in the pool, throbbing as if the pool were breathing through me. A purple snake glided over my image and Christy shot it, tearing my image into pieces.

And then he sat down on a stump, looking as tired as if he had lived all the ages, and with such a longing and such an ageing in his face that I backed away . . . for he looked like a beast in the woods, shaggy and gray and fierce. Yet some enormous tenderness was rising out of him. His look asked for something that I could not give because I had not learned how to give it.

I backed away, backed away and he sat still on the stump. He pointed his gun at me to shoot me like a bird; and I backed away. And then he lowered his gun and watched me and let me get away; and then I ran.

I ran and ran and felt myself melting down as I ran, but I would not cry. It was toward twilight and soon it would be dark. O which way was home? The sun was setting. I ran and ran.

All the woods were now saying the same things to me that I had heard during the long timeless hunt with Christy. Something like stars was twinkling in my loins. I prayed. Moss hung from trees like long hair and I saw the little green fuzz on rocks. What would I ever do with all this that had been said to me, now that Christy knew I knew all this? I would pray against it. I walked praying through the woods. O which way was home? The sad dusk was falling, and I was lost, lost. There was a kind of purring of the woods before dark. Which way was home? I had left Christy alone in the woods and night was coming. I called Christy Christy! but only the woods, faraway, called him too; and he did not answer. Then I cried Christy Christy come home, come ho-o-me! Only an echo answered and no answer from Christy came. Some burden weighed upon me, some yoke around me.

I was by the river. There, in a place, I suddenly saw the print of Christy's body in the sand where he had kneeled down to drink, and I kneeled into it and drank as Christy had and felt at that moment that I was Christy drinking from our River. As I kneeled something swung against my face like petals of flowers and it was the birds Christy had shot and I had tied by their legs to a string, as fishermen do fish, and had laid them round my neck. I saw that I was dappled by the blood of birds and that the beaks had beaten against my bare arms as I had run and brought my blood there, mixed with the blood of the birds.

I ran on again with his yoke of birds swinging against me, Christy's message to me. I ran blessed with his yoke of loves, of words, his long sentence in words of birds, bloody and broken and speechless, enchained in links of colored feathers and closed little eyes and beaks and limp frail feet, sentences of his language shot out of his air and off his trees' boughs that were his words' vocabulary: flying words that call at twilight and twilight, nest and hatch and fly free, yet caged in his own birdcage mind, freed by hand, brought down solid and sullied by beebee shot from his air by his own aim and fire (misfire!).

I ran with his yoke of birds quivering upon me blessing me and marking me. How would I ever wash away all this blood of birds? O now he was bird and I was bird, he was my truth and my untruth, he was my victim, he contained me, I possessed him.

Now it was dark and I was full of fears. In a pond I passed, the moon lay fallen and small and mean among weeds and fallen branches. All birds were calling and returning to bough or nest without Christy there to try to shoot them, safe and homing at nightfall. O who would welcome me home when I finally got home?

Now the woods seemed a huge web that held Christy like a caught insect in it. Now I really *loved* Christy, longed for him, calling to him (O where was he?). We had come to the woods in a dream and in a quick dream he had faded away from me. The ripe cracking of his gunshot like the splitting of a ripe tree fired in my head. That I betrayed

Christy! That I failed him in the woods, he who gave me all these gifts of birds, who spoke for the first time to me and waited for me to answer. To whom would I answer, to whom in the House would I answer when I came back, over the sea of bitterweeds of Bailey's Pasture riding in home, bottled news to be broken against the hands of the House that sealed it? What he had put into me, through my eyes, through my ears, and marked and strained upon my body was to be carried *away*, through the bitterweeds, across the River and into the world to be read out to the world. If I could only find him again to tell him this, for he would want to know. I called his name into the woods that he had called his own names into—Christy! Christy!—but no answer came back, only my own calling hurled back into my ears.

I was by the river and so tired with all the weight of the birds. And then I knew what I must do with the birds . . . I flung them into the river. They went down, a flotilla of feathers, like a floating garden, like a wreath to the river drowned, for Otey for Christy for all of us. I washed in the river. And then I felt so light with all my burden and I lay down close to the river's side, and slept.

Suddenly I woke in touch with something in the air. Something called, something hovered, hard and real and whole as a soaring bird. O birdcursed, birdblessed, birddrenched me . . . he is all my Sin and all my Vision and all my searching calling back to me, claiming me. Just when I am free and clean and myself again I hear this voice, I know this hovering . . . in my ascensions like wings from a bough that I think are up and away from him I am only soaring up to him . . . he is my net, he is my air, he receives me, I fly back to him.

For I am in these woods again (but there is a clearing ahead where the river turns and flows, cuts through the trees, shall I follow it?) where there seems and seemed to be no time nor past nor future, where once I was lost for the first time away from the House and Kin—homing! how homing? O home me! where?—and thought of all them, back there, Granny and Aunty and Malley and all the rest. Who am I, separated from all of them and from home, yet with the idea of them and the idea of home in my mind, claimed and cursed by these, blessed and marked, sent somewhere?

There is the river, over I must . . . across I'll go.

Oh Christy make us real, make us hard and real in our sorrow: we who walk up and down in this autumn, trying to make ourselves real.

WILLIAM GOYEN   109

We are involved, we are involved; and we cannot break away. All the history that we saw on the map in the kitchen pours into us and we contain it, display it like a map for others to look at and be history. Go into the world, go build cities, go discover countries; go spread love, go give, go make magnificence, get and give light, save and join and piece together (as you did the bits of string and cloth and whittled wood to make your ship) and show a whole and put it, combined and formed and shaped, into the world like a bottle with a ship in it. Gather the broken pieces, connect them: these are the only things we have to work with. For we have been given a broken world to live in—make like a map a world where all things are linked together and murmur through each other like a line of whispering people like a chain of whispers a full clear statement, a singing, a round strong clear song of total meaning, a language within language, responding each to each forever in the memory of each man.

It was morning and a new, known world. I walked straight home, and as I came through Bailey's Pasture, stained with all my stains and feathers in my hair and clinging to my clothes, the wind blew the feathers from me over the pasture and the feathers fell on the bitterweeds. Ahead, in the woodshed, I saw Christy sitting there and whittling. He did not even look up as I came through the gate and went into the House. In the House Malley was sitting by the window and Granny was nowhere to be found. No one even seemed to know that I had ever been away, and Christy never mentioned it. We never went hunting again.

Spoonbread on a Woodstove

ALICE MARRIOTT

Drawings by MARGARET LEFRANC

MY highly personalized alarm clock goes off at seven every morning. Precisely on the moment of the hour, Elsie de Wolfe, Lady Mendl, who is a small blue Persian cat only to strangers, comes to the door that separates my bedroom from the kitchen and hall where she spends the night. Elsie scratches with the point of one claw on the lower panel of the door and retires expectantly to the kitchen. Our day has begun.

It's a regular New Mexico kitchen that I enter as I still struggle sleepily with the other sleeve of my dressing gown. The room is sixteen feet square, and its walls are whitewashed clean twice a year. The ceiling is supported on stripped trunks of white pine, and the boards above the rafters are the same as the boards in the floor. Between the sink-worktable and the window, Queen Christina sits majestically, waiting for me.

I bitterly refute the people who refer to Queen Christina as "your quaint, old-fashioned wood range." In the first place, Her Majesty of the Kitchen is not at all old-fashioned; she is the very latest model in white enamel and black iron, set off with the twinkling costume jewelry of chromium handles. She is anything but quaint; she is built exactly like the gas ranges in the city apartments of those same patronizing friends. And, most of all, Queen Christina is not, to me, merely a stove. She is a personality; she is militantly and unpredictably feminine as her namesake.

I shake down the ashes and fill the firebox with paper, kindling, chips, and a few sticks of juniper wood. I fill the teakettle with water and set it on the hottest spot on the stove top. I measure the coffee into the drip pot; a spoonful for a cup and one for the pot. Christina begins to produce small, pleasant, crackling sounds, and there are sparks of light flashing along her side where the draft of the firebox stands open.

Elsie gets the first meal of the day. Water from the teakettle, as soon as the first chill is off, poured over dog meal or Pablum, and stirred well. As soon as she begins to eat, I leave the kitchen and crawl back into bed. There's nothing else for me to do till the stove heats and the kettle boils.

Elsie finishes her breakfast and comes to sit on my chest. Together we wait dozily until there is a humming sound from the kitchen, a noise that pierces through and dominates the fire-sounds. Elsie and I roll out of bed, for keeps this time, and each of us takes up her day's work. Elsie goes into the next room to Martha's bed and knocks politely for the second time in the morning, drawing one claw along the footboard. She keeps this up until Martha turns back the covers. Then Elsie jumps up and sits for exactly ten minutes on Martha's chest.

Meanwhile I pour the boiling water into the top of the coffeepot. Then, while it drips, I raise the blind on the kitchen door and look out at the mountains to the east. This morning there is a slight haze of coming snow on the twin peaks of Truchas Mountain, and I decide that breakfast shall be eggs.

The coffee has dripped, and I pour myself a cup—that first, wonderful, half-stolen cup of coffee that is the best thing I shall taste all day. Then I get down to business.

I put little heavy earthenware bowls in a flat pan of water. Then a teaspoonful of butter goes in each bowl, and over the butter cut chives from the pot on the windowsill. Those are remarkable chives. I brought the parent plant from the East at Christmastime, as a present to a friend. The little pot of herbs survived three days of freezing weather in the car, and within a week it had put out so many shoots that my friend separated the plants and gave me back half of what I had given her. Wonderful things, chives, you can't kill them. So they grow and flourish on the windowsill.

Herbs and butter go, in their earthenware bowls, into the oven to warm. I squeeze orange juice and slice homemade bread for toast. Elsie canters through the doorway, her skunklike tail waving as a banner. Martha follows her, yawning. The family is assembled. Breakfast can begin.

The butter and herbs are bubbling just a little in the bowls. I break the eggs into the mixture and slide the pan back into the oven. The slices of bread go on the rack above the eggs. We drink our orange juice and Martha pours coffee. Then I lift out the pan that holds the egg bowls and place the ramekins on the table.*

Martha and I work for our livings, and we keep as close and as careful a schedule as if we went to offices, instead of going into separate rooms and shutting all communicating doors. We do our work in the country instead of in the city because our material is here, but we were city-living office-going wage-earners long before we became free-lancers, and certain habits persist. As soon as breakfast is over and the dishes are washed, we dress for the day, make our beds, and get busy.

*Eggs cooked this way taste better than fried eggs, and dietitians say that they are better for you. They have a taste of their own, and, with the bowls, you are never in danger of breaking the yolks and having them trickle dismally across the plates. You can vary the seasonings with these eggs; use basil or tarragon or parsley instead of chives, or sprinkle a little grated cheese and a dust of paprika over the tops of the eggs, or cut bits of bacon into the bowls to brown and get crisp before the eggs are added.

ALICE MARRIOTT   113

My office is in the kitchen, close by Christina's warm side. I add wood to the fire—slow-burning roots this time—and close the drafts. Then I start the lunch and settle down to work.

Lunch is usually soup, and it is the kind of soup you can't buy in cans. It is an old-fashioned *pot-au-feu*, with the bones of the roast and all the leftover vegetables in the pot, along with odd spoonfuls of gravy and a cup of tomato juice and the liquid from last week's ham—and more herbs. The soup pot stands on the very back edge of the stove and bubbles slowly, slowly. It is an iron pot that came over the Cumberland Trail from Tidewater Virginia to Tennessee a long time ago, and then kept on traveling west with generation-long stopovers in Arkansas and Oklahoma, until it reached New Mexico. It is still the most wonderful pot in the world for making soup.

It is now nine o'clock in the morning. We are at our respective offices and buried in the day's work, Martha at her easel and I at the typewriter. Elsie has settled herself in an armchair in the living room. She knows our working hours as well as we do, and she will be quiet as long as the work goes on.

At ten-thirty there is a knock at the kitchen door. This is the time for the midmorning break anyway, and I welcome the interruption. I open the door and behold our eighty-year-old Spanish neighbor from next door. Her black *reboso* is wrapped around her head and shoulders, but I can see that her hand, under the folds of cloth, holds something. I speak to her in my clumsy kitchen Spanish, because she has no English.

"Good morning, señora. Come in, for a favor."

"Good morning, señora. Thank you. I will come in."

I present her with a chair. "Sit down, as a favor."

"Very many thanks, señora. Have you a taste for dried meat?"

"Certainly, very certainly, we have, señora." I raise my voice in a call for Martha. A present must be acknowledged, with full ceremony, by both of us. Besides, Martha really speaks Spanish. I can stagger conversationally through these polite preliminaries to a visit, but after the phrases I know have been exhausted, I must revert to hand-waving and smiles. Martha emerges from the studio and we all sit down for a cigarette and a cup of coffee. We give the señora a bowl of sugar and she departs, going, as we instruct her to, with God.

Martha goes out to the mailbox by the gate and brings back three letters, a bill for me from the American Anthropological Association, and a folder setting forth glittering bargains at Sears Roebuck's Albuquerque store, eighty miles away. We firmly resist the temptation to leap into the car and gallop off to Albuquerque in order to acquire such highly essential articles as bicycle lamps and feather dusters—two of each for the price of one. We sternly return to work.

Nowadays I know what to do with Spanish dried meat. The first time I was confronted with a sun-blackened, sun-hardened, paper-thin slab of it, I had recourse to the only Spanish cookbook in the house, one

that told of the foods of the conquistadores. The recipes had not, apparently, been revised since 1650.

The book said that there was no substitute for pounding dried meat, so I dutifully pounded it with a hammer on a brick, wrapping the piece of jerky in a clean cloth when I saw fragments begin to fly all over the kitchen. I pounded and pounded and pounded, and our neighbor heard the noise and came over to investigate.

"Señora, have you a machine?"

"Certainly I have a machine," I said, waving at the typewriter on the kitchen table.

"No, no, señora. A MACHINE." She made violent grinding motions with her arm, and light dawned on me.

"But certainly." From a drawer I produced the meat chopper.

"Ah, yes. A machine." She showed me how to cut through the meat with the grain and then grind it quickly and easily to a fine powder to

ALICE MARRIOTT   115 be added to soup. I blessed the Age of Mechanics and mentally wrapped the Conquistadores' Cookbook to mail to an eastern friend for Christmas. She would consider it a quaint bit of Americana and she, I knew well, would never encounter dried meat in the flesh.

So now I add a cupful of ground dried meat to the soup and go back to work. At twelve I hear a small sound. Elsie has come to the kitchen door and is doing two elaborate, ballet-stretching steps across its sill, her eyes gleaming like amber balls as she looks meaningly at Christina.

Plates, soup bowls, crackers, cheese, apples, and coffee cups go on a tray with silver and glasses. Then I carry it all into the living room, where Martha has lighted a fire in the semicircular corner fireplace. I bring in the soup and fill the bowls, then set the pot by the fire to keep warm. Cedar crackles and piñon glows; Elsie eats fragments of crackers and cheese, and we enjoy our lunch and the rest that it brings.

The afternoon passes like the morning, quickly and busily. At five Martha lays down her brushes and comes out in the kitchen. Elsie, who has spent the afternoon at her own pursuits in the alfalfa field behind the house, returns to have tea with us. She wants a nibble of ginger cookie, and a sip of milk poured into her blue pottery bowl.

Now the workday is over, and we become people who have returned from their offices and are thoroughly domestic. Martha fills a can with kerosene from the drum at the side of the house, and then fills the tanks of the circulating heaters. She brings in armloads of wood to stack in the woodbox that has been my desk chair all day. I tidy up and put away all traces of my work. Elsie patters busily after us, supervising our activities.

Then I sweep and dust the living room, quickly, not too thoroughly, but sufficiently. We are having guests to dinner, so, while Martha makes sure there is extra wood heaped by the fireplace, I wash the noon dishes. With the chores out of the way, we prepare to become social.

Once I thought that entertaining was hard work; that you had to do something special about meals when you had guests. I am past that point. Martha puts a bottle of sherry and the wine glasses on a tray, with salted nuts and crisp crackers. I mix one spoonful of cider vinegar with two of olive oil, add salt and pepper, a pinch of sugar, a shake of paprika, and twigs of fresh dill and tarragon from the window garden. We lay out the steaks that we froze in the icebox weeks ago, to thaw. And I begin to mix the spoonbread.

Every housekeeper has her specialty, and spoonbread is mine. One cup of yellow cornmeal and three of hot water, with a teaspoonful of salt, brought to a boil and stirred smooth, makes the basic mush. While it cools, I put a pat of butter in a flat, oblong earthenware pan, and set it on the back of the stove to warm. I give Christina a dose of small, quickly-heating juniper sticks, and raise the temperature from the even 250 degrees the oven thermometer has shown all day to 400. Everything is ready for the final touches.

Our guests arrive. They have driven twenty miles over snowy dirt roads, and they come in crackling with cold and hungry laughter. While Martha takes their coats and settles people in the living room, I add a cup of milk, three egg yolks, and a teaspoonful of baking powder to the cornmeal mush. I whip the whites of the eggs till they are stiff and fold the batter into them. The mixture is in the buttered pan and the pan is in the oven at the precise moment that Martha finishes pouring the sherry.

Spoonbread is a soufflé, and like all soufflés it has one exact moment of perfection when it should be served and eaten. For that reason, knowing all the things that can happen on country roads in a New Mexico winter, I won't put the spoonbread in the oven until I know my guests are settled before the fire.

Halfway through the thirty minutes that the spoonbread bakes, Martha brings the longhandled grill and the steaks into the living room. The fire in the fireplace is just right now. She lays the steaks on the grill —just plain, without salt or pepper or butter or anything to *do* anything

to them—and holds the grill in the flames for a quick searing. I take Elsie out in the kitchen and give her a generous helping of canned dog food. If she is stuffed, the rest of us can eat in peace.

Now Martha moves the grill over the piñon smoke. This is the moment when the meat is seasoned. I toss lettuce, tomatoes, and green pepper into the wooden salad bowl with the dressing and bring it into the living room. Martha looks over her shoulder at me and announces, "They're ready."

NOW is my moment. While she lays the steaks on the plates that have been warming by the fireplace, I open the oven door and take out the spoonbread. It is puffed a quarter-inch above the edge of the pan; gold dusted with copper brown in color, steaming a little bit, and popping like the juniper wood that baked it as it cools.

Quick, onto the hot plates beside the hot steaks. Quick, butter all around, on meat and spoonbread alike. No time to pour more wine. This must all be eaten, now, this minute. Salad can come later, to fill in the cracks.

Salad does come later, and so does coffee, and so does dessert. Dessert is fruit. We have tried serving other things, but nobody seems to want them. Many people say they never ate whole steaks in their lives, and most men say at least once that steak calls for potatoes. But we have never yet served potatoes with our steaks, and only once have we taken a piece of meat back to the kitchen. And the lady who left it on her plate had been sick a long time, so she wasn't really responsible.

There is good talk in the evenings following these dinners. Everybody is relaxed and warm and full. If there is a gusty wind, with a tang of snow in its breath, outside, so much the better. All the more reason to draw a little closer to the fire. The radio is jerky on such nights, so we play records on the phonograph side of the combination. Any records! Burl Ives, or Corelli, or Leadbelly blues, or Indian dances; whatever we and our guests are in a mood to hear.

Everybody goes home by ten o'clock. They, like us, will have to be in their offices and studios at nine in the morning. We carry the plates to the kitchen and wash the dishes quickly in hot water from the tank on the side of the stove. As we tidy the kitchen we discuss the evening with each other and with Elsie, who has decided views on our guests. She respects those who bring their steak bones into the kitchen for her, but she passionately loves those who put their bones on paper napkins on the living room floor. Elsie, like all good cats, is house-proud. She takes pains to keep the bones on the napkins, always.

And then it is ten-thirty. The house is tidy and aired and quiet. Martha opens the beds in our rooms, and I make up Elsie's on the woodbox. What she and I would do without that piece of furniture, I do not know. Elsie has a malted milk tablet then, because she has been a good cat. She licks it daintily while Martha holds it for her.

Finally I give Christina her last two big solid chunks of piñon wood and close the dampers. She and I have been in company all day, and we are both ready to settle down for the night. Martha has already gone to her bedroom. I close the kitchen door. The day is over.

In Touch's Kingdom

WILLIAM STAFFORD

We use the stupid self:
a touch at a time are moved,
and we save each other—
from drift, from loss,
from Hell's deep gulf
that being alone would open.

We hold each other safe.
Refuse touch, you fall,
a loss too steep for thought,
too quick for light.
Hell has flames that leave you:
you go out.

Endzone

MARSHALL TERRY

THE SKY was Greek blue.

An hour before the contest the endzone was filled. Then it was filled so tightly, much over capacity, that there was no room to move up and down the steps. Everyone was crushed into the other, like a wriggling coiled caterpillar breathing in and out in fuzzy jerky ripples with one heart. No one could move. It was packed tight. The walls of the Cotton Bowl were shining white in the sun, looming around the pockets and smears of people like a great sparkling lavatory bowl. It was late August, brilliant blue sky-domed day of intense heat, full of the packed stirring smell of black and brown and rank white sweat, day of the hungry dog. Hot. It was an afternoon game, with the hated Packers. It was the Salesmanship exhibition game. The field below was a gorgeous striped green. The people jammed into the endzone sat and quietly laughed and talked and drank Coke and orange and Dr Pepper until they could no longer bring it down the aisles in iced papercups, making the great snake in the bowl writhe, the colors of the beach change, the water shift its mood. Or ate meat sandwiches for lunch from sacks. Black and Latin, a few whites, they watched the side-stands fill up with the highrollers, gaining a further sense of self, endzoners, looking up toward harsh bright sky to see the time tick off on the great blue and silver-starred Republic clock, waiting for the moment when the Cowboys would come out onto the lush striped field to kill Green Bay.

I was there with the chairman of Philosophy and another friend. We ate hard white bread and dark spiced oily meat, and were drinking Cokes from iced papercups, chewing on the ice. It was terribly hot. I wore a folded cardboard eyeshield that said, in green, HORNED FROGS, on its visor. The chairman of Philosophy wore one marked HOGS. It was red. The man on the left and just out of the lap of the chairman of Philosophy offered him a look through his binoculars. He had a Fu, was a simmering

red-brown in color. Looking through the glasses my friend the philosopher noted and remarked that the grass on the field was in good shape. Several all around us affirmed that this was so. Up the aisle a young thin po-
liceman in blue with a large belt and pistol and a visor on his cap that
cocked down humorously to his nose tried to clear the steps. Everyone
laughed at him good-humoredly; flesh separated in a narrow line, came
back together. The fellow with the Fu found the young cop in his binoculars, then took them off him, shouted to him that he should desecrate his
mother, in Tex-Mex. It was hot. A piece of ice from my papercup dropped upon the raised shirttail of a very large black man just in front of
me. It began to slide down his shirt and onto his sweating skin and I
watched it slide slowly down into the dark crevice below his belt. But
he did not seem to notice or perhaps he was grateful. I was glad of that.

Then Green Bay came out. There was a roar.

There were the hideous mothers, the sons of dogs and pigs and goats,
the living hunks of massive bone muscle and shit that had beaten Dallas
in the championship game. They were Nemesis. Had Dallas ever beaten
them? Would Dallas emerge fully erect one day and smash them, screw
them down into the ground, gut them on the green lush turf? Would it
be today? We rose, all fully up, endzone presenting the point of hate
and noise at them.

On both sides of the stands the honkies also rose and howled whitely
at them.

They split in phalanxes, came down the field to us in units, in their
fancy gold and green, dispersed, pranced to throw and catch the golden
balls in air. They came right down to the endzone rail, a few of them,
catching the ball on fingertips, gracefully turning on the runback to
grin green and gold at us.

One came, who had been a hero of the game; made a gesture to us.
We howled, howled, howled.

Then they left the turf. Then the Cowboys came. We roared again.
Our blue and silver boys. Linemen of massive thighs and arms, the weight
of whose genitals could not be guessed. Black Pugh, while Lilly, fierce
lithesome Lee Roy. Backs fleet as wind, strong and bold as horny bulls.
Flankers, splits, and safeties. The Lance, cool and slim and sure. Bob
Hayes danced before us, zephyr-footed, swiftest human in the world. We
roared for Bobby Hayes, winged of foot, fastest man alive. Surely we
would win today.

The band played. Some stood, or sang, watching the flag lie still and hot over the shimmering silver clock that said that it was nearly time. Someone yelled, at the hymn's end: "Beat Russia." The chairman of Philosophy and I, we chuckled.

Kickoff came. They got the kick; and in a few plays then they scored. Later in the half they scored again. From the endzone hate and papercups were thrown out on the field.

Meredith kept screwing up. The stands howled, raged, screamed bloody-eyed at him. The endzone did not mind so much. They were more loyal to their players, also hated the others more. They did not join in shouting, chanting: "Morton. Morton."

But when Hayes—Mister Speed, man—took a pass and began to turn it on, with a clear lane down the sidestripe, moving on so fast he left the ball behind him up the field in the grass, a dirty Easter egg, then they choked, strangled. The hydra found its voice, its rage: here was a proper goat, who was supposed to be so good.

They would have killed Bob Hayes, eaten his black flesh if they had had him then.

And with minutes shearing from the clock Green Bay came down to us to grin again and kick a field goal. The ball came arcing beautifully through the silver goals over the rail and fence into the endzone to us. It landed just two first downs to the right and above where my friends and I sat squashed together like three gray follicles in an epiderm.

They fought for it. It disappeared, as if eaten by a mouth. Police came down two aisles, three of them, after it. You could not keep the balls, they were property. Then the police disappeared too: just disappeared. Feet kicked out from under them, here, there, tumbling humorously down the aisles, blue legs here, blue arm, cap knocked off in air, to fall and merge with the mass. The endzone heaved, strained, laughed darkly. The tremors came along the flesh, to us.

We sat there. I think we watched the game, for it went on. No, we did not move, the three of us.

Police came, a legion of them, to the top of the endzone, then moving down. The scrambling continued to our right. "Kill them pigs!" I heard above. "Don't let them mothers come in here!" came the cry. On the field Dallas had the ball. The side-stands cheered. Young Morton trotted in the game.

Look at all them police, the large man in front of me said to his white-toothed companion as they both shifted heads around to see. We should go rob a bank, man, with all them police here. They should go and desecrate their mothers, them police, said the man beside us.

Just up from us arose a strange man, an albino man who had two young albino children with him, his sons. He was albino and had red eyes and looked strange there amongst us, like a freak. You better cool it, he said. You better not do anything to the law. You better have some sense. You need the law. They laughed and hooted at him, but he said it all again and stood there, stood up among us with his sons, who also stood, so they could see him and said not to mess with the law, to cool it: off-color, sport, a freak.

The police above were coming down. The huge man in front of us stood up, turned, and looked into my eye. All around the people got up. The endzone flexed, began to writhe and turn its head up to the policemen coming down. The albino shrieked again, to let them come; and the chairman of Philosophy sank down upon his seat and began to wipe the moisture from his glasses and I stood turned toward the field and prayed for a miracle and then I saw it and, with others, shouted, shouted, and the head of the snake turned back to the field and I had seen it thrown and it was a terrible pass and bounced off someone's helmet, gold or silver, and up into the air, golden apple, free for the plucking, and he was there—Hayes, Jesus, baby—*Hayes*— and had it and as the endzone came around to it had dodged the remaining secondary and was gone and was even now in the endzone, leaping up and dancing down with clapping hands, tossing the sphere of pig away, and scored, and the Cowboys came to kiss him in the endzone at the far end of the field from us, in that good clean beautiful other endzone. Morton had thrown a crazy touchdown pass and Hayes, man Hayes—Oh Goddamn beautiful Bullet Bob!

And the kick was good.

And, in the endzone, no one recalled the police but everyone smiled and turned to suck the blood from the throat of the one next to him.

And We, Borne Along

WILSON CLOUGH

The western light withdraws, retreats; the hills face westward and wait;
    The cool night-stars emerge, confirmers of space, in clusters, or
        shining apart;
The great granite boulders draw closer, dark, heavy; the aspens pause
    in their whispering;
    The evening breeze rests; there is no sound.

    The east now is glowing, dimly suffused; the sun's moon-mirror is
        coming,
The ghost of daytime, following on day, the revenant, making familiar
    unfamiliar;
And the eastern ridge is a bar against light, a barrier opposing the glow;
And duskily etched, remote, a lone pine is lifted, signaler, apprizer,
    A measurer of moons, awaiting the comer.

    Look! The yellow dim-disk is rising; and the pine is an arrow,
        its shaft
Feathered, obscuring; then cleaving the golden gong; then a hand on
    a dial, saying twelve;
And almost one catches the pine-point's time-clocking, the upgoing,
    the moon's progress measured,
    The silent, conjunctive spheres, the balance of planets.

    But hold! It is earth, our earth, that so spins; and we, borne along,
        are in motion;
And the pine finger drifts like a pilot's rod at the prow, stately in pace
    by the cliff,
The horizon rising as the ship comes to harbor, as the hill-circled harbor
    comes forward;

Old earth gliding on its elder, swift track, heaving on its keel toward the
   disk,
   Its pine prow dipping, like a mast on a deck.

For earth-ball is pressing around on its course, steadily pivoting
   eastward;
And we, the passengers, on its dervish bulk whirling, we are forever
   unheedful;
But the lone pine announces it, timing, reminding, then dropping below
   the moon-dial,
   Ready for the sun, and the morning star.

And we the forgetful, assuming all fixed, unable to hold to the fact,
Repeat the old myth of Dian, and of moon's motion, and of rising and
   setting of suns . . .
And behind us the granite is glittering with crystals of mica, winking and
   twinkling,
Till the boulders seem buoyant like massy balloons, hardly anchored in
   the golden-dim mist,
   Hardly freighting this moon-struck globe, this earth.

Carnival   WILLARD MARSH

Meet yourself in mirrors in the Laff House:
Examine your prehensile snout with nightmare
Appendages and laugh, while Ralph the Alligator Boy
Dreams of himself and the barker's wife together
In a world where freaks lack scales, and love
Slides like a glacier on webbed feet:
Laugh while the ferris wheel unpetals thighs
Above the homesick sailor, and adolescents
Crank pubic mysteries past a lighted slot
As painted horses circle to a hearsetime tune.

The Pacific Spring

CHARLES OLIVER

WE ARE NOT *strangers to blood. It recalls a warm grief. We call it our own and say it flows excited with the triumphs of our honored dead through eternal caverns. We do not talk so much about the wild dark bubbling and spewing, though that is ours, too. But also there is an underground spring, bright and blue, that in some of us becomes, strangely, a torrent to reach the Pacific, the great ocean, and that spring is older and deeper than the blood streams.*

Not long ago I visited the small southern town in which I was born and lived for the first nine years of my life. My father had owned twenty acres about a mile southeast of town, not far from the riverbottoms. As I drove out the gravel road, I recognized some of the old houses, and the lay of the countryside was vaguely familiar, but it was the recognition and familiarity of a remembered dream. I parked by the side of the road and looked at the house of my youth, the surrounding fields—there was the great oak. Then I recalled the spring of my sixth year and all that had happened was once again vivid—*O, Ginny!*

Our house sat about fifty yards off the gravel road, almost in the middle of the acreage. It was a small white frame house, rather pretty and pert on the top of the rise from the road. The barn was behind the house at the edge of the cornfield. On either side of the house the fields had been neglected for several years. Now those fields were thick with matted weeds and grass higher than our heads and myriad saplings and evergreen bushes among the few old oak and elm trees. Because Daddy worked in a furniture factory in town, he did not have time to care for all the land, and Mama had to take care of three children; so we only had the ten acres of corn, which were enough to hoe.

That spring when I was six years old a neighbor boy, Dean Lee Hall, who was two years older than my big brother Tommy, had taught us how to cuss and to make a rubbergun. Tommy and I practiced cussing and we soon had three or four rubberguns apiece. We had even made our baby sister Ginny a little one.

It took a long time—sometimes a whole day—to make a good rubbergun. On a plank you drew the shape of the gun and then sawed it out. That was harder than it seemed; it took practice to saw straight and keep the barrel or handle from breaking off. Once you had the gun in one piece you sandpapered it. The backside of the handle had to be flat so you could nail on the clothespin which became the trigger. Then you notched the end of the barrel. If you had some paint, you could make the gun pretty, as Tommy did once.

For bullets you cut a strip of innertube. The strip was doubled and knotted. To load the gun you dropped the loop into the notched end of the barrel and stretched the rubber till it could be vised in the lips of the clothespin. You fired it by pressing your palm against the clothespin, opening the lips and letting the rubber zip just like a real bullet.

When we began to play war with rubberguns, we had to have hideouts and paths down which to chase each other, barefooted and barebacked, and from which to advance to meet the enemy, which most of the time was just Tommy, Ginny, or I because the Halls, our nearest neighbor with a kid big enough to play with us, lived a mile away.

Tommy and I both wanted to make a hideout with the bales of hay in the old unpainted barn; so we had a fight. Tommy was bigger and heavier than I; when my lip was bleeding, he furiously said I could have the damned hell hay. He was afraid I would tell Mama on him. He had been whipping me a lot that year, and Mama had warned him about it. So Tommy took Ginny and went down into the unused field, toward the great oak, and I got busy rearranging the hay. Before suppertime I had a fine hideout, a warm little room with the good smell of hay. But it was too dark, and I could not figure out how to get any light in there except by cutting a hole in the wall, which would have got me in more trouble than I wanted. Daddy would have whipped the dickens out of me if I had taken a saw to the wall.

The next day I sat in my hideout for a long time, more than thirty minutes, but I got tired of the darkness and I wanted something else to do, dammit to hell. I thought I might sneak up on Tommy and Ginny and see what they were building. It was no trouble at all because the grass was higher than my head, and being barefooted, I could move along as quiet as a spy. Just as I had figured, they were making a hideout near the old oak. Ginny, three years younger than even I and still fat like a baby, was not much help. She carried the tiny branches Tommy had broken off for her. She waddled along with her little load as though she were toting a hundred-pound sack of flour, her eyes wide and blue as the deep ocean. Tommy had closed the holes at the bottom of a clump of bushes and had used sapling branches for rafters. Now he and Ginny were gathering brush to cover the roof. I had to admit that it was a good hideout, shaded inside but not dark like mine. As I lay there watching them, I wished Tommy had taken the hay when he whipped me, because already I did not have anything to do and time was heavy on my hands. I wanted to help, but I knew Tommy would get mad if he found out I had sneaked up on them.

That night as we lay in bed I asked Tommy if he wanted to see my hideout. He said sonofabitch no. Then I asked him if there was anything I could do to help him make his. He said he was not even making a hide-out and for me to go to sleep because he was sleepy. Though I knew he was fibbing, I could not say so. I lay there and thought. When I got my idea about making paths, I tried to wake him up, but he slept deep. I thought a long time before I went to sleep. I woke up before dawn, still thinking about the same thing.

Because he was two years older than I, Tommy never liked to do anything I suggested, but when Mama finally got him out of bed, I asked him anyway. He said he had things to do. While we ate breakfast, I tried to get back at him by saying I was going to get Ginny to help me today because she had been helping him all the time. I told Ginny how much fun we would have, her eyes getting bigger and her cheeks, smeared with oatmeal, fat with a baby smile. She said she would go with me. We were going to make a path, a secret one; we were going to make it personally, by ourselves.

Ginny and I wandered down to the barn, looking for a place to start. I kept watch out of the corner of my eye and saw Tommy trying to ease unseen into the field to head for his hideout. From the barnyard we went out into the cornfield, now scuffing our shoes along the dirt and knocking down a cornstalk when we crossed rows, which would have gotten us in trouble if anyone had ever found out who did it. In that way we made a meandering trail through the field. When we were far out in the corn, we turned around and tried to retrace our path, still raking the ground with our shoes to make the path more distinct. Those times that we could not tell by which way we had come, we laid down rocks or sticks so the next time there would be no problem.

After three days Ginny and I ran the course of the path without having once to stop and figure out which way to go. It is true that I did not run fast that afternoon because Ginny had plump, short legs, and I was her leader. That evening, though, I went back by myself and ran as fast as I could, carrying a rubbergun, zigzagging through the cornstalks without missing a turn in the falling darkness, which was sweet and gentle that busy spring.

Then Tommy finished his hideout and began to make paths, too. Once we worked together for almost an hour, but then Tommy and I started to cuss and fight about which way the path was to go; so he took his direction and I took mine, by myself, Ginny going with Tommy because he was bigger than I. Tommy liked to pick out a place and then make a path as straight as he could to it. I made mine harder. Mine curved in and out among the trees and saplings, ran along gullies and the roadside ditches, came steeply up the sides, and struck out through the thickest weeds and brush. Even with a lot of markers, sometimes I could not tell where the path went next, which would make me mad.

In the days that followed Ginny went with me a few times, but I was having to work hard and did not have much time to bother with her when she would feel lost or tired. She would want to go back to the house, and if I refused to take her back, tears would leap out of those deep blue eyes—*like the ocean*, I remember, *great tears from two blue eyes of a child.*

Tommy made straight paths; he stayed in his hideout more; and I do not think he worked as hard. Anyway, Ginny liked helping Tommy better than running through the fields every which way again and again and carrying rocks and branches to show the way; so finally she stayed with Tommy all the time, which was all right with me because I was working hard and beginning to see my paths form. It took a lot of running and tramping before the grass and weeds were beaten down, and I came home at night many times tired to my bones. But the next morning I would feel a need to get out of the house and busy. Mama would make me eat my breakfast first, but I eventually got around that by getting up when Daddy did. In the morning's darkness he milked the cows while Mama was still asleep, and at the breaking of dawn I would be running a path.

I would eat breakfast before Tommy and Ginny were awakened, and I would be at my work again while they were eating.

Finally I had so many paths that some crossed others. One even ran under the barbwire fence back of our cornfield and into the thicket on Halls' land, which might have gotten me in trouble if anyone had found out.

I would not show Tommy or Ginny my paths because I had made them by myself. Tommy got mad and with Ginny helping him started moving my markers. One day I caught them at it, and I had a fight with Tommy. Because he was bigger than I, he got me down and pinned my arms to the ground. Ginny started crying and hitting Tommy, the blue tears dropping from her eyes as she bawled. I did not need to be let up and Tommy was afraid Mama would hear; so we both tried to quieten her down. She would not stop, though, till Tommy got off me. As soon as we were on our feet, I tackled Tommy, and he got me down again. Ginny cried, and he let me up. It made me hellfire mad, especially at Ginny, but it was no use. She would not quit bawling unless we were not fighting. So I said to Tommy: "I dare you to bother my rocks and paths. Leave my things alone!"

"What if I don't?" Tommy said.

I almost went at him again, but Ginny was puckering up to cry. "Crybaby!" I said to her.

"Sonofabitch, she's crying for you," Tommy said. "You ought to be glad, or I'd whip you up right."

I walked up real close to Tommy, even though he was bigger than I. "Say that again and I'll make your nose bleed."

Tommy said it again, and Ginny started to cry, her eyes now darkly blue encircled by white—*like the ocean, the ocean within the springtime sky*, I recall.

"Wait till she's not around," I said. "Now I dare you to—"

"I take it," Tommy said. He went over and picked up a sapling branch that I had laid out to point the way. There was nothing I could do. I was mad, but I told Tommy I would show him all my paths if he would put the branch down. Then we spent the afternoon going over my paths. It would not have been so bad, but Tommy kept saying I was silly for curving them around so much.

What Tommy did not know was that when I got mad I decided to keep the best two paths secret. One of them ran right behind his hideout by the great oak, which would have gotten me in trouble if Tommy had found out.

Now that Tommy knew almost all my paths, it was not near so much fun running them, dammit to hell. So we played rubberguns more.

But it was not long, a whole day, before I needed something else to keep me busy. Then I decided to build the biggest rubbergun ever seen. Tommy had a Long Tom—what we called the long-barreled guns—but soon after he had finished it and had painted it red he had shot me at close range and raised a blister on the calf of my leg. I had not been able to keep from crying, and Mama had made Tommy put up the Long Tom. So I knew that if anyone caught me making mine I would be in a lot of trouble.

Materials for rubberguns were harder and harder to come by. Because we had used so many of Daddy's planks he had warned us not to saw up any more, and because we had lost so many rubbers in the brush we had cut up all the good tubes. And Mama had even begun to complain about our using so many clothespins. So I knew from the beginning it would be hard, but I had done other hard things that spring. I could get the materials if I was willing to take the chances of getting in trouble, and I was.

In two mornings' time I had let the air out of the spare tire in the trunk of Daddy's old Chevrolet and pulled out the tube. By the time Daddy came back from the barn with the pail of milk the second morning I was spying from the side of the house. Daylight was coming fast, and I barely had time to run down to the barn and hide the tube in the hay before Mama started calling me.

Getting the lumber was even harder, because it had to come from inside the house. None of the old pieces that we had left was anywhere near long enough for the gun I was going to build. Besides, they were warped and weathered, and I knew where there was a bright new board over four feet long. It was in the closet in my and Tommy's bedroom. The closet shelf was three planks wide, and I figured that if I took the back one it would not be noticed. But I had to wait till Mama was outside before I could get my hammer out from under the mattress and give the plank a few good licks on the bottom. Twice while I was pounding at the plank Mama came running back into the house. She had heard me, and I had to say that I was trying to fix the windowsill. Neither time she found anything that required fixing, and so she sent me outside with my hammer, the last time with a scolding, a warning, and a smack on my rump. Goddammit.

But one day I finished the job in less than an hour. Mama intended to take all three of us kids to visit the Halls, but I played like I was feeling bad. She came close to not going; so I said I would get better soon and come on over by myself. She would not agree to that, but she finally made Tommy stay with me.

Tommy was mad because he had wanted to play rubberguns with Dean Lee Hall, who was even bigger than Tommy. He said he wished he did not have a little brother like me. He said that if I said I was sick one more time he was going to hit me in my dammit to hell mouth. He said he could whip me with one hand tied behind his back and he wished I would say something so he could. I kept quiet, but I was thinking and planning. I figured it out, and then I propped my head up on my elbow and said I was feeling better and was about ready to go. I lay back down. Tommy walked around and around, but now he was not saying anything bad to me. When I saw he was tired of waiting again, I sat up in bed. "I'm about ready now."

"Let's go," he said, leaning toward the door already.

I looked down at my shoes on the floor. "It'll take a while yet. I don't even have my shoes on," I said, slow enough to make him wonder if I was going to be sick again. That worried him. "Why don't you start on?" I said. "I'll probably catch you by the time you get there."

A rabbit could not have caught him if he kept going the way he left. I jumped up, got my hammer out, and went to work, tickled—I did not even intend to wear shoes today.

Soon I had my plank with three gleaming nails sticking through each end. It was pine wood, and lucky for me it was not warped and had only two knots, which I could easily cut around. Just gazing at the board. I could see in my mind the mightiest gun ever built by man. It would not have taken me as long as it did to get to the Halls if I had not bothered to drive the nails out of my plank, pick three of Mama's best clothespins, and round up the saw, nails, scissors, and hammer. All of these I hid in the barn with the tube.

From then on I worked on my Long Tom every chance I got. In a way it was like making paths. It was all I could think of, and when I could not be working on the gun, I was planning how to get more sandpaper or something else, or I was worrying about being caught.

Then one day I finished it. It was bigger and finer than any other gun in the whole world. The handle sloped out of the barrel like the polished stock of a rifle, and the barrel was over three feet long and smooth as real steel. I decided to paint it so that in all ways it would be better than Tommy's red Long Tom, and it took me a long time, more than an hour even, to figure out where I could get the paint. But I remembered that Daddy had a can of blue touchup paint for his old Chevrolet. The next morning I got it out of his glove compartment and that afternoon I painted the long barrel. The handle I left pine white. All I had to do then was to cut and knot my rubbers, and by suppertime I had three good ones—and the paint was drying.

I almost told Tommy that night as we lay in bed together. I could not keep from hinting about it, but I wanted to see his face as he looked at my Long Tom for the first time. So I just kept saying I would show him something he had never seen before if he would get up when I did in the morning. He asked me a couple of times what it was, but I just said: "Nothing. You got to see it."

"I don't want to see any damned thing that early in the morning," he said. "Don't wake me up or you'll be in trouble."

"All right," I said. "But you never seen anything like this."

He said I had better shut up and leave him alone, but I was excited and could not sleep; so in a while I said: "Yours is not nearly so good as mine."

He lay quiet for a moment. and then he asked me what I meant.

"Nothing. But if you'll get up in the morning I'll show you."

He jumped up in bed and cocked his fist at his shoulder, pointing it down at my face. I was a little afraid. "I'm not going to tell you again," he said. I lay quiet. He brought his fist down to about an inch from my nose and held it there. I lay still. Then he said: "You can wake me up this one time, but you better not be fibbing if you know what's good for you." He took his fist away, and I turned over on my stomach and tried to sleep. I was too happy. Like at Christmas, I did not think I could wait all through the night till morning.

It was still dark when I woke up, but I remembered almost that same instant what day it was, and suddenly the sleep passed away with a thrill. I started shaking Tommy, telling him to get up.

Daddy had not even gotten up to milk the cow as Tommy and I went down to the barn. Tommy was still rubbing the sleep from his eyes and muttering at me as I hopped and jumped along beside him. He was still saying he was going to whip me if I was fibbing when we reached the barnyard. I said I would help him whip me if he was not surprised. I told him to stay outside, and I went into the barn. Even in the deep darkness I thought I could see the blue barrel and the pearl white handle flashing with light. I stuffed the three rubbers into my pocket—as though I knew even then what would happen when Tommy saw my Long Tom.

Tommy was about to enter the door when I pushed it open with my foot. So I was standing above him holding out the gun toward him with both hands. He came closer and I pulled the gun back. He peered at the gun and then reached for it. I held it tight and jerked it back against my chest. "It's my Long Tom," I said. He reached again and I stepped back. He was getting mad now, and I thought he might either try to take it away from me or tell Mama and Daddy, which would have gotten me in trouble. "I made it," I said. "It's mine. I made it all by myself." I wanted to say that it was bigger than his Long Tom, but I thought that might make him too mad. He stood there for a long time, his eyes moving from the gun to my eyes back to the gun. I clutched the gun tightly, hoping that if it had to be one, it would be to fight me for it, because I did not think he could whip me, not the way I felt now. The longer we faced each other unspeaking, the more I thought he would tell on me. Then I was surprised when he said solemnly: "Take out. I'll go get my Long Tom and come after you. All hell's going to break loose."

We stared at each other for several moments, the blood hatred rising like a mushroom cloud over us there in the quiet and final darkness of the night.

Tommy whirled about like a soldier and went toward the house, not running but walking with quick steady determination. I waited till I could not see him any more before I moved. Now that I was alone I was afraid I was trying to think where I should go and hide when I remembered that my Long Tom was greater than his. If he had had any sense, I thought, he would have gone to hide and I would have gone after him.

My hands were shaking as I sat down on the milk stool to load the gun. When I tried to pull a rubber from my pocket, all three came out, and I scratched about the ground till I found them. I learned something from that; I put one rubber in each of my front pockets so that they would not become entangled and I could load quicker. The gun between my knees, I looped the rubber over the end of the barrel, jigged it into the notch. and drew it back toward the clothespin. But I had not figured one thing; as tight as the clothespin lips were, they would not hold the rubber. I could see the rubber slowly slipping, and it would have fired if I had not grabbed it. Now I was really afraid. I wanted to run after Tommy and shout for him to wait till I could get my gun fixed, but I knew he was mad enough that whether I had a gun would make no difference. O, dammit, dammit.

The sky was already beginning to lighten, and Tommy would be coming soon. I jumped up and started running, not thinking where I was going or which way Tommy would come. In and out of the rows of corn I ran, following my old path, bearing my gun with both hands in front of me, almost crying. I remember that Tommy knew the cornfield path, but I did not dare go back to the barn. I veered off the path and rammed through wall after wall of cornstalks, now making a new and furious course.

Tommy saw me before I reached the high grass. In the first faint light of dawn I glanced toward the barn as I came out of the cornfield. He was standing in the barnyard, gazing about him slowly and cautiously. With a desperate lunge I tried to get to cover before he saw me, but maybe I was making too much noise, because he suddenly jerked his head around. As I scrambled to get to my feet, I saw him start to run, his legs pumping faster and faster and one arm churning the air. In the other hand he carried the red Long Tom, and I knew his was loaded.

I was running as fast as I could, certain that at any moment he would come sweeping up behind me like a hawk from the sky, the blow from his gun knocking me headlong—and I would never get up again. It was my luck then that as I flogged my way through the grass and weeds and brush I came upon a path I recognized. I hesitated for just a moment, and then my senses came back. Now I could run faster and think at the same time. I followed the winding course of the path, whirling and bending through the waste of the field, thinking faster. As long as he was behind me, I thought, he might be able to watch my flight by the movement of the grass. Then by taking a straight line, as was his nature, he could head me off eventually. So I bent over and ran slower and slower, till I was barely trotting, and now thinking faster and faster. It was then that I figured out how to load my Long Tom, which let me hope once again that I could get Tommy first. All I needed was a little time and a place, and right off I had a good idea. The path I was following would lead me behind Tommy's hideout near the big oak, and he did not know that I had watched him build a part of it, that was a place he would not think of searching for me.

More and more carefully I made my way till finally I burrowed into the hideout. I lay still and listened. Closer than I had expected, Tommy was wading strongly through the grass, hurrying.

My hands shaking, I put the gun between my knees, looped the end, stretched the rubber back to the clothespin, and held the clothespin tightly closed with the press of my hand. It worked. The rubber did not slip, and now I was armed.

Twice Tommy came within a few feet of me, without hearing my hard and furious breathing, without seeing the quivering barrel of my gun as I aimed at the small low entrance, the grass thrashing as he passed. But the sound died away, and figuring that Tommy was cutting across the field to hunt me elsewhere, I almost giggled at how I had fooled him —Goddammit! But I could not leave the hideout right then because I wanted more time to get over being afraid and to plan how to sneak up on him. My hand was beginning to ache as the dawn brightened the sky, cracking the spring night open.

Away off now I heard Ginny calling—*like the ocean, the ocean, her eyes*—calling for Tommy and me to come to breakfast. I listened for Tommy's answer, but I heard nothing. So I kept quiet and still. Then I heard Tommy holler out to Ginny that we would be in right away. He was not as far from me as I had thought, and my blood was quickening once again, my hand aching, my head thinking faster. Tommy and Ginny were hollering back and forth, louder, coming closer. Ginny kept saying come on now. Tommy was saying in a minute.

Now I heard someone approaching the hideout—Tommy, of course, I thought. This time he just might come in. Softly and quietly I scooted as close as I could to the evergreens, hoping to be hidden in their shadows. Tommy came nearer, and I aimed my gun at the hole through which he would enter. He was beneath the oak now, walking lightly, and he was coming toward the hideout. I was afraid, panting, but I held as still as I could. Yet the blue and white gun was shaking so much that I slowly brought up my legs, rested the barrel in the notch of my knees, and with my other hand steadied the gun as I aimed down the long, long barrel. I heard him drop to his hands and knees, crawling toward me, and my heart was furious and terrible. I saw him, cried out, and let go of the trigger.

Ginny screamed in pain and terror and fell forward. I saw the blood flowing, bubbling it seemed, all along one side of her face. I jumped up, my head pounding, watching silently for a moment the blood pouring from about Ginny's eye. Then I was wailing out—*Ginny! Ginny!*—again and again, while in my fury I tried to get more light into the hideout by hacking at the makeshift roof with my gun. I crashed out of the hideout yelling for Mama and Daddy, wanting to run, to run and never cease running till the sight of Ginny lying before me, her eye slashed open, letting in the lasting darkness, by the rubber from my gun, disappeared forever from my mind.

O, Ginny! How many years ago was it that Daddy and Mama and Tommy came running to help you, while my heart thundered, while I screamed—and in my torment I took the gun that was stained with the blood of an ocean-blue eye and with a rage beat it again and again against the trunk of the oak, struck harder and harder, till that gun and all those guns in our benighted world were broken and splintered. And I left them there and walked to the house, crying for you.

Climbers

STEPHEN MALIN

It is said of men, lost in mountain woods,
That conscious effort must be put to keep
Upon the downward way; that, not on guard,
A man will start the climb again toward
Faces sheer and white from where the ancient
Echo keens, calling out of dark bone cages
Up to cliff-slung, wind-swung places,
Into mazes carved of rock and vapor,
Even those who would as lief have stayed behind.

CHARLES OLIVER

The Poet and the Laboratory

LAURENCE PERRINE

WE LIVE, we are often told, in an age of science. We have seen during our lifetimes the invention of the hydrogen bomb and the first landings of men on the moon. There may be a connection between these events.

In the hydrogen bomb, scientists have invented a means of destruction capable of eliminating one of the planets from the universe as a place fit for human habitation. Having done this, it's appropriate that they should look for some place else for man to go. Space exploration seems the necessary corollary of the discovery of nuclear fusion.

A frequent deduction from this situation is that we must educate more engineers and scientists, in order to keep up, or catch up, with Russia. The reason for this need is obvious; it's so that we can blow the Russians up before they blow us up. Nowhere, on the other hand, do we hear it said that what we need is more poets and readers of poetry. Yet if America and Russia were engaged in a race to see which could turn out the more first-rate poets rather than the more nuclear scientists, the world might be a far safer place to live in.

What is the need for poetry in an age of science? I'd like to explore some of the differences between science and poetry and to explain why I think both are necessary. I won't claim that we don't need more engineers and scientists. I *will* claim that, more imperatively, we need more good poets and readers of poetry. What do we need fewer of? Well, salesmen possibly—juvenile delinquents certainly.

What do I mean by poetry? I do not necessarily mean that peculiar kind of writing which is printed in lines of irregular length going down the page instead of that neater kind which always keeps equal margins. I mean rather a kind of writing whose primary concern is to extend and deepen the range of human experience, whose function is to make us more alive, and by doing so to make us more human.

I ask children sometimes, "What is the opposite of poetry?" The answer comes back, "Prose." But the opposite of prose and poetry is a false one. The opposite of prose is not poetry, but verse. Prose is the well-scrubbed, well-behaved kind of writing that keeps equal margins. Verse has more internal order, but has no respect for margins. Poetry may be written in prose or verse. *Moby-Dick* and *The Old Man and the Sea* are poetry; and so, by my definition, are *Huckleberry Finn* and *The Death of a Salesman.* When a piece of writing conveys some aspect of human experience with intensity or passion, it becomes poetry.

If the opposite of prose is verse, then what is the opposite of poetry? Let me suggest just a tentative answer. The opposite of poetry is science.

Science and poetry take opposite approaches to experience. Science is the *analysis* of experience, poetry is the *synthesis* of experience. Science is the taking apart of experience in order to know it piece by piece. Poetry is the putting together of experience in order to know it in its totality.

How, for instance, might the poet and the scientist approach the experience of water? The poet might tell you a number of things about water. Water is clear and silvery; it sparkles in the sunlight. Water is transparent: you can see the face of your sweetheart through a glass of it. Water reflects: you can look into a pool of water and see your own face in it. Water is cool to the skin; when you dip an arm into it, it mats the hair and leaves your skin wet. Water is refreshing: you can quench your thirst with it. When water is gathered in lakes or oceans, it becomes blue or green in color. It reflects the sky and the clouds. Water bears you up: you can swim in it. Sometimes water becomes wrinkled or gathered in waves which pound on the rocks and break up in spray. Water may be cruel: a man can drown in it.

And how does the scientist approach water? For the scientist, water is a chemical compound of which the individual molecules consist of two atoms of hydrogen and one of oxygen. In scientific shorthand, water equals H_2O.

Of course, the scientist can tell us other things about water, too. He tells us its density and specific gravity, its boiling point and its freezing point, its refraction index, its coefficient of thermometric conductivity, and its dielectric constant—whatever that is. But in all cases, the scientist is interested in something less than the total experience of water, and is interested in it one aspect at a time. As far as possible he holds all the variables constant except one, so that he can study that one variable, that one abstracted aspect, in isolation. And what he finally gives us is a fact *about* water, or a series of facts about water; he does not, like the poet, reproduce the whole shining experience of water intact and alive in the imagination. When the scientist tells us that water is H_2O, he tells us something that no poet would ever have discovered. But when Tennyson writes,

> All night
> The plunging seas draw backward from the land
> Their moon-led waters white,

or when Matthew Arnold describes how

> the stars perform their shining,
> And the sea its long moon-silvered roll,

they are equally describing a truth about water—a truth beyond the reach of the scientist as scientist.

"Science," says Robert Louis Stevenson,

writes of the world as if with the cold finger of a starfish; it is all true; but what is it when compared to the reality of which it discourses? where hearts beat high in April, and death strikes, and hills totter in the earthquake, and there is a glamour over all the objects of sight, and a thrill in all noises for the ear, and Romance herself has made her dwelling among men?

Here, then, is a first difference between science and poetry. But there is another important difference. The poet, when he tells us about water, tells us how it appears to the human being. You can see your face reflected in it or your sweetheart's face refracted through it. It is cool to your skin, it mats your hair, it quenches your thirst, it bears you up, it can drown you. What color is water? Is water blue? Not for the scientist. For the scientist water reflects light waves of certain frequencies and absorbs light waves of other frequencies. Its *blueness*, the experience of blueness, originates in the observer's head. And so science tries to separate the thing observed from the observer; it is interested only in the thingness of the thing, while poetry is interested in it as it affects our humanity.

The human being, indeed, is an embarrassment to the scientist. It would be best if he could be eliminated. The scientist must be objective. He must measure and weigh and count. And so the scientist always introduces an instrument between himself and the thing studied; he has to separate himself from it, to get as distant from it as he can. At the least he uses a ruler or a scale or a thermometer. More elaborately he may use a telescope, a microscope, a complicated electrical apparatus, a photoelectric eye, a test-tube jungle. Increasingly the scientist has to devise instruments to use his instruments, and other instruments to read his instruments. He finds, in his most delicate experiments with heat, for example, that he can no longer go up and read a thermometer, for the very approach of the human body to the thermometer violates the accuracy of the reading. Somehow he has to eliminate the human body, or keep it at a distance.

Do our astronomers walk out into the "mystical, moist night air" and look up at the stars with unaided eye? No; they use a telescope. But do they take the telescope in their hands and aim it at the stars? No; they attach the telescope to a clock and let the clock aim the telescope. Do they then look through the telescope and see the starlight as it falls through the lenses directly on the eye? No; the lens of the telescope is at right angles to its barrel, and the light reaches the lens only after it has been reflected by several mirrors. But do the astronomers even look *into* the telescope? No; today they put a camera at the eyepiece of the telescope and let *it* look at the stars.

And how does the scientist deal with radioactive materials? He puts the materials in one room, puts himself in another room with thick glass windows between, works the controls of a mechanical crane that lifts and moves the materials, then puts his arms into a pair of heavily insulated sleeves extending into the other room, grasps some sort of tool through the heavy gloves, and with this tool does something to the materials, stirs them perhaps. In this case the scientist has to separate himself from his materials lest the human factor be eliminated in a way displeasing even to him.

For ultimately, of course, the scientist cannot entirely eliminate the human observer, as much as he might like to. There must be somebody to read and interpret the data transcribed on the smoked revolving drum. But if the scientist cannot eliminate the human being—cannot eliminate himself—he must eliminate a good part of the human being. For if science presents but one aspect at a time of the thing it studies, it also presents it to the consideration of but one aspect of human consciousness —the intellect. All other human faculties are disturbing elements; the human factor must be minimized. Emotions are irrelevant: they upset the validity of experiments and vitiate the interpretation of results. Errors of the senses must be corrected by the use of instruments. Imagination, though useful for suggesting a procedure or a hypothesis, must be rigidly checked and counterchecked. Fancy is a wild thing and must be restrained; it might substitute a unicorn for the corpse on the dissecting table; it might picture, as Hamlet does, a camel in a cloud; or, reversing things, it might see the evening stretched out against the sky as a patient etherized upon a table.

And how wrongheaded the poet is, after all! He looks up at the sky and mutters, "The moon [is] a ghostly galleon tossed upon cloudy seas." Galleon indeed! Or he may look down into a pool and see hanging there another sky. How twisted up can one get? In a moment of greater clarity, he may look up and say with Coleridge's ancient mariner:

> The moving moon went up the sky,
> And nowhere did abide;
> Softly she was going up,
> And a star or two beside.

But even this is nonsense! When the moon seems to be moving among the clouds, the clouds are really moving in front of the moon. When the moon seems to climb up the sky, the earth is really turning past an unmoving moon, though the moon too has a motion which must be taken into scientific account. Surely Shakespeare did have one moment of scientific insight: when he classified the lunatic, the lover, and the poet as being all of one kind.

And yet, though so precise and accurate the scientific account, how false it is to all human experience! For the farther science advances, the farther it takes us away from the truth of human experience. The very chair on which I sit dissolves under the examination of science into a swarm of atoms, each a miniature solar system with electrons revolving like miniature planes around its central body, and each system separated from its neighbor by vast distances of space. The scientist presents us this conception as fact. I acknowledge the fact, but wonder how it manages to hold me up. For truth I return to the poet and his "moving moon."

But I would leave a wrong impression if I let it be thought that I think ill of scientists, or that I think of science and poetry as antagonistic. Some of my best friends are scientists.

It is true that some individuals, among both scientists and poets, have thought of the two activities as antagonistic. Sir Issac Newton is reported to have dismissed poetry as "ingenious fiddle-faddle." And William Wordsworth described a scientist as "one that would peep and botanize/ Upon his mother's grave." John Keats accused Newton of reducing the rainbow to commonplaceness by reporting it as a prismatic phenomenon, and Edgar Allan Poe pictured science as a vulture, preying on the poet's heart. But wiser heads among both parties have prevailed. Tennyson, speaking of scientific knowledge in *In Memoriam* as "a beam in darkness," said, "Let it grow!/Let knowledge grow from more to more." And Charles Darwin said that if he had his life to live again, he would make it a rule to read some poetry and listen to some music at least once a week, because "the loss of these tastes is a loss of happiness, and may possibly be injurious to the intellect and more probably to the moral character, by enfeebling the emotional part of our nature."

Science and poetry are complementary, not antagonistic, activities. They should be partners, not enemies. And life is always in danger when this partnership is threatened, as it is, indeed, today. Science is, or should be, an aid *to* life. Poetry is, and ought to be, a means *of* life. Science—though it may lead to destruction—is necessary for survival. Poetry makes us worthy of survival, and makes survival worthwhile. Without science we should probably not be able to exist, or not for long. Without poetry, and music, and art, many of us should not much *want* to exist. For art makes worthwhile the extensions of life that science gives us. The use of poetry is to make us human.

To the medieval mind, interestingly enough, the poet and the scientist both figured as necromancers. Virgil, for many centuries, was set down as a mighty magician. He was supposed to have fabricated a brazen fly and an ever-blooming orchard, to have beguiled the devil, and to have built for the emperor a marvelous castle in which the emperor could see and hear everything done or said in Rome. Aristotle and Roger Bacon, the thirteenth-century scientist, were similarly regarded as magicians. Roger Bacon was supposed to have constructed a brazen head capable of talking and delivering lectures on philosophy. He also controlled devils and meant to use them to build a wall of brass about England so that no enemy might "touch a grass of English ground." And there is little to wonder at in either superstition. For poets and scientists and magicians are all people who exercise extraordinary powers by means of spells or verbal formulas. "Abracadabra, hocus pocus," says the necromancer, and a beautiful woman is suddenly make invisible. "Arma virumque canto," begins Virgil, and the living past is conjured up before us. "E=MC²," says Einstein, and Hiroshima disappears in a mushroom cloud. The people of the middle ages were not so mistaken after all. For Virgil, in a very real sense, may be said to have made "an ever-blooming garden." And scientists today have constructed brazen heads that not only speak but think. Instead of commanding devils to do their bidding, they command machines; and the machines do not only their housework, but their homework.

But machines, though they may perform complicated problems in mathematics, cannot write *King Lear*. And they cannot read it. Poetry is not outmoded by the inventions and discoveries of the age of science. It is rendered even more necessary by these discoveries. Science, as an activity of analysis, disintegrates our experience. Poetry integrates. Science splits our experience into fragments—into densities, specific gravities, molecular weights, chemical components, refraction indexes, and conductivity coefficients. Poetry reaffirms the wholeness of experience. Science finds man almost an excrescence in an alien universe; he is an embarrassment in its experiments, and in its results he is seen as a knatlike creature against the almost limitless immensities of empty space. Poetry reasserts the primacy of the human being and makes a universe of the human mind and heart. Science enables us to control the outer world: Boom! and we blow up Hiroshima. Poetry enables us to control the inner world—so move men to "thoughts too deep for tears."

Science today is justly proud of having landed men on the moon and begun the process of exploring it. But the poets had been there already and explored it long ago. Homer explored it. Sir Philip Sidney explored it. Keats and Shelley explored it. Edmund Rostand's Cyrano de Bergerac most notably explored it. At a time when no man had yet seen the other side of the moon, Browning told us unforgettably what it was like coming out on that other side:

> But the best is when I glide from out them,
> Cross a step or two of dubious twilight,
> Come out on the other side, the novel
> Silent silver lights and darks undreamed of,
> Where I hush and bless myself with silence.

Yes, the poets long ago explored the moon, and are still exploring it. It is encouraging that there the scientists have at last begun to catch up with them.

But poetry has explored other places that science hasn't even discovered yet. The Garden of Eden, the pleasure-dome of Kubla Khan, the Isles of the Blest, Camelot—a city which Tennyson describes as

> built
> To music, therefore never built at all,
> And therefore built forever—

Lilliput, Vanity Fair, Purgatory, Heaven, Hell. Science has been doing a thorough job of exploring the interior of the atom. Poetry, above all, enables us to explore the interior of the heart.

Why poetry in an age of science? To reaffirm the wholeness of experience and the primacy of man; to tell the whole truth about our experience, not just describe its facts; to let us sail on rivers unmapped by any scientist—the inland rivers of the human heart.

Warning

JAMES HAINING

Pulling a child by his arm
can be dangerous, Chief;

I wouldn't do that if I
were you. The arms will
swell quickly and drop

to the sides for years.

Señor Payroll

WILLIAM E. BARRETT

LARRY AND I were Junior Engineers in the gas plant, which means that we were clerks. Anything that could be classified as paper work came to the flat double desk across which we faced each other. The Main Office downtown sent us a bewildering array of orders and rules that were to be put into effect.

Junior Engineers were beneath the notice of everyone except the Mexican laborers at the plant. To them we were the visible form of a distant, unknowable paymaster. We were Señor Payroll.

Those Mexicans were great workmen; the aristocrats among them were the stokers, big men who worked Herculean eight-hour shifts in the fierce heat of the retorts. They scooped coal with huge shovels and hurled it with uncanny aim at tiny doors. The coal streamed out from the shovels like black water from a high pressure nozzle, and never missed the narrow opening. The stokers worked stripped to the waist, and there was pride and dignity in them. Few men could do such work, and they were the few.

The Company paid its men only twice a month, on the fifth and on the twentieth. To a Mexican, this was absurd. What man with money will make it last fifteen days? If he hoarded money beyond the spending of three days, he was a miser—and when, Señor, did the blood of Spain flow in the veins of misers? Hence it was the custom for our stokers to appear every third or fourth day to draw the money due to them.

There was a certain elasticity in the Company rules, and Larry and I sent the necessary forms to the Main Office and received an "advance" against a man's paycheck. Then, one day, Downtown favored us with a memorandum:

"There have been too many abuses of the advance-against-wages privilege. Hereafter, no advance against wages will be made to any employee except in a case of genuine emergency."

146

We had no sooner posted the notice when in came stoker Juan Garcia. He asked for an advance. I pointed to the notice. He spelled it through slowly, then said, "What does this mean, this 'genuine emergency'?"

I explained to him patiently that the Company was kind and sympathetic, but that it was a great nuisance to have to pay wages every few days. If someone was ill or if money was urgently needed for some other good reason, then the Company would make an exception to the rule.

Juan Garcia turned his hat over and over slowly in his big hands. "I do not get my money?"

"Next payday, Juan. On the twentieth."

He went out silently, and I felt a little ashamed of myself. I looked across the desk at Larry. He avoided my eyes.

In the next hour two other stokers came in, looked at the notice, had it explained, and walked solemnly out; then no more came. What we did not know was that Juan Garcia, Pete Mendoza, and Francisco Gonzalez had spread the word and that every Mexican in the plant was explaining the order to every other Mexican. "To get the money now, the wife must be sick. There must be medicine for the baby."

The next morning Juan Garcia's wife was practically dying, Pete Mendoza's mother would hardly last the day, there was a veritable epidemic among children and, just for variety, there was one sick father. We always suspected that the old man was really sick; no Mexican would otherwise have thought of him. At any rate, nobody paid Larry and me to examine private lives; we made out our forms with an added line describing the "genuine emergency." Our people got paid.

That went on for a week. Then came a new order, curt and to the point: "Hereafter, employees will be paid ONLY on the fifth and twentieth of the month. No exceptions will be made except in the cases of employees leaving the service of the Company."

The notice went up on the board and we explained its significance gravely. "No, Juan Garcia, we cannot advance your wages. We are sorry. It is too bad about your wife and your cousins and your aunts, but there is a new rule."

Juan Garcia went out and thought it over. He thought out loud with Mendoza and Gonzalez and Ayala, then, in the morning, he was back. "I am quitting this company for different job. You pay me now?"

We argued that it was a good company and that it loved its employees like children, but in the end we paid off, because Juan Garcia quit. And so did Gonzalez, Mendoza, Obregon, Ayala, and Ortez, the best stokers, men who could not be replaced.

Larry and I looked at each other; we knew what was coming in about three days. One of our duties was to sit on the hiring line early each morning, engaging transient workers for the handy gangs. Any man was accepted who could walk up and ask for a job without falling down. Never before had we been called upon to hire such skilled virtuosos as stokers for handy gang work, but we were called upon to hire them now.

The day foreman was wringing his hands and asking the Almighty if he was personally supposed to shove this condemned coal, while there in a stolid, patient line were skilled men—Garcia, Mendoza, and others—waiting to be hired. We hired them, of course. There was nothing else to do.

Every day we had a line of resigning stokers, and another line of stokers seeking work. Our paper work became very complicated. At the Main Office they were jumping up and down. The procession of forms showing Juan Garcia's resigning and being hired over and over again was too much for them. Sometimes Downtown had Garcia on the payroll twice at the same time when someone down there was slow in entering a resignation. Our phone rang early and often.

Tolerantly and patiently we explained: "There's nothing we can do if a man wants to quit, and if there are stokers available when the plant needs stokers, we hire them."

Out of chaos, Downtown issued another order. I read it and whistled. Larry looked at it and said, "It is going to be very quiet around here."

The order read: "Hereafter, no employee who resigns may be rehired within a period of 30 days."

Juan Garcia was due for another resignation, and when he came in we showed him the order and explained that standing in line the next day would do him no good if he resigned today. "Thirty days is a long time, Juan."

It was a grave matter and he took time to reflect on it. So did Gonzalez, Mendoza, Ayala, and Ortez. Ultimately, however, they were all back—and all resigned.

We did our best to dissuade them, and we were sad about the parting. This time it was for keeps, and they shook hands with us solemnly. It was very nice knowing us. Larry and I looked at each other when they were gone, and we both knew that neither of us had been pulling for Downtown to win this duel. It was a blue day.

In the morning, however, they were all back in line. With the utmost gravity, Juan Garcia informed me that he was a stoker looking for a job.

"No dice, Juan," I said. "Come back in thirty days. I warned you."

His eyes looked straight into mine without a flicker. "There is some mistake, Señor," he said. "I am Manuel Hernandez. I work as the stoker in Pueblo, in Santa Fe, in many places."

I stared back at him, remembering the sick wife and the babies without medicine, the mother-in-law in the hospital, the many resignations and the rehirings. I knew that there was a gas plant in Pueblo, and that there wasn't any in Santa Fe; but who was I to argue with a man about his own name? A stoker is a stoker.

So I hired him. I hired Gonzalez, too, who swore that his name was Carrera, and Ayala, who had shamelessly become Smith.

Three days later, the resigning started.

Within a week our payroll read like a history of Latin America. Everyone was on it: Lopez and Obregon, Villa, Diaz, Batista, Gomez, and even San Martin and Bolivar. Finally Larry and I, growing weary of staring at familiar faces and writing unfamiliar names, went to the Superintendent and told him the whole story. He tried not to grin, and said, "Damned nonsense!"

The next day the orders were taken down. We called our most prominent stokers into the office and pointed to the board. No rules any more.

"The next time we hire you *hombres*," Larry said grimly, "come in under the names you like best, because that's the way you are going to stay on the books."

They looked at us and they looked at the board; then for the first time in the long duel, their teeth flashed white. "*Sí, Señores*," they said.

And so it was.

Four Indian Poems

NORMAN H. RUSSELL

The World Has Many Places Many Ways

in the forest hearing
the anger of the black and yellow
wasp in the old tree going
down the sky to the eating
mouth of the earth i walk
a new path around i cannot
speak friend words to
this creature who
only speaks war

in the black night coming
out of the black lake water
mists of mosquitoes seeking
blood of my body i cover
myself with the blanket waiting
the sun of the morning which sends
the night creatures flying
into the trees and the waters
their secret homes to hide

one goes his way with wise feet
one walks with open eyes
one sleeps in his own places
the man has his place in the world
the world has many places many ways
only the creature who leaves his own place
only the creature who walks anothers way
will be killed will be eaten.

The Eyes of the Child Do Not See Me

i look into the eyes of the child
the eyes of the child do not see me
the eyes of the child look somewhere else

i look down at the sand
the child has a stick in his hand
the child makes pictures in the sand

what do the pictures mean?
what do the eyes of the child see?

i speak to the child
i ask him what he draws in the sand
the child looks at me and says nothing

the child arises and runs into the forest
i sit still looking a long time at his pictures
something in the sand is speaking to me.

The Tree

the wind comes like a heavy beast
and sits upon the limb of the tree
the wind comes like a hungry mouth
and chews and spits the leaves of the tree
the tree turns and twists and whistling screams
the leaves fall and rise and beat each other
the wind is death searching among the leaves
the wind is torture turning the trunks
the wind is as hungry as an army of wolves

when the wind goes away
the limbs of the tree reach out again
the leaves turn their faces to the sun again

nothing is as strong as the tree
nothing is as brave as the tree
nothing will live as long as the tree
for the tree always returns
for the tree never goes away
for the tree can never hide.

It Is All the Same It Is Nothing

he who spoke against me in the camp
sits smiling now in the council
speaks not of me or to me
speaks to the others of his plan

i sit quietly looking at this one
thinking of the sound of his voice
speaking against me in the camp
in the night when i was not there

it is all the same it is as nothing
i do not fear the words of his voice
i too will smile i will pretend
such a small one has not spoken at all

it is all the same it is as nothing
i do not think the hate will leave my heart
i will see this evil one alone
i will speak to him in the blackness of the night.

Lost Sandstones and Lonely Skies

JESSE STUART

FROM THE RIDGE ROAD I had seen the blue slate dumps where my father used to dig coal. When I saw them I knew not many days would pass until I would return. Now, with a stick in my hand, I walked up the path. I carried the stick for copperheads; this was copperhead country. Sweat ran down my face and dripped from my nose and chin. Sweat soaked my shirt collar until it felt wet and limp around my neck. But I was happy to be on my way back to a desolate part of this community. I was happy my health permitted me to walk here. This was a forsaken section of sandstones, scrawny pines, greenbrier, pennyrile, and high lonely skies. The only vegetation that would grow here were the kinds that survived in a thin, starved soil. But fortunately for my father and his father, when they moved here there was coal under these sandstone hills to be mined.

I wanted to return to the place where I was born. I wanted to see once more the ugly mouths of the gaping mines in the slopes of these high desolate hills. Now I climbed up a path wagonloads of coal had once rolled over. Cattle, mule, and horse teams had pulled the jolt wagons of coal, heaped high with big black lumps, over the winding indentation that was only a bare trace now. Once it was filled with tracks where animals had dug deep with their feet as they strained at their heavy loads. I followed this old road to the top of the ridge. Then I followed the ridge to a sand gap. Here I took the old wagon road to my right down the sandy point.

This old road had grown up in poison vine, bittersweet, bull grass, and briers. This was the first time since I could remember that this road had been overgrown. The ground had never had sufficient rain before to grow such heavy vegetation. But this season we had had plenty of rain. And through the years past, the dwarfed bushy-topped oaks growing along the banks of this ancient road had shed their leaves season after season, and these had rotted on the infertile land. These few old trees had done a splendid job of fertilizing the barren earth. Now the forest of worthless trees and briers was closing in. Soon this old road would be a part of the jungle.

I broke grapevines and bittersweet with my hands and pushed through this jungle growing in the middle of the old road. Often I had to lay my weight against the vegetation and push. Once I sat on the exposed roots of one of the old trees that had shaded the hot oxen many a time as they had toiled up this point with a load of coal from the mines below. This tree had shaded the mules and horses, too. Not many would think this bushy-topped oak had served a purpose in its earlier years. Well, it had. I could remember the long trains of mule and horse teams that left these mines with wagons of coal when I was a small boy. They went up this point, and they could go either right or left when they reached the ridge road. If they went right, they had to go over the hill by the Collins house and down W-Hollow to the E. K. Road and on to Greenup. If they went left, they had to go over and down the hill to the Womack Hollow Road, then to the Little Sandy River Road on to Greenup.

I walked down to the bushy-topped white oak. This tree stood in the yard of the house where I was born. But that one-room structure was in ashes now. In the spring of 1954 a forest fire, which burned over more than two thousand acres, got this little shack. This was my first time back to the scene since it had burned. And where this house had once stood, the ashes had helped to refertilize the ground and the weeds had grown taller. I could measure the exact spot where it had stood. Where the old garden was, someone had planted corn. This corn wasn't up to my shoulder. This was not land for corn. This was starvation land. It had always been. The Stuarts starved out when they moved here from Big Sandy. Everybody else had starved from this land. No one could have half-existed from the sustenance of this infertile land had he not mined the coal from under the sandstones.

Here I could smell the pennyrile, that aromatic herb which is death on insects, especially mosquitoes. But mosquitoes would never come to this hilltop where there isn't any water. There was a sulfur spring near the coal mine when my father and mother lived here. But this water was too full of minerals to use. My mother used to climb this mountain with a lard can of water on one hip and a child on the other. How my parents were ever able to live here, I never knew. And what was I doing here? Why had I returned?

The rabbit returns to the place where it nested in the ground. When dogs follow its tracks and hunters shoot, the rabbit returns to its place of nativity. This was the reason I was returning. I was born on this desolate spot of infertile earth, in a one-room shack without a doctor. In how many places upon this American earth, now desolate, forsaken, and forgotten, have America's children been born? America's ambitious children who have gone forward with starlight in their eyes, a dream in their hearts, and a prayer on their lips? Many of these have come from the inaccessible places, lost coves and hollows, beneath the high, spacious, lonely American skies.

No one passing could now tell that people had once lived here. The jungle had moved in. But people had once pushed the jungle back, mined the coal, and raised gardens here among these sandstones beneath these high unfriendly skies. They had cut the sassafras, greenbrier, and saw brier with their garden hoes. They had salted the earth with their sweat to get only a meager pittance in return. Now they had mined out all the coal, and my people had helped. My people's sweat had salted the sterile earth of these sandstone hills. They moved away and other people came. They mined coal and worked the land for a bare existence. Now, all had moved away. All were gone. And the saw brier, greenbier, wild grapevine, sassafras, persimmon, and scrubby pine were moving in.

I turned away from where the shack had once stood. I walked down the old wagon road toward the mines. The jungle had come over this too. But there were still prints of the load the way my father had walked. I found the place where scales used to be. Here was where they had weighed the coal when it left the mines.

From here, I broke vines with my hands and pushed my weight against the everlasting jungle. Finally I reached a high blue cone where vegetation didn't grow. Here was a clean place surrounded by bush, thorn, and vine. This was the old blue slate dump I had seen from a distance. My father had wheeled much of this slate from the coal mine above. Now the coal mine's mouth was a dark cavity, surrounded by earth's woolly jungle lips. The lips of this mouth were sealed tight. Vegetation would soon cover the mouth of this mine. I wondered how many times my father had gone back under the hill here. How many times had he lain on his side, on his back face up, and on his belly face down, and picked the coal from the seam in the days of long ago? How many times had he come out into the sweltering heat of a summer day? How many times had he made a fire of coal outside the mine and sharpened his coal picks on an anvil? How many dreams he must have had here!

Now, this was a land where dreams were buried. They were under this hill, in all directions the coal mine ran. They were every place under this hill where there was a mine entry. There were the old bank ties and wooden rails, turned dust or still preserved. Their dreams were deep deep down in this hollowed-out hill. Somewhere far away, men had burned this coal in the long ago. They, too, had sat before their blazing fires and dreamed. Giant teams had strained as the big wheels rocked under the heavy weight on the sandstone road. My father had seen the drivers leave the mine with loaded wagons for the scales. My mother had seen the teams pass on their way up the sandstone point to the ridge. And I, as a small boy, perhaps, had waved to the drivers when they passed. I never remembered these drivers. I might have met them as strangers in city streets in other towns in the later years of my life. And over this land I had walked with my father. He had held my hand in those years and led me to the scales and to the mine.

Now life once lived here, as in other parts of American earth, was a buried dream. Once it was a living dream that expanded, lived, breathed, and helped to build America. But now only the wind sighs lonesome songs, and the crows caw, and the sulfur stream of water flowing from a hole in the hill where the mine used to be mumbles sounds for those who once were here but who are now lost forever.

Freeway to Wherever

MAURICE OGDEN

RAPID as spilled mercury, the freeway flowed west in a gay pattern of shifting pastels.

With easy motions Tom wove a brilliant way through the pattern, mildly intoxicated with power and combativeness. Beside him Mary lolled on the luxurious leather, breathing the rich new-car smell and trying hard to maintain a countenance of bored unconcern.

The children, momentarily subdued by the sweeping wallop Tom had aimed at Janey for bouncing on the rear cushion, had recovered enough to stand with arms braced on the back of the front seat.

No one knew where the freeway went—no one was curious.

"Will our car go faster than the Powers's?" Bobby demanded.

"Sure, I told you," Tom said.

"Is it a better car?"

"I told you twice. It cost a thousand dollars more, it's got fifty horse-power more, it's five inches longer, and it has an extra strip of chrome on the side."

"You children shouldn't worry about things like that," Mary put in mechanically.

"After the way Jim Powers lorded it over everybody when he bought that monstrosity?" Tom demanded. "You just tell Jimmy your folks wouldn't pay out good money for a car as cheap as theirs."

"We did get a prettier color combination," Mary said complacently. "It was the first thing I noticed."

Ahead of them, the traffic moved like a school of gaudy minnows, its common motion dramatically varied with angular darts and surges. A canary hardtop in the slower lane to their right challenged alertly as a brief opening appeared magically in front of them. Tom touched the accelerator, gratified at the smooth burst of power.

"Ah, you joker you!" he chuckled triumphantly.

Frustrated, the hardtop dropped back into its own lane.

A powder-blue convertible slid alongside and paced them on the right. The driver, a well-fed man with a large stone on the little finger of his near hand, grinned floridly around his cigar.

"Anybody know where this thing goes?" he asked across the few inches separating him from Mary. "I got on it by mistake."

Mary continued to stare ahead coldly, but her hands began a nervous fumbling in her purse for a cigarette. Tom leaned across her and called, "Search me, buddy. We must have made a wrong turn back there some-place, too."

Everybody laughed—even Mary, who had found a cigarette and re-covered her composure now that Tom had taken the situation in hand.

"Who cares?" the man said, laughing. "Easiest-riding durn road I ever drove. Wonder where the eastbound is?"

"Probably on another level," Mary said, fumbling for a match.

"Be my guest . . ." The man extended a folder across the wind-whipped space. Mary took it and lit her cigarette.

"Look, Tom," she said, "real little sulfur matches!"

"Read the cover," their owner called over to her.

Obediently, she read:

DICK BLUE'S DRIVE-INS.
Matchless food wherever you are!

"That's me, Dick Blue," the man said. "Big blue signs, get it? And I do mean wherever. When we get to where this thing goes, I bet the first thing you recognize will be a big blue sign."

"I've seen them around," Tom said vaguely.

"Keep 'em," the man said expansively as Mary started to return the matches. "I got a ton of 'em."

A horn sounded impatiently behind him.

"Well, see you folks in wherever-it-is." He touched his hat jauntily and surged ahead.

"Character," Tom commented.

"Awfully common," Mary said.

"Worth a mint, though, I bet."

"I'm hungry," Janey announced from the back seat.

"Me too," Bobby seconded.

"We'll take the next turnoff and get a hot dog," Tom promised.

"There don't seem to be too many turnoffs."

"We passed one back there while you were talking to that man," Mary said.

"I saw it, but it would have caused a royal foulup if I'd tried to cut over."

"There must be plenty of turn-*ons*," Mary observed. "I don't think there's anybody in the world driving anyplace else."

"Maybe a few clowns in model T's that can't make the speed," Tom said, and the children laughed. Cutting speed, he eased lane by lane to the slow-flowing file on the right.

"This is what I hate about the outside," he said. "Over here you always get stuck behind some clunk, and on the inside there's always some joker with two carburetors trying to blast you out of the way. The middle's easier on your nerves."

"Just an old middle-of-the-freewayer," Mary said, craning her neck to peer down the outside of the roadbed.

"I can't see a turnoff on this side," she announced, withdrawing behind the windshield. "Maybe there's one on the other side."

Whipping along at the furious pace of the inside lane, Tom leaned out with the wind beating at his hair. He retreated quickly, rubbing his eyes. No exit was visible.

"You'd think there'd be signs of some kind," Mary complained.

"There generally are," he said. "I guess they haven't got around to it yet."

The children had started a game, counting the lavender-flowering crests of jacaranda trees, rising from invisible landscaping below the roadbed, with points for the first to spy each one.

"Remember how we used to do that with white horses?" Mary said. Tom nodded absently.

"You'd of thought there'd be big headlines when they opened up a stretch this big," he said thoughtfully. "I can't figure out where it could go."

"Free ride to Fateville," Mary said in a singsong voice.

"What?"

"My sister," she explained, giggling a little. "I hadn't thought of it in years. Every Saturday we used to go into Fayetteville, and she'd be ready hours before anybody else, standing out by the car and yelling 'Free ride to Fateville!' every time anybody looked out the door."

"Your sister's a real cute kid," Tom said in a flat voice.

"You don't have to be snotty."

"Who's snotty?" Tom braked violently as a pert sports car whipped saucily in front of him. "Damn smart aleck!"

"Caught you napping, didn't he?"

"There's one too many drivers in this car," Tom said tightly.

As the traffic increased, the freeway's holiday mood slipped imperceptibly into irritable impatience. The current flowed slower and more tensely, and the fluid shifting of the pastel pattern became skittish and erratic. Now the greetings and laughter exchanged between strangers an hour earlier had become the grim silence between antagonists, broken by an occasional hysterical protest of rubber on cement or the momentary grate of metal against metal. From behind sunglazed windows, faces peered out in attitudes of anxiety and hostility.

"We're finally coming to something," Tom said, pointing to a yellow pall of smog hanging along the horizon.

"I hope we can turn off before then," Mary protested. "It doesn't look very inviting."

"Oh, la-de-da!" Tom said in resigned disgust.

Suddenly he wrestled the wheel over frantically, shouting something incoherent at the driver on his left, who shouted back in flushed fury. Mary, thrown against Tom, pushed herself away and screamed as they caromed against the car on the right with a brief metallic screech. Tom and the other driver snarled at each other.

"There goes a hundred dollars' worth of paint," he groaned.

"Well, la-de-da!" Mary said viciously.

"Shut up!" he said. "Just shut up!"

"You too!" he added savagely as the children started to whimper chorally.

"I'm hungry!" Janey whined.

"I wanta get home before dark so Jimmy can see the car," Bobby complained.

"You two want another wallop?" Tom bellowed. They subsided resentfully.

"It beats me," he said, "why kids can't enjoy a ride without feeling mistreated if there's not a whole bunch of added attractions."

"They're only children," Mary said loftily.

"What kind of an alibi is that?"

"It's so *hot*." She ignored the question, passing her hands under her hair in a gesture he had always found particularly offensive. She touched the button, and the glass beside her slid down.

"It's just as hot out there," Tom grumbled.

"Maybe we should have got the one with the air-conditioner."

Ahead, the sun rested on the horizon, saffron and unreal behind the smog.

"I wonder." Mary stared fixedly through the windshield, half hypnotized by the sluggish shuttling of the traffic. "Is a new car really so much?"

"So much?" he demanded indignantly. "So much! I just wish I had a nickel for every time you've said, 'When we get the furniture paid for, and drive the best car on the block, we'll be fixed for life.' I just wish, that's all. What do you mean, 'so much'?"

"Oh, I don't know. But it seems like when what you want most is . . . is a *thing* . . . well, you always feel a little bit disappointed when you actually get it. Like a big part was just having something to want. Don't you ever feel that way?"

He concentrated stubbornly on his driving, refusing to commit himself. She sensed suddenly that he was bewildered and hurt, touched in some secret place. It was a new and unexpected insight, maliciously gratifying.

"Here we are, thirty years old, and we've got what we always said we wanted. It almost seems like we didn't have anything left to live for."

She was too tired to pursue it, too much caught up in a vague, critical uneasiness to relax.

"All those people out there." She glanced around at the montage of sullen and anxious faces behind their transparent shields. "What are they thinking about? I bet you could write an awful story about every one of them if you knew what they know about themselves."

"What are you all of a sudden?" he demanded irritably. "A philosopher or somebody?"

"I don't know." She stretched and yawned. "I guess I'm just tired and bored. How much longer do you think it will be before we can turn off?"

"How should I know?"

"I said how long do you *think*—but just skip it." Absently, she looked into the back seat. The children were asleep, their plump faces sullen and unattractive.

"Looks like an intersection up there."

Mary looked. The yellow smog had grown, reaching halfway up the evening sky now. Below it, she could make out the gray line of an elevation at right angles to the freeway, and what appeared to be a mammoth overpass.

"Well, thank heavens we're getting someplace finally," she breathed.

They drove for thirty minutes in blank silence.

"Tom!" Mary clutched his arm in sudden alarm. "That's not another freeway. It's some kind of a wall."

He nodded absently. "I've been watching it. Maybe it's a military setup or something."

Without warning, she began to cry weakly.

"Tom, couldn't we just pull over to the side and stop? We could climb down the embankment and find out where we are, or get directions or something. We could walk someplace if we had to."

"Are you crazy? One car stopped here would either get clobbered or jam things up clear back to the beginning. The one thing we can't do is stop."

The traffic moved slowly and orderly now, like a lava-flow. In the gathering twilight, like the sound of disturbed crickets, anxious voices and snatches of frightened questions floated to them from the surrounding automobiles.

Then, trapped and pressed forward in the relentless flow, they were crossing to the mighty gate, between the grim, smoke-blackened battlements reared against the black sky, and the scarred, ageless granite of ponderous walls.

Beyond, the indestructible city burned luridly.

The pastel pattern moved steadily into it, and all of a sudden nobody was very surprised, and nobody asked any more questions.

Palominos

JOHN GOULD FLETCHER

These slipped from the Spaniards' hold;
The golden horses—to go where ranges sleepy blue
Burned high above the poppied valleys. On they easily flew
Careering over earth, flashes of startling gold.

They were lost, lost for a season;
As booted miners combed their lice and swore
Huge nuggets into each sack, the hillslopes bore
Faint hoofmarks going on beyond all reason

Into the high aisles of the redwood standing somber
And cool above the sage and chaparral;
Where still the chipmunks flourished and the call
Of the loud jay awakened green ferns to remember

How the golden horses had passed. The land grew proud
Without them. Fortunes flourished, cities gleamed
Amid the palms. Afar off, white manes streamed
Above long glowing necks, as they vanished from the crowd.

Now once again, since gold is of little worth,
Being dead metal, fit to fill cold ranks
Of steel-protected vaults:—but fiery on these flanks
Rippling in power, they run afresh on earth.

The golden horses are here, not to breed true,
But beautiful as a seawind or a song
Upon these shores of time that stretch along
Beyond these leaden walls of fear that humans knew.

May they, in steadfastness or in flaming power,
Take hence the message of too many misspent years:
As long as the sons of men pile high the cold arrears
Of self, they shall not thrive, nor flourish for an hour.

The Return

JOHN TAYLOR

*There will come other horrible workers: they will
begin at the horizons where he has succumbed.*
—RIMBAUD

He has come out of the jungle and he still looks only
A little way before. His face is yellow
And his feet are painted with antifungicide inside his new shoes;
His shoulders move strangely in his suit,
Still bent by a pack, and when he sits at a table
Under a café awning and watches the crowd pass
He lets his wine go untasted while his yellow eyes
Still march through prison-cell after prison-cell of vines.
He hardly recognizes these other faces,
As foreign as the jaguar and the tapir who were his companions.
Appetite, all appetite. He drinks at last;
It tastes strange, like rust or water purified by tablets
In a canteen, and yet that was all he had for months—
Already strange to where he has been and not yet used
To where he is, he listens to the howling of the taxihorns
And wonders if he is a ghost come back or is this place
A ghost. His eyes stain all the streets epidemic green
And toucans are crying from the chimneypots.

Davis Mountains Holiday

ROY BEDICHEK

TOWARD THE END of each August I have an attack of Davis Mountain-fever. Nothing will do it any good except a visit for a week or two weeks or just as long as I feel that I can afford to stay.

I was introduced to these green and pleasant elevations in the summer of 1920. Ever since then, in the fag-end of our Central Texas dog days (period of milignant influences, as classical superstition had it, and quite correctly, I think)—ever since 1920, as the pounding of the late summer sun and the succession of sultry nights begin to get unendurable, I think of the Davis Mountains as a cool finger of the Rockies thrust southeastward into our Texas desert, beckoning lowland sufferers to come up out of the sweltering heat.

I have been told that it is only contrast which makes the Davis Mountains seem desirable; that any kind of refuge would be a relief from the road one must travel to get there; that this lowly and limited range, rather bare and almost waterless, is merely a "rock in a weary land"; and that, but for the "weary land" within which the haven is isolated, the mountains themselves would be found commonplace. Well, well, one may admit this: if we eliminate the element of contrast, enthusiasm for any pleasure dwindles down to the apathy with which an indifferent appetite regards the hash of yesterday.

The point is that the summer vacationist bound for the Davis Mountains is forced into an enjoyment of immediate and quite surprising contrasts, since every approach (except by air) is so guarded that he is fairly exhausted by the time he gets there. For literally hundreds of miles he has been traveling in repulsive intimacy with three soft, fat giants whose names are, respectively, Fatigue, Heat, and Monotony. Each one by turns has lolled and wallowed over him, and so worn down his resistence that he is fairly gasping for relief from any quarter.

It's a long pilgrimage from any one of the more populous centers of

Texas. I have tried every route, and I prefer the one presenting the most violent contrasts: the Bankhead Highway, U. S. 80 to Pecos, thence south to Balmorrhea and on up Limpia Canyon into the mountains.

I can assure the August tourist that if he takes this route, he will arrive well baked, so weary from looking over plains alternating with greasewood flats glazed with alkali, and into the mirage shimmering down long stretches of pavement, that his eyes will welcome anything to lean upon. I can give him the further assurance that when the mountains are recognized, first mistaken for a bank of cloud along the southwestern horizon, his vacation will begin, since anticipation now has something tangible to take hold of.

I camped in a valley about ten miles southwest of Fort Davis, in sight of the famous Bloys Campmeeting Grounds at an elevation of about six thousand feet.

The first animal acquaintance I made there was a squirrel; not the red fox squirrel of the Central Texas creek and river bottoms, nor the large black one of the Edwards Plateau, but the half-black and slightly smaller rock squirrel. It is curious that the same variation in color occurs in European countries. Thus, while squirrels of north and west Europe are of a bright red color, those of the mountainous regions of southern Europe are a deep blackish gray.

This animal approached my camp after very little reconnoitering and began digging a burrow within ten feet of my cot. I lay perfectly still, he proceeded with confidence. If I made the slightest motion, however, even to turn the page of a book, he scampered away, and returned only after the great beast (as he doubtless considered me) had gone back to sleep.

When he had excavated enough of a hole to hide his head and shoulders, he evidenced his misgiving by backing out every now and then to look me over and see that I had not changed position. Sometimes he would study me for two or three minutes before recovering sufficient assurance to resume his digging. It took him two days to complete the burrow, and from then on he improved each shining hour, storing in the deep-delved earth the little acorns of the gray and Emory oaks nearby which bore a heavy mast.

He came in from his excursions with cheeks puffed out, giving his whole physiognomy a blowsy, bloated, dissipated look. A few moments later he would emerge with his face not "lifted," but, on the other hand, considerably let down. He made the same round many, many times: first a short gallop to a small oak tree, up to its topmost branches to feed a while, then a leap to a larger tree—sampling, sampling, sampling—finally gathering a supply of fruit proper for storing. Then down he came, and, by another route, back to his burrow. At the entrance he would pause for a moment with his cheeks ridiculously inflated, take a good, long look at me out of his large, lustrous eyes, and dive in. I think he repeated exactly this routine a dozen times in one morning.

I was told that often the squirrel is ousted from his painfully dug den by a skunk, who prefers evicting others to digging a place for himself. My friend Ross Graves, who has been a professional trapper in the Davis Mountains for many years, doubts this story, especially in so far as concerns the hognose skunk, which is too large to enter the burrow of a rock squirrel. If any skunk does this, he says, it must be the Texas spotted skunk. In summer months this skunk avails himself of a variety of shelters, such as packrat dens, brush piles, or prickly pear bunches. In extremely cold weather, he occupies abandoned prairie dog holes, an armadillo den, or a burrow of his own making. Mr. Graves is of the opinion that he is able to take over a den from any small animal, provided it is large enough for him to enter. He apparently makes the mistake sometimes of intruding upon coyotes or even upon red wolves. Says this trapper, "I have seen a number of instances when a coyote or a red wolf had killed a skunk near his den." Whether the skunk was attempting an eviction or just happened to come along, innocently inspecting the mouth of the wolf's burrow to see whether or not anybody was home, the record does not make clear.

The rock squirrel seemed to prefer acorns from the topmost branches. He sampled the lower ones, but took those from the top for his hoard. The band-tailed pigeons in a nearby oak fed from the topmost branches also, but not so daintily as the squirrel, or with such discrimination either. They gobbled up these small acorns voraciously, cup and all.

The feeding and hoarding habits of the rock squirrel made a great impression on me, for I had been watching recently the way of our own fox squirrel with a much more valuable nut, the pecan. The contrast is quite painful, especially to the pecan-grower. Our fox squirrel begins operations in July while pecans are still green with husk tightly sealed to the nut and, apparently impatient for his favorite food, tears into them with a vengeance.

He gnaws the green husk down to the shell of the nut where the bitter juice bites his thievish tongue, and then throws it down. Not only does he cast away this one, but also the two or three or half a dozen others growing on the same twig—rejecting them after having tasted only one out of the whole cluster. About one in fifty of these green pecans the squirrel seems to find a little palatable, for he eats about a third of it. I sat under a tree in which two were feeding one afternoon in early August, watch in hand, and counted the pecans they discarded in five minutes—forty-six.

On a peak a couple of miles west of the Campmeeting Grounds I had my first encounter with the Mearns quail. I had read a dozen descriptions by competent ornithologists of the the antics of this creature, and should have known just what to expect. And still she took me completely by surprise. There is no warning adequate to prepare one for the impersonation which this miscalled "fool quail" puts on when startled from her hiding.

I had reached the summit after a long climb, leg-weary and winded, and was about to seat myself on a boulder when, from right under my feet, the bird flounced out of the grass. She shattered the armor of my suspicion at a stroke and made an open-mouthed, wide-eyed gull of me before I knew it. I am glad there was no one looking on. Indeed, for the moment I didn't even identify the bird. I saw only a flapping ball of feathers emitting a variety of nerve-shattering sounds like the clamor of protesting guinea fowl mingled with the squawks and cackling of excited hens.

She flounced around me just barely out of reach of my hand for several minutes, often lying on her side in the grass and fluttering her upper wing as if mortally wounded.

Finally, it dawned upon me that this was a Mearns quail. I walked over to a boulder and sat down to see her finish out her little comedy. She seemed puzzled for a moment, like an actress who begins getting boos instead of the applause she expects. She flew away about twenty steps and again began her unearthly vociferation. In about three minutes there appeared nearby a young bird, perhaps half grown. It took its stand on a stone about ten feet away from me and began answering its mother. Both were greatly excited, but neither showed any disposition to run.

I then had a good opportunity to study the markings of the old bird and compare them item for item with my memory of the famous painting Fuertes made of one in the Chisos Mountains. Here I saw the "wall-paper pattern" of the head, the dark front, the streaks, dots and dapplings of the sides, all said to make up one of the most remarkable pieces of camouflage in nature.

Presently both birds quieted down. The youngling rejoined its mother, who, after pausing just a moment to "mushroom" her crest, led her darling quietly away into the tall grass.

Of course this bird was not as crazy as she appeared to be. "Though this be madness, yet there is method in it." It is not unusual to find feigning in the bird world as a device for luring an enemy away from young or from a nest. The killdeer puts on a pitiful show, trailing a wing and uttering a cry like that of a lost soul. The mourning dove's act is not quite so convincing, but the intent to deceive is still apparent. This "crazy quail," however, takes you by storm, startles and confounds, finally excites compassion, and then wanders away unconcernedly, leaving the observer feeling rather silly that he should have been taken in by such a synthetic tantrum.

Another time I climbed the same peak again, hoping to find another crazy quail; but no such luck. I did get to see a pair of *paisanos* posing on a granite boulder, outlined against the sky, the male's crest flushed and his tail raised at just about the angle at which, in his jauntiest mood, the late President Roosevelt was wont to tilt upward his long cigarette-holder.

I found also on the high tabletop a pair of Townsend warblers, early migrants, cousin to the golden-cheeked warbler and rivaling the golden-cheek in startling patterns of yellow and black. Then, off a cliff, dashing by at lightning speed, I saw for the first time in these mountains the white-patched form of the white-throated swift.

Any swift anywhere always excites me. There is one species of the swift family that is the fastest animal which wears wings;* it has been

---

* According to A. C. Bent (*Life Histories of North American Birds of Prey,* Part II, Bulletin 170, pp. 59-60, U. S. Nat. Museum), the utmost speed of the duck hawk "has been estimated as ranging between 150 and 200 miles per hour; it may attain or even exceed such speed in its swift plunges, but no such speed could be maintained for any great distance. D. D. McLean timed with a stop watch a hunting duck hawk and estimated its speed as between 165 and 180 miles per hour. The same authority reports a duck hawk passing an airplane which was in a nose dive at an estimated 175 miles per hour. The aviator reported that the hawk diving at a duck 'passed me like I was standing still.' " But that was a "stoop" and hardly to be counted as flight proper. The "stoop" of the bearded eagle has been estimated, also, at 200 miles per hour.

clocked by airplane at two hundred miles per hour in sustained flight. The swift is the only bird that flies with alternate wingbeats and has a continual fever raging in his body (111 degrees Fahrenheit); and, whereas man's eye has only one area of acute vision, the swift's eye has three.

Swifts have always been mystery birds. The older ornithologist classified them as swallows; now they are put into the same family with goatsuckers and hummingbirds. The disappearance in the fall of the common chimney swift is so sudden as to seem almost magical. Today hundreds are squeaking in your chimney; tomorrow there is not one to be found anywhere, high or low—gone they are until the insects fly again in the spring. This abrupt disappearance so puzzled the delightfully cautious Gilbert White that he flirted all his life with the theory, widely accepted at the time, that the English swifts simply crawled into the mud and hibernated for the winter.

With all the research of the past fifty years on the migration of birds, tracing their routes and destinations out in minutest detail, the common chimney swift outwitted the researchers until quite recently. Only within the past year was his winter residence discovered to be on the upper reaches of a tributary of the Amazon in a far corner of northern Peru. Chapman had guessed "Amazonia" in 1931—certainly wide of a bull's-eye, but at that the nearest mark of any guess until the winter resort was definitely determined.

I made a note on September 10, 1942, of seeing many swifts coning up hundreds of feet in the air at 7th Street and East Avenue in Austin with the City Market serving approximately as the base of the cone. A year later, seeing the same exhibition, I added the following: "Probably catching insects rising from the fruits and vegetables of the City Market."

Late one spring afternoon I was sitting with a friend on a window-balcony of the southeast corner room, third floor, of the Driskill Hotel in Austin, watching the nuptial flights of swifts. Suddenly two came together in the air and maintained contact throughout a fall straight down of about three hundred feet before separating. This may have been the consummation of the nuptial flight, or it may have been two rivals fighting for the favor of a female, or mere play. Anyway, it was quite startling.

The climax of my bird-watching on my most recent trip to the Davis Mountains occurred in the lowlands at a ground-tank near the Fort

Davis-Marfa Road where a fork leads off to Valentine. Here for the first time, although I have hunted for him arduously along the Mexican border both in Texas and in New Mexico, I saw at last the famous phainopepla—not only one, but a whole family. There is no mistaking the male of this species. He is velvet black with a greenish sheen upon his shoulders; has a tall, slender crest, curved forward, and a reddish iris. He is not quite as long as a mockingbird, carries himself with great pride, and, in flight, shows white spots on the wings. The books I have read don't do this bird justice.

The female and young are of a dirty brownish color with little to attract the attention except the crest. I returned to the pond the following morning and had the pleasure of seeing the whole family again. The morning following that, however, was cold and drizzly, and, although I waited two hours, they didn't show up. The phainopepla is called a flycatcher, but he is no kin to our flycatchers. He takes his prey with the same technique, that is, he darts after flying insects from a perch and snaps them in flight; but there the resemblance ends. He is the only species of his family, the silky flycatchers, to breed within the borders of the United States. Indeed, there are only four species of this family in the world, and they are all peculiar to Mexico and Central America. The taxonomists place them near our waxwings; and there is a forward curve to the crest of the phainopepla which does suggest the waxwing's crest rather than that of any other of our crested species.

On the way home I made only one overnight camp, and that was in a mesquite pasture about halfway between Odessa and Midland. Except for the mesquite, all vegetation was in a bad way. There had been only two inches of rainfall in the last seven months.

As no birds appeared around the camp next morning, I strolled over to a windmill about a mile away where I found a ground-tank nearly dry. At its margin, flourishing like the proverbial green bay tree, was an immense bois d'arc.

Here I surprised a whole family of Bullock orioles bathing in the dirty water; also scissor-tailed flycatchers. A pair of these elegant birds were swooping down and breasting the water just enough to cause a little splash. Time and again, until their feathers must have been quite wet, these two bathers dashed their pearly gray breasts against the still water and fluttered out, each time flashing a glimpse of the delicate salmon pink with which the underwing surface is lined.

ROY BEDICHEK

A solitary mockingbird had taken possession of the luxurious bois d'arc and would permit no other bird to come near. Even the scissor-tailed flycatchers avoided his fierce and ill-humored dives. Thus, true to his character, he monopolized this one oasis of green in a wide and withered landscape. A white-necked raven flew past, in appearance hardly to be told from a crow. He betrays himself, however, the moment he opens his mouth. His voice is ragged and sore-throated in comparison with the brisk, rasping "caw" of the American crow.

I trailed back to camp with my heart still in the highlands. There was no birdlife in the sky, and little life of any kind on earth except myriads of millepods which last night's shower had made active. You could hardly walk without stepping on one. I thought what a bonanza this would be for my odd little friend, the armadillo, which is exceedingly fond of the thousand-legged worm and often in the Austin area roots half an hour to turn up *one* such tidbit.

The memory of an experience is pleasanter, sometimes, than the experience itself was. Looking back from this flat expanse of country, I recall one moment which stood out above all others. I had climbed to an altitude of about seven thousand feet. The open character of the mountain permitted the eye to range far and away over great distances punctuated by peaks, scored by bluffs, interspersed here and there with lower elevations, smooth and rounded, which led the eye downward by degrees to long, gradual valleys, peaceful and inviting, dotted with clumps of oaks, some bright green and some a deeper, bluish hue.

On this lookout I experienced the effort of trying to lengthen out the sight, widen its scope, taxing it a little and a little more to extend its reach to the utmost through air so clear that distance did not obscure an object or fuzz up its outline, but only reduced its proportions. At the same time I felt the need of more expansive breathing. The struggle for oxygen and the greater visual effort were really stimulating rather than unpleasant compulsions. It was delightful to feel the tonic effect of deeper inhalations while the eye encompassed the spread and pomp of this far-flung mountain scenery.

Even with no nature-hobby to indulge, if one is enough of an East Indian (as I am) to enjoy periods of pure, undiluted contemplation as opposed to intellectual effort of any kind or character, he may here (comfortably above the torpid life of the lowlands) "fleet the time idly" for a few summer days at least, drifting along such currents of musing as these cool solitudes may set going, and come out the fresher for it. Indeed, if William Wordsworth (as he solemnly assures us he did) cured completely a sore heel by giving up temporarily the rigors of poetical composition, surely the rubs, galls, and abrasions of the spirit may be soothed if not healed by simple abandonment for a time of mental strife —a remedy made particularly easy in these open mountains where one may with a kind of yoga-detachment immerse himself in the silence of sunset or of the rise of stars.

Cave Pictures
Carlsbad Caverns

BERNICE AMES

Two cameras threaten
this brooding in a great gasp of earth.
One, carefully placed
where stalagmites are labeled
flashes brightness with a litter of bulbs.

The other, hesitant,
polar-bear paces
the small choice of angle.
Thinking infinity and taking f5.6
leaves cavernous room for distortion.

Loneliness snuffs the last light.
Soon bats will rise like smoke
from the mouth of the cave,
dragging dusk over darkness.
The only escape is into the lens.

Sanchez

RICHARD DOKEY

THAT SUMMER the son of Juan Sanchez went to work for the Flotill Cannery in Stockton. Juan drove with him to the valley in the old Ford.

While they drove, the boy, whose name was Jesus, told him of the greatness of the cannery, of the great aluminum buildings, the marvelous machines, and the belts of cans that never stopped running. He told him of the building on one side of the road where the cans were made and how the cans ran in a metal tube across the road to the cannery. He described the food machines, the sanitary precautions. He laughed when he spoke of the labeling. His voice was serious about the money.

When they got to Stockton, Jesus directed him to the central district of town, the skidrow where the boy was to live while he worked for the Flotill. It was a cheap hotel on Center Street. The room smelled. There was a table with one chair. The floor was stained like the floor of a public urinal and the bed was soiled, as were the walls. There were no drapes on the windows. A pall spread out from the single light bulb overhead that was worked with a length of grimy string.

"I will not stay much in the room," Jesus said, seeing his father's face. "It is only for sleep. I will be working overtime too. There is also the entertainment."

Jesus led him from the room and they went out into the street. Next to the hotel there was a vacant lot where a building had stood. The hole which was left had that recent, peculiar look of uprootedness. There were the remains of the foundation, the broken flooring, and the cracked bricks of tired red to which the gray blotches of mortar clung like dried phlegm. But the ground had not yet taken on the opaqueness of wear that the air and sun give it. It gleamed dully in the light and held to itself where it had been torn, as earth does behind a plow. Juan studied the hole for a time; then they walked up Center Street to Main, passing other empty lots, and then moved east toward Hunter Street. At the corner of Hunter and Main a wrecking crew was at work. An iron ball was suspended from the end of a cable and a tall machine swung the ball up and back and then whipped it forward against the building. The ball was very thick-looking, and when it struck the wall the building trembled, spurted dust, and seemed to cringe inward. The vertical lines of the building had gone awry. Juan shook each time the iron struck the wall.

"They are tearing down the old buildings," Jesus explained. "Redevelopment," he pronounced. "Even my building is to go someday."

Juan looked at his son. "And what of the men?" he asked. "Where do the men go when there are no buildings?"

Jesus, who was a head taller than his father, looked down at him and then shrugged in that Mexican way, the head descending and cocking while the shoulders rise as though on puppet strings. "*Quien sabe?*"

"And the large building there?" Juan said, looking across the rows of parked cars in Hunter Square. "The one whose roof rubs the sky. Of what significance?"

"That is the new courthouse," Jesus said.

"There are no curtains on the windows."

"They do not put curtains on such windows," Jesus explained.

"No," Juan sighed, "that is true."

They walked north on Hunter past the new Bank of America and entered an old building. They stood to one side of the entrance. Jesus smiled proudly and inhaled the stale air.

"This is the entertainment," he said.

Juan looked about. A bar was at his immediate left and a bald man in a soiled apron stood behind it. Beyond the bar there were many thick-wooded tables covered with green material. Men crouched over them and cone-shaped lights hung low from the ceiling casting broadening cones of light downward upon the men and tables. Smoke drifted and rolled in the light and pursued the men when they moved quickly. There was the breaking noise of balls striking together, the hard wooden rattle of the cues in the racks upon the wall, the hum slither of the scoring disks along the loose wires overhead, the explosive cursing of the men. The room was warm and dirty. Juan shook his head.

"I have become proficient at the game," Jesus said.

"This is the entertainment," Juan said, still moving his head.

Jesus turned and walked outside. Juan followed. The boy pointed across the parked cars past the courthouse to a marquee on Main Street.

"There are also motion pictures," Jesus said.

Juan had seen one movie as a young man working in the fields near Fresno. He had understood no English then. He sat with his friends in the leather seats that had gum under the arms and watched the images move upon the white canvas. The images were dressed in expensive clothes. There was laughing and dancing. One of the men did kissing with two very beautiful women, taking turns with each when the other was absent. This had embarrassed Juan, the embracing and unhesitating submission of the women with so many unfamiliar people to watch. Juan loved his wife, was very tender and gentle with her before she died. He never went to another motion picture, even after he had learned English, and this kept him from the Spanish films as well.

"We will go to the cannery now," Jesus said, taking his father's arm. "I will show you the machines."

Juan permitted himself to be led away, and they moved back past the bank to where the men were destroying the building. A ragged hole, like a wound, had been opened in the wall. Juan stopped and watched. The iron ball came forward tearing at the hole, enlarging it, exposing the empty interior space that had once been a room. The floor of the room teetered at a precarious angle. The wood was splintered and very dry in the noon light.

"I do not think I will go to the cannery," Juan said.

The boy looked at his father like a child who has made a toy out of string and bottle caps only to have it ignored.

"But it is honorable work," Jesus said, suspecting his father. "And it pays well."

"Honor," Juan said. "Honor is a serious matter. It is not a question of honor. You are a man now. All that is needed is a room and a job at the Flotill. Your father is tired, that is all."

"You are disappointed," Jesus said, hanging his head.

"No," Juan said. "I am beyond disappointment. You are my son. Now you have a place in the world. You have the Flotill."

Nothing more was said, and they walked to the car. Juan got in behind the wheel. Jesus stood beside the door, his arms at his sides, the fingers spread. Juan looked up at him. The boy's eyes were big.

"You are my son," Juan said, "and I love you. Do not have disappointment. I am not of the Flotill. Seeing the machines would make it worse. You understand, *niño*?"

"Si, Papa," Jesus said. He put a hand on his father's shoulder.

"It is a strange world, *niñito*," Juan said.

"I will earn money. I will buy a red car and visit you. All in Twin Pines will be envious of the son of Sanchez, and they will say that Juan Sanchez has a son of purpose."

"Of course, Jesus *mio*," Juan said. He bent and placed his lips against the boy's hand. "I will look for the bright car. I will write regardless." He smiled, showing yellowed teeth. "Goodbye, *querido*," he said. He started the car, raced the engine once too high, and drove off up the street.

When Juan Sanchez returned to Twin Pines, he drove the old Ford to the top of Bear Mountain and pushed it over. He then proceeded systematically to burn all that was of importance to him, all that was of nostalgic value, and all else that meant nothing in itself, like the extra chest of drawers he had kept after his wife's death, the small table in the bedroom, and the faded mahogany stand in which he kept his pipe and tobacco and which sat next to the stuffed chair in the front room. He broke all the dishes, cups, plates, discarded all the cooking and eating utensils in the same way. The fire rose in the blue wind carrying dust wafers of ash in quick, breathless spirals and then released them in a panoply of diluted smoke, from which they drifted and spun and fell like burnt snow. The forks, knives, and spoons became very black with a flaky crust of oxidized metal. Then Juan burned his clothing, all that was unnecessary, and the smoke dampened and took on a thick smell. Finally he threw his wife's rosary into the flames. It was a cheap one, made of wood, and disappeared immediately. He went into his house then and lay down on the bed. He went to sleep.

When he awoke, it was dark and cool. He stepped outside, urinated, and then returned, shutting the door. The darkness was like a mammoth held breath, and he felt very awake listening to the beating of his heart. He knew he would not be able to sleep any more now, and so he lay awake thinking.

He thought of his village in Mexico, the baked clay of the small houses spread like little forts against the stillness of the bare mountains, the men with their great wide hats, their wide, white pants, and their naked, brown-skinned feet, splayed against the fine dust of the road. He saw the village cistern and the women all so big and slow, always with child, enervated by the earth and the unbearable sun, the enervation passing into their very wombs like the heat from the yellow sun so that the wombs themselves bred quiet acceptance, slow, silent blood. The men walked bent as though carrying the air or sky, slept against the buildings in the shade like old dogs, ate dry, hot food that dried them inside and seemed to bake the moisture from the flesh, so that the men and women while still young had faces like eroded fields and fingers like stringy, empty stream beds. It was a hard land. It took the life of his father and mother before he was twelve and the life of his aunt, with whom he then lived, before he was sixteen.

When he was seventeen he went to Mexicali because he had heard much of America and the money to be obtained there. They took him in a truck with other men to work in the fields around Bakersfield, then in the fields near Fresno. On his return to Mexicali he met La Belleza, as he came to call her: loveliness. He married her when he was nineteen and she only fifteen. The following year she had a baby girl. It was stillborn and the birth almost killed her, for the doctor said the passage was over-small. The doctor cautioned him (warned him, really) La Belleza could not have children and live, and he went outside into the moonlight and wept.

He had heard much of the loveliness of the Sierra Nevada above what was called the Mother Lode, and because he feared the land, believed almost that it possessed the power to kill him—as it had killed his mother and father, his aunt, was in fact, slow killing so many of his people—he wanted to run away from it to the high white cold of the California mountains, where he believed his heart would grow, his blood run and, perhaps, the passage of La Belleza might open. Two years later he was taken in the trucks to Stockton in the San Joaquin Valley to pick tomatoes and he saw the Sierra Nevada above the Mother Lode.

It was from a distance, of course, and in the summer, so that there was no snow. But when he returned he told La Belleza about the blueness of the mountains in the warm, still dawn, the extension of them, the aristocracy of their unmoving height, and that they were only fifty miles away from where he had stood.

He worked very hard now and saved his money. He took La Belleza back to his village, where he owned the white clay house of his father. It was cheaper to live there while he waited, fearing the sun, the dust, and the dry, airless silence, for the money to accumulate. That fall La Belleza became pregnant again by an accident of passion and the preg-

178   THE SOUTHWEST REVIEW READER

nancy was very difficult. In the fifth month the doctor—who was an atheist—said that the baby would have to be taken or else the mother would die. The village priest, a very loud, dramatic man—an educated man who took pleasure in striking a pose—proclaimed the wrath of God in the face of such sacrilege. It was the child who must live, the priest cried. The pregnancy must go on. There was the immortal soul of the child to consider. But Juan decided for the atheist doctor, who did take the child. La Belleza lost much blood. At one point her heart had stopped beating. When the child was torn from its mother and Juan saw that it was a boy, he ran out of the clay house of his father and up the dusty road straight into a hideous red moon. He cursed the earth, the sky. He cursed his village, himself, the soulless indifference of the burnt mountains. He cursed God.

Juan was very afraid now, and though it cost more money he had himself tied by the atheist doctor so that he could never again put the life of La Belleza in danger, for the next time, he knew with certainty, would kill her.

The following summer he went again on the trucks to the San Joaquin Valley. The mountains were still there, high and blue in the quiet dawn, turned to a milky pastel by the heat swirls and haze of midday. Sometimes at night he stepped outside the shacks in which the men were housed and faced the darkness. It was tragic to be so close to what you wanted, he would think, and be unable to possess it. So strong was the feeling in him, particularly during the hot, windless evenings, that he sometimes went with the other men into Stockton, where he stood on the street corners of skidrow and talked, though he did not get drunk on cheap wine or go to the whores, as did the other men. Nor did he fight.

They rode in old tilted trucks covered with canvas and sat on rude benches staring out over the slats of the tail gate. The white glare of headlights crawled up and lay upon them, waiting to pass. They stared over the whiteness. When the lights swept out and by, the glass of the side windows shone. Behind the windows sometimes there would be the ghost of an upturned face, before the darkness clamped shut. Also, if one of the men had a relative who lived in the area, there was the opportunity to ride in a car.

He had done so once. He had watched the headlights of the car pale then whiten outward and the looks on the faces that seemed to float upon the whiteness of the light. The men sat forward, arms on knees, and looked over the glare into the darkness. After that he always rode in the trucks.

When he returned to his village after that season's harvest, he knew they could wait no longer. He purchased a dress of silk for La Belleza and in a secondhand store bought an American suit for himself. He had worked hard, sold his father's house, saved all his money, and on a bright day in early September they crossed the border at Mexicali and caught the Greyhound for Fresno.

Juan got up from his bed to go outside. He stood looking up at the stars. The stars were pinned to the darkness, uttering little flickering cries of light, and as always he was moved by the nearness and profusion of their agony. His mother had told him the stars were a kind of purgatory in which souls burned in cold, silent repentance. He had wondered after her death if the earth too were not a star burning in loneliness, and he could never look at them later without thinking this and believing that the earth must be the brightest of all stars. He walked over to the remains of the fire. A dull heat came from the ashes and a column of limp smoke rose and then bent against the night wind. He studied the ashes for a time and then looked over the tall pine shapes of the southern sky. It was there all right. He could feel the dry char of its heat, that deeper, dryer burning. He imagined it, of course. But it was there nevertheless. He went back into the cabin and lay down, but now his thoughts were only of La Belleza and the beautiful Sierra Nevada.

From Fresno all the way up the long valley to Stockton they had been full with pride and expectation. They had purchased oranges and chocolate bars and they ate them laughing. The other people on the bus looked at them, shook their heads and slept or read magazines. He and La Belleza gazed out the window at the land.

In Stockton they were helped by a man named Eugenio Mendez. Juan had met him while picking tomatoes in the delta. Eugenio had eight children and a very fat but very kind and tolerant wife named Anilla. He helped them find a cheap room off Center Street, where they stayed while determining their next course of action. Eugenio had access to a car, and it was he who drove them finally to the mountains.

It was a day like no other day in his life: to be sitting in the car with La Belleza, to be in this moving car with his Belleza heading straight toward the high, lovely mountains. The car was traveling from the flat-

180

ness of the valley into the rolling brown swells of the foothills, where hundreds of deciduous and evergreen oaks grew, their puffball shapes still pictures of exploding holiday rockets, only green, but spreading up and out and then around and down in nearly perfect canopies. At Jackson the road turned and began an immediate, constant climb upward.

It was as though his dream about it had materialized. He had never seen so many trees, great with dignity: pines that had bark gray twisted and stringy like hemp; others whose bark resembled dry, flat ginger cookies fastened with black glue about a drum, and others whose bark pulled easily away; and those called redwoods, standing stiff and tall, amber-hued with straight rolls of bark as thick as his fist, flinging out high above great arms of green. And the earth, rich red, as though the blood of scores of Indians had just flowed there and dried. Dark patches of shadow stunned with light, blue flowers, orange flowers, birds, even deer. They saw them all on that first day

"*A donde vamos?*" Eugenio had asked. "Where are we going?"

"*Bellisima,*" Juan replied. "Into much loveliness."

They did not reach Twin Pines that day. But on their return a week later they inquired in Jackson about the opportunity of buying land or a house in the mountains. The man, though surprised, told them of the sawmill town of Twin Pines, where there were houses for sale.

Their continued luck on that day precipitated the feeling in Juan that it was indeed the materialization of a dream. He had been able in all those years to save two thousand dollars and a man had a small shack for sale at the far edge of town. He looked carefully at Juan, at La Belleza and said, "One thousand dollars," believing they could never begin to possess such a sum. When Juan handed him the money, the man was so struck that he made out a bill of sale. Juan Sanchez and his wife had their home in the Sierra.

When Juan saw the cabin close up, he knew the man had stolen their money. It was small, the roof slanted to one side, the door would not close evenly. The cabin was gradually falling downhill. But it was theirs and he could, with work, repair it. Hurriedly they drove back to Jackson, rented a truck, bought some cheap furniture and hauled it back to the cabin. When they had moved in, Juan brought forth a bottle of whiskey and for the first time in his life proceeded to get truly drunk.

Juan was very happy with La Belleza. She accepted his philosophy completely, understood his need, made it her own. In spite of the people of the town, they created a peculiar kind of joy. And anyway Juan had knowledge about the people.

Twin Pines had been founded, he learned, by one Benjamin Carter, who lived with his daughter in a magnificent house on the hill overlooking town. This Benjamin Carter was a very wealthy man. He had come to the mountains thirty years before to save his marriage, for he had been poor once and loved when he was poor, but then he grew very rich because of oil discovered on his father's Ohio farm and he went away to the city and became incapable of love in the pursuit of money and power. When he at last married the woman whom he had loved, a barrier had grown between them, for Ben Carter had changed but the woman had not. Then the woman became ill and Ben Carter promised her he would take her West, all the way West away from the city so that it could be as it had been in the beginning of their love. But the woman was with child. And so Ben Carter rushed to the California mountains, bought a thousand acres of land, and hurried to build his house before the rain and snows came. He hired many men and the house was completed, except for the interior work and the furnishings. All that winter men he had hired worked in the snow to finish the house while Ben Carter waited with his wife in the city. When it was early spring they set out for California, Ben Carter, his wife, and the doctor, who strongly advised against the rough train trip and the still rougher climb by horse and wagon from Jackson to the house. But the woman wanted the child born properly, so they went. The baby came the evening of their arrival at the house, and the woman died all night having it. It was this Ben Carter who lived with that daughter now in the great house on the hill, possessing her to the point, it was said about his madness, that he had murdered a young man who had shown interest in her.

Juan learned all this from a Mexican servant who had worked at the great house from the beginning, and when he told the story to La Belleza she wept because of its sadness. It was a tragedy of love, she explained, and Juan—soaring to the heights of his imagination—believed that the town, all one hundred souls, had somehow been infected with the tragedy, as they were touched by the shadow of the house itself, which crept directly up the highway each night when the sun set. This was why they left dead chickens and fish on the porch of the cabin or dumped garbage into the yard. He believed he understood something profound and so did nothing about these incidents, which, after all, might have been the pranks of boys. He did not want the infection to touch him, nor the deeper infection of their prejudice because he was Mexican. He was not indifferent. He was simply too much in love with La Belleza and the Sierra Nevada. Finally the incidents stopped.

Now the life of Juan Sanchez entered its most beautiful time. When the first snows fell he became delirious, running through the pines, shouting, rolling on the ground, catching the flakes in his open mouth, bringing them in his cupped hands to rub in the hair of La Belleza, who stood in the doorway of their cabin laughing at him. He danced, made up a song about snowflakes falling on a desert and then a prayer which he addressed to the Virgin of Snowflakes. That night while the snow fluttered like wings against the bedroom window, he celebrated the coming of the whiteness with La Belleza.

He understood that first year in the mountains that love was an enlargement of himself, that it enabled him to be somehow more than he had ever been before, as though certain pores of his senses had only just been opened. Whereas before he had desired the Sierra Nevada for its beauty and contrast to his harsh fatherland, now he came to acquire a love for it, and he loved it as he loved La Belleza; he loved it as a woman. Also in that year he came to realize that there was a fear or dread about such love. It was more a feeling than anything else, something which reached thought now and then, particularly in those last moments before sleep. It was an absolutely minor thing. The primary knowledge was of the manner in which this love seemed to assimilate everything, rejecting all that would not yield. This love was a kind of blindness.

That summer Juan left La Belleza at times to pick the crops of the San Joaquin Valley. He had become good friends with the servant of the big house and this man had access to the owner's car, which he always drove down the mountain in a reckless but confident manner. After that summer Juan planned also to buy a car, not out of material desire, but simply because he believed this man would one day kill himself, and also because he did not wish to be dependent.

He worked in the walnuts near the town of Linden and again in the tomatoes of the rich delta. He wanted very much to have La Belleza with him, but that would have meant more money and a hotel room in the skidrow, and that was impossible because of the pimps and whores, the drunks and criminals and the general despair, which the police always tapped at periodic intervals, as one does a vat of fermenting wine. The skidrow was a place his love could not assimilate, but he could not ignore it because so many of his people were lost there. He stayed in the labor camps, which were also bad because of what the men did with themselves, but they were tolerable. He worked hard and as often as he could and gazed at the mountains, which he could always see clearly in the morning light. When tomato season was over he returned to La Belleza.

Though the town would never accept them as equals, it came that summer to tolerate their presence. La Belleza made straw baskets which she sold to the townspeople and which were desired for their beauty and intricacy of design. Juan carved animals, a skill he had acquired from his father, and these were also sold. The activity succeeded so well that Juan took a box of their things to Jackson, where they were readily purchased. The following spring he was able to buy the Ford.

Juan acquired another understanding that second year in the mountains. It was, he believed, that love, his love, was the single greatness of which he was capable, the thing which ennobled him and gave him honor. Love, he became convinced, was his only ability, the one success he had accomplished in a world of insignificance. It was a simple thing, after all, made so painfully simple each time he went to the valley to work with his face toward the ground, every time he saw the men in the fields and listened to their talk and watched them drive off to the skidrow at night. After he had acquired this knowledge, the nights he had to spend away from La Belleza were occupied by a new kind of loneliness, as though a part of his body had been separated from the whole. He began also to understand something more of the fear or dread that seemed to trail behind love.

It happened late in the sixth year of their marriage. It was impossible, of course, and he spent many hours at the fire in their cabin telling La Belleza of the impossibility, for the doctor had assured him that all had been well tied. He had conducted himself on the basis of that assumption. But doctors can be wrong. Doctors can make mistakes. La Belleza was with child.

For the first five months the pregnancy was not difficult, and he came almost to believe that indeed the passage of La Belleza would open. He prayed to God. He prayed to the earth and sky. He prayed to the soul of his mother. But after the fifth month the true sickness began and he discarded prayer completely in favor of blasphemy. There was no God and never could be God in the face of such sickness, such unbelievable human sickness. Even when he had her removed to the hospital in Stockton, the doctors could not stop it, but it continued so terribly that he believed that La Belleza carried sickness itself in her womb.

After seven months the doctors decided to take the child. They brought La Belleza into a room with lights and instruments. They worked on her for a long time and she died there under the lights with the doctors cursing and perspiring above the large wound of her pain. They did not tell him of the child, which they had cleaned and placed in an incubator, until the next day. That night he sat in the Ford and tried to see it all, but he could only remember the eyes of La Belleza in the vortex of pain. They were of an almost eerie calmness. They had possessed calmness, as one possesses the truth. Toward morning he slumped sideways on the seat and went to sleep.

So he put her body away in the red earth of the town cemetery beyond the cabin. The pines came together overhead and in the heat of midday a shadow sprinkled with spires of light lay upon the ground so that the earth was cool and clean to smell. He did not even think of taking her back to Mexico, since, from the very beginning, she had always been part of that dream he had dreamed. Now she would always be in the Sierra Nevada, with the orange and blue flowers, the quiet deep whiteness of winter, and all that he ever was or could be was with her.

But he did not think these last thoughts then, as he did now. He had simply performed them out of instinct for their necessity, as he had performed the years of labor while waiting for the infant Jesus to grow to manhood. Jesus. Why had he named the boy Jesus? That, perhaps, had been instinct too. He had stayed after La Belleza's death for the boy, to be with him until manhood, to show him the loveliness of the Sierra Nevada, to instruct him toward true manhood. But Jesus. Ah, Jesus. Jesus the American. Jesus of the Flotill. Jesus understood nothing. Jesus, he believed, was forever lost to knowledge. That day with Jesus had been his own liberation.

For a truth had come upon him after the years of waiting, the ultimate truth that he understood only because La Belleza had passed through his life. Love was beauty, La Belleza and the Sierra Nevada, a kind of created or made thing. But there was another kind of love, a very profound, embracing love that he had felt of late blowing across the mountains from the south and that, he knew now, had always been there from the beginning of his life, disguised in the sun and wind. In this love there was blood and earth and, yes, even God, some kind of god, at least the power of a god. This love wanted him for its own. He understood it, that it had permitted him to have La Belleza and that without it there could have been no Belleza.

Juan placed an arm over his eyes and turned to face the wall. The old bed sighed. An image went off in his head and he remembered vividly the lovely body of La Belleza. In that instant the sound that loving had produced with the bed was alive in him like a forgotten melody, and his body seemed to swell and press against the ceiling. It was particularly cruel because it was so sudden, so intense, and came from so deep within him that he knew it must all still be alive somewhere, and that was the cruelest part of all. He wept softly and held the arm across his eyes.

In the dark morning the people of the town were awakened by the blaze of fire that was the house of Juan Sanchez. Believing that he had perished in the flames, several of the townspeople placed a marker next to the grave of his wife with his name on it. But, of course, on that score they were mistaken. Juan Sanchez had simply gone home.

Politician

ERNEST KROLL

Speaking on the
(*Integer vitae*)
Honesty
Ticket, he
(*Scelerisque*)
Put one hand
Over his
(*Purus*)
Heart.

The Hunter Rests

DAVID CORNEL DE JONG

The taste of the day
then becomes that of nasturtiums
on buttered toast, its smell
that of waterlilies floating
in burgundy wine, yet it
rustles with the crinkled
meaning of old cassocks worn
by a man of a different faith.

Suddenly I tuck in my muscles,
hold my 80 proof breath, and
accept taste, sound and smell
as judgments passed on those
who would shoot pheasants or
peasants wherever they emerge
from harmless coppices, and
I feel as narrow as a casual
comma set amid the lesson of day.

With my head tucked beneath
a misgiving, I take no chance
with emotions or beliefs, and
my value rests like a turtle's
egg in the palm of my slaying
hand, even if I am ready
to forestall anyone who'd upbraid
me for a taste of nasturtiums and
burgundy so far afield, or
the rustle of a no-ways understood
onus amid the sedges and rills.

Art for Art's Sake

ALBERT GUÉRARD

A SHORT WHILE AGO, nothing could have been more *passé* than Art for Art's Sake. The phrase had a stale savor of aestheticism, decadence, the Yellow Nineties, the Mauve Decade—pink striving to be purple. James Branch Cabell, with a melancholy smile, professed to be the ultimate defender of that outmoded creed; and I, who taught it but never practiced it, felt very lonely in the grimly earnest academic world. My faith has not faltered, and I am able to speak today with greater assurance than a decade ago. Let me first nail a few theses on the door, as Luther did at Wittenberg. It is as fair, and as accurate, to identify Art for Art's Sake with Aubrey Beardsley or Des Esseintes, as it would be to equate Democracy with the Dixiecrats. The philosopher of Art for Art's Sake is not James McNeill Whistler, but Immanuel Kant. The best representative of Art for Art's Sake is not Oscar Wilde, but William Shakespeare. If Art for Art's Sake be escape, there are times when the first duty of man is to escape from tyranny, not to accept defeat. The monks escaped from the corruption of the world, Thomas Mann from Nazi oppression, Borgese from the Fascist yoke, MacArthur from Corregidor. The Ivory Tower is not the abode of the slothful: as in the Litanies of the Virgin, it stands for the strength there is in purity—*Turris Eburnea.* The way out of our tragic confusion—national, political, social—is the spirit of art, which I interpret as absolute disinterestedness and honesty, embracing science, but richer and deeper than science itself.

(By this, I do not mean that practical government should be turned over to the artists, that Messrs. Ezra Pound and Thomas Stearns Eliot should take the places of President Eisenhower and Secretary Dulles. Art would be an admirable guide if it were not for the artists; just as communism, the doctrine and practice of the apostolic age, would be an ideal regime if it were not for the Communists.)

Signs are not wanting that the problem of Art for Art's Sake is very much alive, for all minds that are not primitive. It was in 1926 that Abbé Bremond started a controversy about the nature of pure poetry. Paul Valéry, in his introduction to the French National Encyclopaedia, gave as the distinctive character of art its utter usefulness. Ortega y Gasset refused to submit to "the revolt of the masses"—the masses being not the lower orders, the proletariat, but the mass-minded, the conformists, the eager victims of collective hysteria; and he found in art his supreme refuge. E. M. Forster gave a lecture before the American Academy on that once unpopular subject, and managed to "sell" the address to an excellent middle-brow publication, *Harper's Magazine*. I have on my desk a delightful document which bears on its front page Walter Pater's resounding declaration: "Art comes to you proposing frankly to give nothing but the highest quality to your moments as they pass." This leaflet is issued by the Cambridge Trust Company; it announces that the Fogg Art Museum had loaned a few pictures to the bank, so as to take away the stench of pelf and filthy lucre—a sort of aesthetic Airwick or chlorophyll. To be sure, Cambridge moves with such majestic deliberation that this might not be the dawn of a new day, only the afterglow of Ruskin's gospel—that Ruskin who called Harvard's Memorial Hall the finest Gothic structure in America.

A few caricatures of art need to be brushed aside; we must not forget that most idols are caricatures. Art is not erudition about art. Culture is not acquired by memorizing a catalogue. A young lady—it must have been fully half a century ago—asked one of her swains: "Are you fond of Botticelli?" And he answered after a judicial pause: "Well, I believe I prefer Chianti." His rival gloated: "Now you have done it, you fool: Botticelli is not a wine, it is a cheese." For the pure artist, it matters little whether Botticelli be a wine, a cheese, a prize fighter, a dictator, a mayor of New York City. Von Bode once proudly displayed in the Berlin Museum a wax bust of Flora which he ascribed to Leonardo da Vinci. The bust was found to be stuffed with nineteenth-century newspapers, and contemptuously ejected from the temple of art. If it was of such a quality as to impress an expert like Bode, it deserved a place of honor in any museum. Collecting is not identical with appreciations: Soames Forsyte was a shrewd collector. In this field, I am the merest layman; but I know I have the approval of a friend whose authority is unchallenged: Bernard Berenson.

Art is not technique. On the lowest level, the two words are synonymous: there is an art or a technique of peeling potatoes. In the eighteenth century, a project for the development of Paris was known as *le plan des artistes*, that is to say of the experts or technicians. There is a "gentle art of making enemies," and an immensely more profitable art of making friends and influencing people. Whatever it is you are attempting to do, it is preferably to *know how*. But a clumsy effort in the right direction is better than smooth perfection in futilities or in wrongdoing. If murder, according to De Quincey, is one of the fine arts, it is one of the crudest kind, on a level with musical comedy. If technique be the efficient, the approved manner of manufacturing standardized objects, then art is an eternal rebellion against technique—against tricks of the trade, styles, patterns, *poncifs*, clichés; aye, and against precepts à la Boileau, schools, doctrines, and dogmas as well. Art is the constant reassertion of the artist's freedom.

Finally, art is not artificiality, sophistication, preciosity, the esoteric, the cryptic, the hermetic. All this is merely the snobbishness, the pharisaism of art, a "more-cultured-than-thou" attitude. I fully agree with Peter Viereck that art need not limit itself to the obvious, any more than philosophy or science: Hegel and Einstein are frankly difficult, more difficult than Mallarmé. But their difficulty is not an opaque film meant to conceal shallowness. Let us probe our conscience: how much of our admiration for alleged modern poetry is simply the dread of not being counted among the initiated, of being kept out of the temple with the vulgar profane? At the beginning of any art course, we should read over Hans Christian Andersen's profound apologue, "The Emperor's New Clothes." It took a child to exclaim: "But the Emperor has nothing on at all!" Sturdy Molière might also be our guide. In *The Misanthrope*, Oronte recites to Alceste a sonnet, simple enough according to our present standard, but with a taint of preciosity Alceste damns it in the bluntest terms and offers as a model of true art a naïve folk song. It was the same Molière who gave out as the first and greatest of commandments: "As if the great rule of all rules were not to please!" Aye, but to please whom? Demos? The hucksters? The cliques? The professors? One chosen soul? Or simply one's self?

When, with my students, I battle through the problem of pure art, we traverse the field no less than five times. We first take up the problem theoretically, by discussing a few of the innumerable definitions of art that have been proposed in the past. My aim is that of Montaigne in his "Apology for Raymond de Sebonde": to foster healthy skepticism, to release the critical spirit from any dogmatic bondage. Then we go through the history of the idea, beginning with Homer, Plato, and the Bible, down to Aldous Huxley, Ortega y Gasset, André Gide, André Malraux. Next, we examine the negative aspect of the problem: art for some other sake, utilitarianism, philistinism. Then we take up the positive aesthetic gospel: life for art's sake, beauty as the essential principle, the infallible sign of goodness and truth. We are then ready to face our personal responsibility: theory and history have led us to the rim; what peaks can we, with our own eyes, descry in the mist?

The most cursory historical survey reveals that Art for Art's Sake is not a brief disease which afflicted a few in Western Europe some sixty years ago. It is a recurrent, or rather a permanent, tendency. In ages of harmony—those which Henri de Saint-Simon called *organic periods*, when economics, government, science, religion bear the same stamp— art takes the culture of the time for granted and does not need to assert its autonomy. The result is a truly classical synthesis, of impressive majesty. But such periods are rare in the history of the Western world: there are not more than five or six. And they are fleeting: none lasted more than two generations. In *critical periods*, to use Saint-Simon's phraseology, or in *times out of joint*, if you prefer Shakespeare's, traditions and aspirations, doctrines and practices no longer coincide. As a result, the individual is released, he seeks to frame his own law, he spurns forms which have proved hollow, creeds which are hypocrisy, authorities which, because they are unreasoning, have become capricious and tyrannical. This rejection of outworn rule may take many forms: a sentiment of solitude, deepening into melancholy and despair; rebellion or suicide; cynicism and irony; reveling in mere technique, toying with jeweled phrase or strange subtle chord; or again a flight into Utopia, a vanished Golden Age, a new heaven and a new earth about to be revealed. There is a moment, in the life of the individual or even in that of the group, when these feelings are divorced from action, when their only mode of expression is art.

This would go far to explain two giants of literature, Cervantes and Shakespeare. The tremendous release of energy we call the Renaissance was still sweeping them on. But the faith of that great period had waned. Antiquity rediscovered was no longer a fresh delight: it had become pedantic or commonplace. The *virtú* of the Renaissance man clashed with the stern *virtue* of the Reformer. The Reformation itself had bred theological subtleties, fanaticism, hatred. The tragic stalemate, the mutual cancellation of ideals, had one miraculous result. Not the form merely, but the creative energy of art paradoxically survived the wreck of purposes, and we had, as Kant so quaintly put it, "Zweckmässigkeit ohne Zweck," adequacy to purpose without purpose. This clue may help us to interpret Cervantes. World crusade, world conquest, wealth untold, all the dreams, heroic or brutal of sixteenth-century Spain had ended in weariness. Hence the disenchanted cynicism of the greatest book in Spanish literature; there is but one idealist left in the world, Don Quixote, and he is mad. No hope is to be placed in the clodhopper common sense of Sancho Panza: Sancho can never lead. If Don Quixote wakes up, with sobered mind and body ailing unto death, it is no victory for Sancho, who has lost the light of his dull life. Don Quixote does wake up, penitent and wistful. It *was* a dream, but a beautiful dream. This satire on romance, this farewell to romance, is the highest tribute to romance. Art here does not serve even the shadow of a cause: it is "pure."

And this is true of Shakespeare also. Shakespeare did write for money, and he did write for fame: these were incentives, not sources of inspiration. He shared—sincerely or with the half-sincerity of the dramatist— the patriotic enthusiasm which marked the heyday of Elizabeth's reign. But he is, first of all, the poet of the "cursèd spite," the man who is not, and cannot be, Hellenic without scruple or Hebraic without reserve; the belated fighter who can harbor no faith and serve no purpose, while he feels surging within him the power made intense by the earlier strife of faiths and purposes. In Cervantes and Shakespeare, the very causes which should have precipitated decadence led to unique achievements. Don Quixote wakes up, Prospero breaks his wand. The vision leaves not a rack behind. Not a rack? Only supreme masterpieces.

This "law"—if in art we can utter the word "law" without a shrug and a smile—is excellently illustrated by Coleridge and Keats. By 1797, the youthful Jacobin had lost faith in the Revolution—the Koestler, the Silone of his day. He had not yet found a refuge in German transcendentalism. He was, for a brief season, nothing but a pure and supreme poet. There is no sense in "Kubla Khan," although heavy volumes bursting with sense may be written about it. "Christabel" is a sphinx that does not know the answer to its own riddle. The only "lesson" we can draw from "The Ancient Mariner" is: "Always be kind to an albatross." Such intense activity in the impalpable inane cannot be lasting. Coleridge, like Don Quixote and Prospero, felt poetry waning as sense returned: and in his great ode, "Dejection," he expressed that "grief without a pang, void, dark, and drear."

Keats provided the two most quotable and most overworked formulas of the aesthetic gospel: "A thing of beauty is a joy for ever" and " 'Beauty is truth, truth beauty,'—that is all Ye know on earth and all Ye need to know." With him as with Coleridge twenty years earlier, pure art arose amid the ruins of political ideals. Up to 1815, England had been engaged in a titantic struggle, which, naturally, had been waged for the sake of righteousness. It must have required a heroic effort of make-believe to identify righteousness with the oligarchy presided over by the Prince Regent: but in all great countries national faith is equal to any task. By 1818 or 1819—Keats's brief golden years—the victory which was to make the world safe for liberty had lost much of its glamour. What remained was the First Gentleman in Europe, and Caroline his wife, the Peterloo Massacre, Castlereagh; on the Continent, the Holy Alliance. Keats, although "La Belle Dame sans Merci" is the very essence of Romantic medievalism, is the reverse of a sentimental Tory; but what other way is open to entice him? The Napoleonic Legend is not ripe, even in France; the Revolution is but the fading memory of a nightmare; Keats is not ready yet for Shelley's prophetic vision. Nothing remains but beauty unfettered by any purpose—Art for Art's Sake. Had Keats survived . . . But, as President Roosevelt was fond of saying, that is an *iffy* question.

Even the briefest survey should include Théophile Gautier and the defiant preface to his *Mademoiselle de Maupin*. The bourgeoisie had just triumphed with Louis-Philippe: a crowned Calvin Coolidge, wielding an umbrella instead of sword or scepter, staunch in the belief that France's sole business was Business, and that, if you wanted a share in the government of the country, the proper way to qualify yourself was to get rich. Against this regime of the safe and sane—we called it *normalcy*—Gautier sported his crimson waistcoat, shook his unshorn auburn locks, and raised his battle cry: "Epater le bourgeois!" Anything to flabbergast the philistine.

Two generations later, the Republic, so fair under the Empire, had aged dismally into a sagging, dull-eyed, heavy-jowled matron. Socialism had not recovered from the bloodletting of the Commune; the Legitimists were discouraged; the Revanche spirit—a crude ideal, but still an ideal—was waning. Even the spirit of adventure which had partly redeemed the materialism of the Second Empire had been discouraged by the fiasco of Panama. Another moment when Art for Art's Sake would raise its protest against universal mediocrity. A very minor star in the Decadent galaxy, Laurent Tailhade, hailed an anarchistic outrage in the Chamber of Deputies with the words: "What matters it that vague human beings should perish? The gesture was beautiful." Thus did he launch the unforgettable phrase *Beau Geste*, one of the pithiest expressions of Art for Art's Sake. Four months later, at Foyot's, Laurent Tailhade was himself the victim of another anarchist's bomb. The Demiurge—or is it the Spirit Ironic?—is not so mortally afraid of poetic justice as our modern playwrights.

If Cabell, delicate and aloof, reached in the twenties the uncongenial blatancy of fame, it was because the crusading spirit of World War I had perished in party squabbles and frenzied Republican prosperity. Today, in the clash of two vast fanatical materialisms, both believing in mass production and mass thinking, both drunk with doctrines and power, what path of salvation is left to a proud soul, except that of pure art?

Pure art! What is it that makes art impure? The most obvious *sake* that could sully its integrity is the profit motive. In dedicating my book on *Art for Art's Sake* to a great divine, I used as an epigraph the gospel words: "For what shall it profit a man, if he shall gain the whole world, and lose his own soul?" And the most tangible form of profit is money. The sign of all noble activity—of soldier, statesman, scientist, poet, priest—is to be without price. As soon as the thought of lucre creeps in, politics turns into graft, love into prostitution, religion into simony. A potboiler is a stench in the nostrils of the muses.

The principle is so definite and so universal that we might rest satisfied, if we did not remember that Homer, according to tradition, exchanged ballads for bread; that Shakespeare sang for his supper; and that Dr. Samuel Johnson, sturdiest of Britons avowed: "No man but a blockhead ever wrote except for money." This apparent conflict between facts and theory disproves neither: it only compels us to seek a finer adjustment. The proper method is *casuistry*, which is not quibbling, but scrupulous weighing of all the elements in each case. Morally, the intention counts more than the deed. A man may kill another by accident, in self-defense, in the service of the law, in honorable combat, in anger, in treachery: death remains a fact, *Thou shalt not kill* remains a sacred commandment, yet no sane jury will fail to make the proper distinctions. An author is not guilty of the profit motive, when that motive was not present in his mind. Abbé Dimnet was astounded at the financial success of his *Art of Thinking* and Robert Bridges of his *Testament of Beauty*. An author is blameless too if he provides, frankly for gain, the very best that is in him. Success consists in doing the thing you like, and getting paid for it: there is no particular virtue in failure. Alexandre Dumas hugely enjoyed the products of his romance factory; Harold Bell Wright was persuaded that, with harmless entertainment, he was bringing to the masses a great spiritual message. It is even possible for a writer to offer the public something which falls short of his own ideal, because the *merely good enough* has a larger market. A manufacturer is justified in selling a good cheap car, although he wants a better one for his own use: the Chevrolet is on the same moral plane as the Rolls-Royce. The preacher adjusts his sermons to his congregation, not to an audience of fellow theologians. Victor Hugo wrote in the same decade magnificent Miltonic poems—"The End of Satan," "God"—which he did not publish, and and the truly great popular epic *Les Misérables*, in which he adopted the devices of Alexandre Dumas and Eugene Sue. I believe he was justified.

This leaves us with the plain case of the author who, of malice prepense, sells what he knows to be actually bad, because there is a market for it: jerry-built, pretentious pseudo-history, commercialized optimism, wonder drugs against loneliness, frustration, worry; or, in a different sphere, cynicism at so much per word, "daring" and surefire "unconventionality," strip tease and aphrodisiacs, and all manner of meretriciousness. The artist of this kind is not an honest merchant, like a dozen popular novelists we could name: he is a peddler of noxious drugs. In the earlier and more legitimate meaning of the term, he is a sophisticate.

Art for the sake of prestige is likewise impure. Art does open supercilious gates. It enabled D. H. Lawrence, a miner's son, to hobnob with the British aristocracy and its American *Ersatz*. Literary success made it possible for Rousseau—supreme victory—to spurn the society that was at his feet. Even Voltaire, even Goethe, even Hugo, were in part such *bourgeois gentilshommes*: the social climber may reach his goal on a ladder of masterpieces. Wilde scorned popularity, but courted notoriety, and imposed himself for half a generation upon a staid, reluctant, indignant, helpless Victorian upper class. Between the notorious and the celebrated, there is but a shade; between the obscure and the famous, there is an abyss. The noble thirst for glory, which is so fundamental a motive in art, is of the same nature as the desire for social prestige. To be *recognized*: glory—even Shakespeare's glory—is but prolonged celebrity. Ever since Augustine, we have been told that the Christian should be willing to be damned to the glory of God; the artist likewise should be ready to be damned, that is to say ignored, to the glory of art.

Art for the sake of information? Useful lore properly sugar-coated with fiction? Of this pedagogical device we have innumerable examples. Travel literature, including *Omoo, Typee*, and *Moby Dick* as well as *Around the World in Eighty Days*; romanced history and biography with the honored names of Scott, Manzoni, George Eliot, Hugo, Tolstoy; documentary realism—the twenty-volume encyclopedia of Emile Zola, the best-known works of Frank Norris, a manual of hotel-keeping like Sinclair Lewis's *Work of Art*, a handbook of social Boston like *Joy Street*. Frankly, I prefer my information straight. Information per se never is an artistic element. Shakespeare is an inexhaustible mine of things that are not so; and if sociologists seek in the vision of Balzac and Proust an accurate picture of French society, they are even more naïve than I thought. There are many details about whaling in *Moby Dick*, and I trust they are right. But Ahab is an Elizabethan character, not a Yankee skipper; and the white whale belongs to unnatural history, like the octopus in *Toilers of the Sea*. We are not quite sure Jules Verne (as Dante before him) truthfully reported his *Voyage to the Center of the Earth*. *The Narrative of Arthur Gordon Pym* and *Le Voyage d'Urien* are said to lack authenticity. Art creates its own universe and proclaims its own law. Give a coast to Bohemia, or have stout Cortez stand on a peak in Darien, and we shall not cavil, if by so doing you open a magic casement.

Art for the sake of propaganda? Aye, there is the rub. The French are ardently discussing "engaged literature," literature committed to a nonartistic cause. Patriotic art, social art, religious art? Yes, if the artist is wholly sincere, if the cause and his inmost self are one. But if he is a retained advocate; if he stifles his own misgivings for fear of deviating from the party line or the American way of life; if he twists, suppresses, or fakes evidence *ad majorem Dei gloriam*; if he willfully appeals to ignorance, prejudice, or blind passion—then he ceases to be an artist.

Dante, Pascal, Milton, Péguy, Claudel are free to express their religious beliefs; Shelley, Hugo, their political faith, without losing their standing as artists. Nay, their stature is increased thereby, for a great soul appears in a nobler light when it is wrestling with great problems, and above all with impenetrable mysteries. We respond to their ardor even though we should reject their mythology. If I cannot fall down and worship Ezra Pound as the Dante of our days, it is not because the creed he defended is far more obnoxious to me even than Stalinism; it is because the personality that he revealed seemed to me stunted, warped, ungenerous; and because his form strikes me as blatant even when it is cryptic.

If we applied the condemnation of art for any other sake with the utmost rigor, the temple would be swept clean indeed, but it would be singularly bare and lonely. There might remain only the Dadaist twittering in the rafters, and Gertrude Stein crooning in the crypt. But art is the greatest fellow traveler. It is willing to go, not one step merely, but twain or more, with any sake or cause, profit, prestige, parties, allegiances, moralities, religions, so long as they are going its way. If they deviate, then art lets them depart. For all "sakes" imply Decatur's blasphemy, from which art alone is free: *right or wrong!* My profit, right or wrong! My party, right or wrong! My economic system, right or wrong! My country, right or wrong! My religious tradition, right or wrong!

In this refusal to accept *wrong*, in whatever holy garments it may be tricked out, art and conscience are one. I prefer to call this obstinate loyalty to personal integrity *art* rather than *conscience*; for conscience is more tangled than art with *morality* in the sense of *mores*, customs, conformity. Conscience admirably defends vested values; the values of art are forever in the making. Art is conscience looking ahead.

Art is a monitor: it warns us against the timid, the dull, the petty, the mean, the callous, the stubborn: all that mesh of philistine virtues which make up the type we call "the realist" and Georges Bernanos, more vividly, calls "les salauds." But is it possible for art to be also a guide? Here we encounter the ultimate temptation: art at the service of a system that calls itself aesthetic, art and life for the sake of beauty.

Aestheticism is the subtlest heresy against artistic freedom and integrity. Art is not beauty-worship, the quest and service of beauty. If beauty has any sense, it means harmony and attractiveness: the charm of a fair May morning, of a smiling sea, of a gentle face. Art does seek these; but it seeks much more. If we wanted to preserve the word *beauty*, we should have to add the beauty of ugliness, the beauty of squalor, the beauty of pain and terror, for all these belong to the domain of art; and then the word *beauty* becomes an absurdity. It is sheer calousness to speak of beauty when Oedipus appears, his eyes gouged out and bleeding, symbols of the unutterable horror within. What we have here is not beauty but power, but significance.

Aestheticism—life for the sake of beauty—is an ancient fallacy. We find it in Homer, when the Trojan elders, awed by Helen's perfect loveliness, whisper: "For such a woman, it is meet that a city perish." We find it in the case of Phryne whose sole defense was to reveal her full beauty to the judges. Our Lorelei, the Blonde Preferred, likewise vamped a jury; but the ancient Greeks were from Missouri, and demanded complete evidence. We find it in the eternal fascination of the Fair Ladies of Old, even with sober, elderly, dry-as-dust historians: Cleopatra, Theodora, Mary Stuart, Marie-Antoinette; for any one of them, the world would have been well lost. We find it in war, the most irrational of *beaux gestes*. "We are not all cotton-spinners yet," Tennyson affirmed, half-drawing an imaginary sword. What matters it that half a million vague human beings were wasted in the mud and snow of Russia? The glory is remembered when the cost is forgotten, and the Napoleonic Legend cannot be exorcised. We find it in the aesthetic gospel of Milton, Rousseau, Chateaubriand, Ruskin, Santayana, Cabell: *credo quia pulchrum*, I believe because it is beautiful.

To be sure, if we admit a God of Beauty, a Divine Artist who fashioned the heavens and the earth for our aesthetic delight, we shall have to acknowledge also a God of Ugliness, who created dreary wastes, swamps and marshes, poisonous jungles, slimy creatures, loathsome insects. Ruskin himself told us that the Deity, drawn very much in the image of John Ruskin, "prepared for us, nearly every morning and evening, windows painted with divine Art, in blue and gold and vermilion." *Nearly* every morning and evening! So there are times when Ruskin the art critic would tell the Cosmic Artificer: "This sunset was not one of your best efforts!"—and we are perilously near blasphemy.

Moreover, *credo quia pulchrum* is a doctrine that leads straight to hell; for, as Blake discovered, devils are far more vivid and dramatic than angels, and Milton, being a true poet, was on their side without knowing it. Satan, the prototype of Lord Byron and Baudelaire, was the first of the Romanticists. Aucassin, the lover of Nicolette, in that age of faith which so impressed Henry Adams with its perfect unity, would have none of heaven, with the sniveling monks; give him the rival abode, with the brave knights and the fair ladies. Art passes all too willingly from the *Little Flowers* of St. Francis to Baudelaire's *Flowers of Evil.* Earnest souls have always considered beauty-worship as a snare: the ancient Hebrews, the early Iconoclasts, the religious orders in their pristine integrity, the Puritans, the Jansenists. Strait is the gate, and unadorned.

Art is not the quest of beauty, which is merely the sign or promise of pleasure. Art is that which enhances our consciousness of life. Man, as soon as he rises above the brute, realizes how precious is this divine gift of life, and how precarious. He dreads annihilation: not only physical death, but that death in life that is the loss of personality. He resists every attempt to devitalize him, to turn him into a slave of the state or of the economic system, into a cog in a huge machine, into a digit in an all-embracing statistical table. In its refusal to exist for any other sake but its own, art comes very close to science, which also is not merely debased but destroyed when it is sacrificed to profit, prestige, or propaganda. Science may even reach loftier heights of purity than art. But in their innermost nature they are antagonistic. For sicence views the world as an ineluctable concatenation of causes and effects. Whatever lies beside or beyond that strict determinism, that rigidly disciplined army of facts, measured, numbered, passively obedient to law, science must ignore or deny. When Napoleon asked Laplace, who had presented to him his *Treatise on Celestial Mechanics*: "Where is God in your system?" the great mathematician answered: "Sire, I had no need for that hypothesis." He had no need either for love or art: facts are facts, and laws are laws. And on his own ground, he was right. The integrity of science demands the rejection of nonscientific data. But, to paraphrase Pascal, even if the scientific universe should crush the individual, man would remain to the last greater than that which crushes him; for he has the consciousness of life, and that, by definition, is denied the scientific universe.

The poet, on the contrary, is akin to the lover and the mystic. For art, love, and religion, all three are assertions of life. In their highest manifestations, they merge. All three bring to man not safety, not even comfort, but rapture. The religion that is merely an insurance policy, the love that is simply a marriage of convenience, the art that brings returns in pelf or station, all three are nothing but philistine caricatures. I do not wish to hierarchize them: they are an indivisible trinity. On a lower plane, differences are manifest; and it may be said, even though it sounds like an outrageous paradox, that art is the purest of the three. For love is too often tainted with possessiveness, with jealousy. It desires to stake a claim, "to have and to hold," exclusively. The nature of art is to give, not to receive: to give to all comers, ideally to all men. And we find it hard to separate religion from material organizations with vested interests of their own, the churches; from scientific or historical data which each faith seeks to impose as essential, and which other faiths deny. The Church Universal is still a dream. But the many mansions of art are not inimical. The freest eclecticism is the rule. Man is bidden to enjoy to his full capacity Homer, Job, the Psalms, Lucretius and Dante, Rabelais and Milton, Shakespeare and Voltaire, Goethe and Tolstoy. Man is free to rekindle his sense of life from any flame of the past or present. He is free to start his own fire and invite all men to share its warmth and light.

Art is not elaborate technique, and art is not the quest of beauty. It is the vanguard of life, scouting, pioneering, reaching into the unknown, into that which is not yet amenable to law. It is the thrill of wonder, the gaze from a peak in Darien, the road to Xanadu, the dim Ultima Thule, the solemn joy of voyaging through strange seas of thought alone. It is a venture beyond *organized* truth, beyond *acknowledged* virtue, beyond *recognized* beauty, and, to follow our prophet Cabell to the very end, beyond the dreary dailiness which usurps the name of life. Art, thus interpreted, spurns patterns, standards, values: words which of their very nature are essentially philistine. Thus it cannot exist save for its own sake only. Whoever looks primarily to the true, the good, or the beautiful, with art merely as a mode of approach, is turning his back on the reality of art.

But if the discoverer is lost to the world, the story ends unrecorded, and there is nothing that may be seized upon to be called art. Art implies a report to the rest of mankind: if the artist ventures "behind the beyond," it must be with a return ticket. This requires communication, and communication in its turn means information, education, propaganda, business, all the "sakes" which we have been attempting to eschew. To help his fellowmen, or simply to establish his claims before them, the poet must sell shares in Xanadu.

When the fruits of the mystic land are brought to the marketplace, they have already lost much of their freshness, and their wild fragrance has grown faint. Their strangeness, which is their secret appeal, is also a cause of offense. Sane men have to be reassured and won over; so the prizes from over the border are decorated, doctored, faked, adulterated, made acceptable to existing taste. Is there an artist who has not felt with despair what a parody of his true vision he was offering to the world? But it is the parody alone that can be bought, judged, taught; the pure vision is incommunicable; the sole language of the mystic is silence.

Worst of all, the explorer, wandering home from "an ultimate dim Thule," has to compete with the artistic Dr. Cook, who has never left the precincts of Greenwich Village or Montparnasse, and who can produce a more plausible relation of a trip "behind the beyond"—more plausible for those who have never been there. Art is mostly artifice, and the purest artist is aware of it. Some of the lines which he knew to be "fakes" drew the warmest response; those which to him were snatches of unearthly melodies brought no echo . . . Can he be right against the world? And he comes to wonder whether he too is not a charlatan, like the rest.

For nine-tenths of their lives, poets, mystics, and lovers are philistines like the rest of us, and should be judged by the law of the philistines: decency, honesty, sanity. For nine-tenths or more of what is left, they carry on a desperate game of make-believe, bluffing themselves even more than the world, hoping against hope that if they strike the attitudes and utter the spells of inspiration, inspiration will descend upon them. And, miracuolusly, without desert, without law, a free gift of grace, it may descend. So there is the saving remnant, infinitesimal and of infinite price. Two lines may sound almost alike. Both may have been written primarily for effect, for profit or for praise, for goodness, for beauty, or for truth: yet *one* will convey a tremor. Some great poets have but half a dozen such lines in their voluminous works: yet they have not lived in vain. The haunting memory, the despairing expectancy of such moments pervade literature, carry us through countless pages of sheer sense and mere beauty. The innumerable company of readers and writers exist only for those few men, and those men for those rare flashes of Art for Art's Sake.

This is the Calvinistic doctrine of art: the small number of the elect.

There is an Evangelical doctrine too: salvation freely offered to all men. But to seize upon that great promise, we must look beyond the cliques, destroy the privileges of those who claim to be the sole repositories of the artistic revelation. In art as in love or religion, professionalism is a deadly peril. The ultimate triumph of the artistic spirit might well entail the disappearance of the material work of art, and of its maker. When all men, released from fear and greed, are able to savor the charm of earthly scene and human face, then they will no longer need to daub messily on a canvas, mold a lump of clay, chip a block of stone, or peddle fictitious scandal. Creation will be selection, exploration, understanding. The whole earth will be a museum and a shrine. In Utopia, the showoff and the huckster will have gone home to their fathers. Every man worthy of the name will be a king, an artist, and a priest. And Art for Art's Sake will have full sway in the Lord's Holy Mountain.

Inheritance

ARTHUR M. SAMPLEY

If my son sleeps in mud, then let it be
In roadside ditches, and if he must lie
With no more cover than this quilt of sky
Then be it warmer sky than covers me.
If he must stagger, let it be from drink;
If he must bleed, let blood at county fairs;
Let him lie home at night and get him heirs
That will not curse him when they learn to think.

Thus spoke my father, sobered by the rain
And by the hot steel whistling past his head,
But lived because some shots are bound to miss,
Went home, grew fat, and did not think again
Of me, who in this storm of falling lead
Swear that my son shall never die like this.

Tomaso of the Temblors

MARY AUSTIN

IT WAS the spring shearing at Agua Caliente, and at Agua Caliente there could nothing more delightful happen in a year's time than the spring shearing, unless indeed it were the midsummer rodeo, or the Christmas bear hunt. In fact there was always something delightful going on at Agua Caliente, from the orange picking in January to the fig packing in September. And in the winter—but there never was any winter to speak of at Agua Caliente; just a little nipping of frost in the air, and a little sifting of snow on the highest hills, and no flowers blooming anywhere except in the sunny nook between the wings of the low adobe ranch house.

But of all the good times at Agua Caliente Tomaso liked the spring shearing best. Nearly all the year he was away with his father, tending sheep; sometimes swinging a wide circle with Agua Caliente as a center, sometimes traveling far northward with the flocks into the heart of the Sierras, or across the Temblor hills into the Coast Range, into sight and sound of the great Pacific.

The Temblor hills lie just at the end of the great valley where the Coast Range and the Sierras come together. It can be seen plainly enough on the map how the two ranges swing around the south end of the San Joaquin, the Coast Range trailing off to the southeast like the tail of a letter Y. In the fork of the Y the Temblor hills lie tumbled thick together, sloping down to the valley with the blue lakes twinkling in its leopard-colored hollow.

The shearing sheds at Agua Caliente looked out upon the valley, and back of them, halfway up the broad winding canyon, lay the ranch house, tangled over with grapevines; back of that the homes of the vaqueros, and the herders' huts; last of all the wickiups of half a dozen Indian families who still clung to Agua Caliente; and in the midst of all these the brand-new, unpainted, pine cabin that was the schoolhouse. Nothing of all this could be seen from the shearing sheds even in winter, for between lay the thick shining green of the orange orchards, and the gray veil, like a mist, of bare fig branches; and now at shearing time the almond trees were showing pink along the lower slopes. Below the shearing sheds the warm water from the spring that gave Agua Caliente its name trickled into a kind of bog, where there was always a spot of greenness and brightness; and there were water toads to stone, and killdees for the boys to shoot at with the bows and arrows the Indians taught them to make, and warm soft mud to wade in when they tired of watching the shearing, which was not often.

There were twenty shearers in the sheds, besides packers; and old Felipe, the cook, and his two assistants had all they could do to get ready enough frijoles, tortillas and chili con-carne against mealtime. The Superintendent walked about with his hands in his pockets, and joked with the men as they worked, and sometimes, when the pack was very heavy or the work going off faster than usual, he threw silver bits to the boys for the fun of seeing them scramble.

Tomaso could remember four shearings and this was the best of them all, or would have been but for one thing: something was the matter with Tomaso's father. He was one of the most trusted shepherds at Agua Caliente, and the best shearer. Nobody could turn out a sheep so smoothly shorn, with never a cut or gash. Tomaso would sit on the fence, when the shorn sheep were turned out to pasture, and pick out his father's work by their smooth clean coats. But this time clearly something was the matter. The sheep suffered at his hands as if he had been the newest, awkwardest shearer of the lot, and there were no jokes and songs from Chopo Ramón who used to be the very life of the shearing. His other name was Eschovar, but no one cared very much for last names at Agua Caliente, and if a man's first name did not fit him he was named over again. So Tomaso's father went by the name of "Chopo" Ramón, which means about the same as "Shorty"; Tomaso himself did not know that he had any other name than Chopo's Tomaso.

But withal Tomaso continued to have a very good time at the shearing, and at the dance which followed it; for at Agua Caliente there could never be any half-dozen of them get together but there would be pretty figures swaying on the smooth adobe floors, and in the dusk, guitars playing. The shearing ball was a thing worth staying up for. Tomaso meant to stay up all night for it, but he never knew when he tumbled off his bench in the ballroom and was carried off to bed by his father.

The first thing that came into his mind as he lay among the blankets on the hay in the morning was the way his father had blundered at the shearing. It was very late—nearly nine o'clock—the hired shearers had gone on to the next ranch, and the shepherds were parting out the flocks. Old Felipe was packing his cooking pots and pails, and gave him some cold scraps for his breakfast. Tomaso took the food in his hands and wandered about the empty sheds looking for his father. Chopo came up presently and spoke to him hurriedly. "When you have finished your breakfast, *Muchachito*," he said, come down to the hay corral. I have something to say to thee."

The hay corral was back of the shearing sheds and there was a great litter of alfalfa and barley, and bales of hay lying about. Tomaso clambered over the bales to a sunny corner and wondered, while he munched his bread and meat, what it could be that made his father speak and act so strangely. Chopo Ramón was the best shepherd on the Temblor Range. His lambs were the strongest, his fleeces the thickest, and his flocks the largest of all the hundreds that grazed among those mountains.

When Tomaso was four years old his pretty young mother had dressed him in his best clothes for his father to see when he came home to the spring shearing, and while they laughed together for glee, a storm broke in the mountains above them. The water rushed down the canyon like a wall against the frail houses, and there was little that could be done. The pretty little Mexican mother was found in a thicket of grapevines when the water had gone by, with Tomaso held close in her arms, unhurt, but drenched and gasping. Tomaso had been told these things so often that he thought he remembered them. What he really knew was that from that time on he and his father had never been separated. He could not remember ever sleeping in a house, or any cradle but the high-backed saddle his father had fitted to a little mouse-colored burro, or any other playfellows than the dogs and the lambs. The lambs were stupid things, but the dogs were as fine as could be, and there is no life in the world like the wild free life of the mountains. Thinking these things over Tomaso could see nothing at all to be grave about, and he had grown quite cheerful by the time his father came around the corner of the hay bales and sat down beside him.

Chopo did not at once begin to talk of the matter that brought him to the hay corral. He spoke of the flocks, how well they were looking and how many there were. Then he talked of the shepherds, how Ignacio had lost his lambs in a storm, and that Francisco Ruiz was to have charge of the home flocks because his wife was sick and he did not wish to go far away. "And I, Tomaso, have charge of the largest flocks, as I always have; we go northward into Little Round Valley as far as the Red Butte."

"The Red Butte!" cried Tomaso. "That will be fine! I have never been to the Red Butte, only to the Haiwai meadows and back again."

"By September," Ramón went on, "we will be at the Red Butte and turn southward to reach Los Alamos for the spring shearing. Juan Romero and his brother Alessandro go with me all the way, and three others as far as Los Osos."

"And I too, father. Oh! it will be fine, and Alessandro promised that if he got the place with you he would teach me to shoot with his gun. All the men like to go with you, father, you have always the good luck."

"That is what I wished to speak about," said his father, not looking at Tomaso, but at the wild oats growing upon the farthest hills, for his heart failed him because of the thing he had to do. It was not right of course that the boy should grow up with the sheep; his mother would not have wished it, and the Superintendent had spoken to him about it. But it was a sore thing for Chopo Ramón that his boy must be left behind for the schooling now too long delayed. So Tomaso was told that morning after the shearing ball, and cried, and let himself be comforted with talk of all the fine things school was to do for him. And when the twilight fires began to glow all down the slope where the departing shepherds lay with their flocks, Chopo Ramón held the boy in his arms saying, "Until I come again, *Muchachito*," and *"Adios mi Tomaso,"* and went sorrowfully away.

Tomaso did not get on well at Agua Caliente. He boarded with Mrs. Hanchet, an *Americana*, who could not make tortillas, who put no chilis in her beans, and quarreled with him because he would sleep always out of doors on a rawhide cot under the grapevine arbor, with the dogs sprawling beside him for company. Besides, Tomaso hated the school where he stood in class with boys much smaller than himself, and most of all he hated sitting at his desk now that spring had come.

Spring comes very quickly at Agua Caliente. You see it first on the hilltops starting the wild oats and alfilaria. Within a week it runs down all the little gullies and spreads far out into the valley. Poppies come up singly here and there, like lambent flames that spread till the farthest hills are all afire. With the poppies come the lupines. You might look out some morning upon the little hollows and see not one, and in a day or two look again, and if you did not know the lupines, think that pieces of the sky had fallen, so blue and thick are they.

After the lupines there are acres of white forget-me-nots in the canyons. Then there are lizards and horned toads, not so active as in the summer months, but spry enough to make it good fun catching them. The plowshares in the long mellow furrows of the wheat lands turn up nests full of gophers and chipmunks; and little rabbits run everywhere through the chaparral. These Tomaso took to school and played with secretly under his desk, for which, as often as the teacher found him out, she punished him. And at school the American boys called him "greaser." Tomaso was very angry, but the other little Mexican boys would not take any notice of it.

"White people always call you that; they do not mean anything, they simply do not know any better."

All these things made Tomaso very unhappy, and he cried at night in his rawhide cot under the grapevine, where the dogs came and put their cold noses against him for sympathy. And lying there, under the same stars that his father watched by some coyote-scaring fire, it came into his mind that he should leave Caliente and go to his father. He would go by the supply wagon which he knew must be starting soon. The shepherds of the Sierras in their year-long wanderings could not take with them food enough to last the whole time, but were supplied by the wagon sent out from headquarters to meet them at places agreed upon. When Tomaso had been a month at Agua Caliente he saw Hank Sturgess, the teamster, greasing the wheels of the big supply wagon down by the hay corral. That night at supper he was unusually quiet, but his eyes were big with excitement and his hands trembled. Mrs. Hanchet gave him some biscuits and cold meat to feed the dogs, but Tomaso took them out to his bed under the grapevine and made them into a bundle with his chiefest treasures—his bow and arrows, the four-bladed knife that was his prize in the footrace, and a bright silk handkerchief that his father had given him. Then he lay down wide-eyed to wait for dawn, for Tomaso had made up his mind; he was going to his father.

He thought he should lie awake all night, but before the lights were out in all the houses he was fast asleep. When at last he woke it was very dark in the canyon, but by the whitening of the stars and the freshening of the air he knew the morning was not far off. He slipped out with his bundle past the silent ranch house. The dogs followed him with questioning whine, and Tomaso dared not drive them back for fear of rousing someone. His plan was to cross the hills by a sheep-trail to a point which he knew Hank must pass late in the afternoon. The wagon road wound about a long spur of the hill, miles and miles farther than the trail, and by the time the teamster reached the point it would be too late to turn back. Once past the spring and safe from the fear of rousing anyone, Tomaso broke into a long swinging trot like the gait of the gray coyote, with the two dogs running noiselessly on the long smooth road that sloped down from the ranch house. Tomaso had no more fear of the night than has any other wild thing that has slept unhoused through all its changes. Finally, when he came to the end of the slope, he drove back the dogs and turned out of the road to find the trail for the shortcut.

It ran slantwise across a long even slope, but if Tomaso had been less accustomed to the night and to finding his way along faint trails, he must surely have lost it in the sagebrush. As it was he followed it slowly until the sky lightened enough to show him the black rim of the valley. Its great hollow filled slowly with pinkish pearly mist; the highest peaks grew rosy white, but deep blackness lay in the canyons. By the time the sun had climbed far enough up behind the Sierras to throw their long, jagged shadows quite across the valley, Tomaso had come to the badlands. These were barren, sandy acres streaked with alkali. Springs oozed out of the hillsides and trickled down from bog to bog in a broad shallow pool ringed round with a white rim of alkali. The badlands were honeycombed with the holes of small furry things, and among their little hillocks tall blue herons stalked slowly, or stood on their long stilts of legs, looking bigger in the misty morning, their long necks drawn down between their shoulders, like little, old humpbacks. The herons seemed not to mind Tomaso; they winked sleepily at him as they changed from one leg to the other, and now and then one stretched himself, neck and legs together, and went on looking for his breakfast among the gopher houses. This reminded Tomaso of his own breakfast, so he ate a biscuit, and thought that Hank must be starting now and presently Mrs. Hanchet would be going out to call him.

So the morning wore on, and Tomaso trotted along the sheep-trail toward his father and away from Agua Caliente. About the middle of the afternoon the driver of the supply wagon stopped his team in sheer amazement at sight of a small dusty figure resting in the shadow of a rock on the Los Vinos road. Tomaso climbed into the back of the wagon and made himself comfortable among the bales and boxes.

"I go to my father," he said with dignity. "I came away in the night by the sheep-trail. The Señora Hanchet does not know," he added by way of explanation.

Hank looked back over the road and up at the sun.

"You kin go as fur as Los Vinos," he said at last. "It's too late to turn back now. What do you s'pose your paw'll say?"

Tomaso had no answer. He was gnawing a piece of *jerke* he had found in a bag under the seat. If he got as far as Los Vinos he would manage to get the rest of the way. Of course his father would be glad to see him. So the wagon jogged on and presently Tomaso fell asleep, utterly content. He was going to his father.

The grazing land at Los Vinos is the best of all the Temblor Range. It lies in a wide deep curve of the hills, acres and acres of it, now all pink with blossoms of alfilaria and spangled over with poppies and lupines. Three canyons open into it: Los Vinos, Los Robles, and Pasteria. Through Los Vinos runs the public highway, turning and twisting its way into other canyons, all the way to Los Angeles and the coast. Through Pasteria you might find your way with scarcely any turnings into the lonely desert of Mojave, but through Los Robles you reach nothing but higher hills and deeper canyons, more and more of them, until you are quite lost. Through Los Vinos rumbles the four-horse stage to Summerfield, and the eighteen- and twenty-mule teams from Salt Creek, long caravans of wood wagons, and whitetopped "travelers." Through Pasteria come the winds, rolling mighty sand blasts down the valley, but through Los Robles comes nothing at all, except now and then a stray deer, or a hungry bear to the sheepfolds. This happens seldom, and the shepherds are counted lucky who have charge of the flocks at Los Vinos. There they pasture for weeks without changing camp, and for weeks longer without going beyond the point of hills that shut it in on either side.

Tomaso did not much mind being left at Los Vinos; Hank had positively refused to take him any farther. The shepherds, whom he knew, were kind and, except for keeping a sharp lookout that he did not follow the teamster away as he did at Agua Caliente, left him very much at liberty. And with the shepherds at Los Vinos he found the little, lame, mouse-colored burro that had carried him on his back for three years. Ladronito could travel farther in a day than most men in spite of his limp, but he had fairly earned his title of "Little Thief." Ladronito could steal and eat anything from a bag of beans to a pair of boots, and do it so cleverly that you could never be properly angry with him.

Tomaso played the weeks away at Los Vinos, glad just to have the sound of the flock in his ear and the taste of familiar food. He watched the eagle poised over against Mount Pinos, and the herd of antelope running heads up against the purple twilight hills; heard the *whit!* and *whir!* of the burrowing owls thicken around him as dusk drew into dark and the stars came out, and the coyotes began to howl their long-drawn howl. He saw the rains playing among the hills and the brown soil crack and break into a riot of growing things, and ran as wild himself as the wild rabbits that ran in the chaparral.

But all this time he had not forgotten his father. On a night after he had been all day over the hills digging wild hyacinth roots to eat, Tomaso, lying in the tent wrapped in a pair of Antonio's blankets, heard the shepherds talking by the fire. Now he learned that his father was on the way to Pajaro, where he was expected to be at midsummer, a prospector who had passed through Los Vinos the day before having seen him at Greenfields within a week. Tomaso was not to be told of this, but was to be sent back to Agua Caliente with the vaqueros who were branding calves in Pasteria, and would be returning in a few days. Tomaso lay awake long after the men were asleep, thinking it high time that he should be gone from Los Vinos.

The next day he began his preparation. He took a bag that had beans and chilis in it and cached it in an old badger's hole, where he kept his bow and arrows and his private treasures. He felt very sorry about it afterward, for Ladronito was blamed for it, and Manuel beat him, calling him hard names. Tomaso went out and explained the matter to Ladronito when no one was looking, but the burro looked so reproachful that suddenly it came into Tomaso's mind that the only amends he could make would be to take Ladronito with him. None of the animals or supplies belonged to the shepherds personally; all were furnished by the Superintendent. Tomaso, who had had the freedom of the sheepcamps all his life, did not hesitate to take all he thought he might need, only Manuel and Antonio must not suspect what he was about. Ladronito came in for more than his share of beatings that week.

Tomaso left Los Vinos as he left Agua Caliente, trusting to the dark and the friendliness of the dogs, and making haste to cross the open before daylight. But long before morning Tomaso knew that he was safe, for he felt the stirring of the air at dawn; and when it was day at last he could not see the sun, for the valley was filled up to its jagged rim with the yellow murk of sand, flying before the strong wind that came out of Pasteria.

Antonio and Manuel had all they could do to manage the flocks in the face of the terrible gusts of sand and wind, so that it was hours before they realized that Tomaso was gone. The next day they were obliged to move camp, for the feed was quite spoiled, beaten down and covered by the shifting sand. After all they were not much troubled about Tomaso, for the boy had been reared to the life. They knew that he had taken Ladronito, and guessed that he had taken supplies.

While the shepherds were worrying the trembling flocks through the blinding, blustering storm, Tomaso and Ladronito were trudging steadily along the upper trail toward Pajaro meadows. The foothills broke through the fringe of the storm, the sun showed a feeble yellow murk, and all the peaks above stood sunlit and clear. Nothing stirred on the hills, not even a coyote. Hawks squatted in the crumbling holes of their sometime victims, wings canted and feathers ruffling to the wind. Cattle turned tail and drooped and browsed with shut eyes. Tomaso traveled with the wind away from Pasteria, picking his way among the fresh and fading trails to put an end as soon as possible to the seventy miles that lay between him and Pajaro. The foothill trails, to one who can read them, are as safe and sure as village roads, and provided his food held out Tomaso risked only the unusual which sometimes meets us in the safest places.

The trail by which Tomaso had come from Los Vinos led up to the river canyons on the west. It skirted the foothills, winding with their shallow canyons, but it never crossed the highland that lay between them and the Sierras. In the third day Tomaso, following a dim, worn path, struck across this mesa heading for the south of the pass by which the sheep went up toward Greenhorn. It was fifty miles to Pajaro, and golden weather. Spring lingered in the canyons after the rains until she had gathered the last vestige of green from the shadeless, crisping hills. Gray squirrels frisked and gossiped there, and now and then a little fox squirrel, running on the low-spreading branches of the oaks, answered the boy's shouts with sharp derisive barks, and from hill to hill sounded the soft *wah! wah!* of the nesting quail.

Tomaso fared heartily enough on the food he had and such things as the road afforded, roots and bulbs, of which he knew as much as any wild thing, and squirrels and quail now and then, which he shot with his bow and arrows. He fed, too, at the mines, the Nugget and Indian Queen, the men laughing to see him fill and fill past any known capacity for a boy of his age. He was skillful, as anyone of his race, in evading questions. Oh! he was Tomaso, he said, of the Temblors, and he went to his father; and with that the miners had to be satisfied.

So rejoicing and unafraid, now walking and now riding, knowing the trails by heart, Tomaso of the Temblors came with hardly a mishap to the foot of the pass that divided him from Pajaro. He spent the night in the ravine at the upper limit of the oaks, and made his camp between two fallen pines wide apart, setting fire to both as a protection against cold and wild animals. Even as late as June it is quite cold in the high altitudes. He lay at dusk in the ravine hearing the *Whoo-oo* of the owls and the querulous twittering of the jays getting themselves comfortably to bed. The light slipped softly from the highest, farthest peaks and the smoke of the campfire wavered up through the deepening shadows. At the head of the ravine a wildcat parted the buckthorn thicket noiselessly and led her four small kittens down the hill. So softly they went that not a twig snapped, four little white bobtail tabbies, so soft and fubsy as to their white and tawny bodies, so fierce as to their sharp ears and yellow eyes. A slender spar of pine had fallen across the stream from bank to bank of the narrow ravine. Over this the mother went step by step, coaxing the kittens safely across. Then at a word the whole family bounded away to their hunting, and Tomaso, watching, was not afraid but dozed and fell asleep between his smoldering logs while Labronito browsed along the stream.

On the next day, which was the sixth after leaving Los Vinos, Tomaso came upon fresh sheep tracks, and that night he camped in what had been the camping place of the shepherds. He was very glad of the rude shelter of pine boughs they had left, for all night big drops of rain pattered at intervals among the soughing pines. The next morning was dull and damp, the streams were muddy and swollen, and woolly clouds hung down from all the peaks that were his landmarks and locked hands across the canyons. Twice that morning Tomaso was startled by the crash of underbrush, and saw dun-colored deer breaking the cover of buckthorn thickets.

As the day wore on the clouds settled more and more, nosing stealthily into all the steep-walled canyons, until he could see no more than the trail under his feet and the dark looming shapes of the nearest trees. In the mysterious, voiceless mist nothing seemed strange or unusual. Once a gray coyote met him face to face upon the trail and hardly slunk aside to let him pass. Tomaso might have struck him where he stood, but his hands were numbed by the creeping chill and mist.

So Tomaso and Ladronito traveled all day in the heart of a cloud, cold and hungry, but quite content, for the trail freshened at every mile, and the burro knew as well as the boy that it was the trail of their own people. Late in the afternoon the cold wind cut the clouds into ribbons and sent them trailing off through one of the great windy passes between the ranges, and the westward wheeling sun, slanting through the canyons, lit up the camp and huddling sheep in Pajaro meadows.

Tomaso, sighting the camp from the top of the divide, struck Ladronito sharply with his stick and plunged shouting down the trail toward the meadows. But Ladronito had seen also and did not need the bastinado. He picked his way more cautiously but not less rapidly than Tomaso among the boulders. Before they had gone much beyond the lowest line of pines that circled the open meadow they had both checked their hurrying descent, Ladronito to feed upon the thick rank grasses, Tomaso to skirt the open like a shy wild animal.

Already he had seen that his father was not among the shepherds at the campfire, and he hoped to find him in some little tongue of the meadow that licked up among the pines along the watercourse. When the men saw him and called he came slowly and with great outward show of indifference, for this half-wild creature had the instinct of his kind to hide what was in him. The men told him soon enough, as the best comfort they could give him, that his father, because there was not feed enough at Pajaro for all the sheep, had taken a part of them and gone on to Manzanita, where he probably was now. Tomaso said no word at all, for if he had spoken he must have cried, so as the next best thing the men gave him some supper. That was a supper to be remembered: camp bread from the bake kettle, beans with chilis, fresh mutton chops broiled on the coals, and canned sweet stuff.

After supper Tomaso told them all the news of Caliente, how he had run away and all the incidents of the journey, and fell asleep before he had quite finished. The men talked of him as he slept.

"He must go to his father," said Alessandro, who was in authority.

"But if he should come to harm," said Juan, "his father would never forgive us."

"What harm can come to him? It is but two days and he has already come ten. The Saints watch over such as he; besides, if he would not stay at Los Vinos he will not stay here. It is better to send him away again with all that he needs. *Santa María!* There is but a handful of beans left in his bag; if the boy had not found us he must have starved. I myself will go with him as far as Passowai to show him the way."

So it was settled and told to Tomaso in the morning, only he must wait at Pajaro until the weather was entirely cleared. On the third day Alessandro packed his saddlebags with food for three days and filled all the remaining space with *jerke* of mutton.

"Your father will not have had time to make any," he said.

Alessandro went as far as Passowai, as he had promised. Passowai is an Indian name meaning "place of springs," a grassy meadow as big as a garden plot set round with trickling springs, and downy all over with the catkins of dwarf willow. From here the trail went up and over a great ragged crest and down and up again and so into the heart of the Sierras. All in between the open places, thick with turf of meadow and wild flowers, twinkling streams curved and crisscrossed aimlessly until they closed in again for the leap down some long gorge to a lower meadow. In these meadows the sheep, grazing as they go from one to another across the broken ranges, feed on the young pines and underbrush and all the little flowering things between. Their tinkling bells on all the hills ring doom to countless blossomings and forests of the time to come.

Tomaso was in great spirits as he lighted his fire that night and toasted his *jerke*. The fatigue of his long journey had slipped away during his rest at Pajaro, and the certainty of being near his father gave him a great sense of security. Alessandro had given him hobbles to put on Ladronito lest the burro should conclude that he belonged to the camp he had just left and go back in the night. As soon as he had made all things secure for the night Tomaso lay down to watch the leaping flames in the resinous pine logs. Excitement kept him awake for a long time. Far off he could hear the crashing of underbrush that was perhaps a bear. A huge night moth boomed clumsily among the pine boughs. From time to time he could hear the clink of Ladronito's hobbles as he stumbled about the meadow, and in the intervals of silence the soft swish of the skunk cabbage pushing out its broad leaves to make room for the growing flower stalk within.

The next day brought Tomaso with scarcely any trouble at all to the stony hill that dropped away directly to Manzanita meadows, but when he came to the top of it and looked down his heart failed him and he leaned gasping against the burro. The meadow was empty; it was quite empty.

When Ramón Eschovar left Pajaro with the flocks he had no thought but to go on to Manzanita meadows, where he would remain as long as the feed was good. Before going down into the meadows, however, he learned that a party of Basques, shepherding for one of the great ranches of the south, had been camped there with their sheep for some time; and the feed was now nearly gone. When Ramon heard of the Basques and their sheep he turned off to the right, by a trail he knew; and at the time Tomaso stood panting at the top of Manzanita Pass his father was camped in a broad ravine three days' journey to the northeast, and was moving northward every day.

Still Tomaso, only half believing the fact of his disappointment, and not understanding it at all, wandered about the meadow calling and peering among the pines for some trace of his father. But Ladronito, who had not known what to expect and was not therefore disappointed, went quickly about the business of getting his supper from the close-cropped grass. Everything gave evidence that a large flock had been pastured there: the short grass nibbled down almost to the roots, the hoof-beaten margins of the stream and the quantity of pine-wood ashes about the camping place.

From other signs Tomaso judged that the meadow had not been deserted more than two days; but there was nothing to tell him that strangers, not his father, had left these traces. At last when it was nearly dark he remembered to put the hobbles on Ladronito, and by a great effort pulled up to the deserted camp wood enough to make his fire for the night. There were plenty of spaces where dead trees lay closer at hand, but it seemed less lonely in the great meadow to be near the old camp.

In the morning Tomaso went about with great care to discover, if possible, what had become of his father and the sheep. He found without much difficulty the trail by which they had gone out at the north end of the meadow; he had no misgivings about its being his father's trail. So at the hour when Ramón Eschovar was moving his flocks down the ravine toward Little Round Valley, Tomaso with many blows and adjurations was urging Ladronito over a rugged trail in an opposite direction.

A boy and a burro can move much faster over a mountain trail than can a band of sheep who must feed as they go, so that allowing the Basques who had pastured at Manzanita two days' start on Tomaso, he had a fair chance of overtaking them in the same time; especially as they would make as long a stay as possible in any meadow they might cross. Tomaso had as much *jerke* as would last him twice as long, and the burro would subsist on anything. The second day he shot a grouse that sat stupidly facing him as he beat up a pathless ravine. Often before he had been startled early mornings and late afternoons as the gray feathered balls whirred past him, but this was his first shot at one. The grouse was very good eating, and Tomaso did not much mind doing without bread.

Several times he woke in the night to hear the patter of big drops from a passing cloud. The morning cleared beautifully but clouded over again, and when Tomaso was halfway up the crest of the range he was crossing, the storm broke suddenly over his head. Lightning flashed from all the jagged points of the ridge and ran like a live thing among the boulders. The rain came down everywhere; little rills trickling among the pine needles ran together and whirled into the stream that rose up between its banks muddy and frothing.

Tomaso left the shelter of the tall pines for a thicket of buckthorn higher up from the swollen stream, as his mountain training taught him to do; but before he could gather himself together a rill broke out farther up, broadened a foot or two, and almost carried him off his feet. While he crouched clinging in the thicket there was a check in the fury of the rain; then it began again in a sharp patter of hail that beat down the blue gentians and the monkey flowers among the grass. This drifted into snow at last, wet and clogging, weighting the pine boughs and covering the hill clear up to the tops of the yellow coreopsis. It was over in an hour but the sky still lowered, and Tomaso, chilled to the bone, pulled Ladronito out of the thicket and went on bravely over the hill.

The trail was quite covered but still well defined by the smooth streak of snow among the undershrubs. Northward along the range the storm moved slowly off, trailing snow as it went along the thick black heads of the pines. All about Tomaso the flowers stood bravely up, knee-deep or neck-deep in the snow, and butterflies folded their wings on the sheltered sides of the pines. If the sun came out the snow would be gone as quickly as it had come, but in the meantime it was bitter cold.

The pines shook their wet branches over him and great balls of sodden snow and earth clogged his feet. So he blundered along, crying a little and shivering a great deal, but getting lower down out of the reach of the storm. About the middle of the afternoon he found a pleasant place where he could build a fire and dry himself. He toasted some *jerke* and gathered nearly a hatful of berries. When he had eaten and warmed himself and begun to look about, he found that he was lost. The neighborhood he guessed well enough, for he had been near it before. It was a long wide canyon or narrow valley, whichever way you chose to look at it, known generally as Little Long Valley; but the Mexican shepherds of Agua Caliente called it Angustora. It was from a half to three-quarters of a mile wide in places, and a stream ran the whole length of it.

Doubtless Tomaso could have found his way through it to any of the well-known trails that are the highways through the mountains, or he could have gone back the way he came to Pajaro. But he was not now on any trail; he had lost all trace of the sheep he had been following, and he did not know whether to go up the valley or down to find them. He mounted Ladronito and set off somewhat aimlessly, keeping well to the middle of the valley and looking sharply out for sheep. He kept on even after dusk had fallen, for Ladronito for the last quarter of an hour had been traveling steadily ahead in one direction as if he knew where he was going. Just before it became quite dark they heard the bleating of flocks and the barking of dogs, and finally came upon the camp of the Basques in a little cove between the hills on the left side of the canyon.

Tomaso's disappointment at not finding his father here was not too great, for he did not realize that these were the sheep whose trail he had been following, and that Ramón had never been at Manzanita. He merely thought it very fortunate that he had met these men who could give him a warm meal and a bed, and perhaps news of his father. The Basques themselves were astonished to see a ten-year-old boy riding a lame burro into their camp at nightfall, but they were simpleminded men who had seen strange sights in the hills and were not much given to conjecture. They gave him supper, but the chance of coming to an understanding was small; they knew little Spanish and Tomaso no French, and none of them very much English. Agua Caliente and Truxton Range they had heard of, but had met no flocks of that brand during the season. They looked at Tomaso's torn clothing—he had had nothing new since leaving Caliente—and at the handful of food in his saddlebags, and agreed that he must be far away from his home and friends.

Early in the morning, before Tomaso was awake, one of the men took Ladronito with him as he went to feed his flocks far down the canyon; and Tomaso guessed by the way the dogs followed him about that they had been told to watch him. This the Basques meant in kindness, for they did not think it best for the boy to be wandering alone in the mountains. Tomaso was very angry at first, but after he began to understand that his father had never been at Manzanita he did not know what to do. By this time he knew that his friends had gone from Pajaro, but where there was no finding out.

The Basques were kind to him and when they saw how well he understood the ways of sheep and the life of sheep-camps, they began to think it profitable to keep him. There is no animal so stupid as a sheep, but Tomaso, who had grown up with them, knew how to take advantage of their stupidity. He knew how to build cunning bridges of sticks and sods over the foot-wide gullies they were too timid to cross, and outdid the dogs in nimbleness when there was need to scatter them out or gather them together. Many shepherds take goats with their flocks to set an example to the timid sheep in crossing streams and foraging in steep places but Chopo Ramón had always declared that Tomaso was better than three goats. It was Tomaso who when the streams were too wide to leap, could find the place where two tall pines grew close together so they could be felled across the stream, and when the place had been filled with sticks and stones Tomaso could best urge the bleating ewes to cross.

Of all the shepherds they met they asked and gave news concerning him, so that word began to spread that Tomaso of the Temblors was to be found in the camp of the Basques at Little Long Valley.

The sheep had fed down one side of Angustora and up the other and in all the little rifts between the hills. Now in midsummer they passed out at the farther end northward into the heart of the high Sierras. The Basques did not keep so close a watch on Tomaso, but he was not anxious now to run away. He did not at this time know where his father or any of his friends might be. Really, since the Basques were traveling northeast, they were all the time getting nearer to Eschovar, but this Tomaso did not know. They had passed into the country of the short-leaved pines, and the stillness of those miles of trees was never broken except by the bleating of the flocks or the harsh clamor of an eagle. The Basques had been north as far as Windy Meadows and were returning by way of Rock Creek, and now Tomaso began to feel very blue indeed, for he knew that in a few weeks at most his father would reach Red Butte and begin to return by way of the eastern slope of Los Vinos.

Tomaso decided that he must get to Red Butte by some means and remain there until his father came. There was a trail that he knew led up from Rock Creek, and if from there he could find a trail across the Querisa he could not miss Red Butte.

Tomaso knew several days before at what time the men intended to leave Rock Creek, and made as much preparation as possible. He took all the food he dared and cached it in a hollow tree near the trail. It was not very much nor very choice, for he was afraid the Basques might suspect what he was about and prevent him.

When shepherds break camp one of them goes ahead to spy out the way: after him come the burros carrying the camp kit, sometimes following close, sometimes dropping back with the sheep, feeding as they go; and after the sheep the men and dogs bring up the stragglers and keep the flock from straying. Tomaso took the upper side of the meadow where the trail went off toward Red Butte. It was nearly eleven when the moving flocks crossed this trail. All this time Tomaso was getting farther and farther away from the sheep, only showing himself occasionally lest his designs should be suspected. Besides the food which he had hidden in the tree Tomaso had his lunch for the day, for the shepherds did not wish to unpack the camp kit until night, and each man carried his dinner in his blouse.

Tomaso would have liked to take his burro, but Ladronito was in the lead with the others, packed with Tomaso's blankets and a few odds and ends of camp furniture. He was afraid to call him off, though the burro often followed at his heels all day like a dog. The shepherds were far apart now and in the thick pines did not often see each other, and if they missed Tomaso they thought that he was perhaps chasing squirrels. In fact they did not realize that he was gone until they came together at night, for each had thought that he was with the other, or lingering along the trail with his bow and arrows. All night they kept a fire burning and one or another of them kept watch for the boy. But Tomaso trudged steadily all that day and at night made himself as comfortable as possible with pine boughs and fire, and happily fell asleep before he had time to think much about the situation.

About the middle of the night he was awakened by a cold nose and a hot breath passing over his face. He lay still in deadly fear and felt himself fumbled over by something huge and hairy. Presently it left him, but he could hear it still moving about in the underbrush. His fire had burned down to a dull red glow, but Tomaso knew that there is nothing wild beasts dread so much as fire. Very cautiously he lifted one of the boughs that covered him and laid it on the fire, rolling over on the ground to reach it. How long it seemed before the needles kindled! At any moment the beast, which he could still hear stumbling about in the darkness, might return and eat him. Then it broke out into a dreadful roar—*Ah-hee-aw!*—and a little flicker of flame ran through the pine needles, flashed into brightness, and showed him—Ladronito!

The faithful burro, missing Tomaso before any of the others, had drawn out of the flock to find him, and coming across the trail to Pajaro, which he also knew, had taken it of his own fancy. Tomaso always believed that Ladronito had followed him with knowledge and intent, and this may have been so, for it is said that a burro can follow a scent like a dog. He was still packed, as he had been on leaving Rock Creek, with Tomaso's blankets, the sheepskins on which he slept, an empty kettle, a bag containing lentils, and best of all a large piece of partly dried mutton. It had been taken down from the tree where it hung the last thing that morning, and put upon Ladronito who was the least heavily loaded of all the burros.

Of all that happened to Tomaso and Ladronito during the next month I can tell you very little, and Tomaso was never willing to talk much about it. Perhaps it was not very clear in his own mind, for it was a time of confusion and trouble. He struck out bravely enough from Pajaro in the direction he supposed Red Butte to be, and as long as his food lasted, things went very well; but afterward when he could not always go the way that seemed shortest, but must take the way that promised the most food, he lost his bearing every little while.

How many times he crossed his own trail he never knew. Several times, when he found himself going about in a circle as lost people do, he would beat out a new trail in an opposite direction with no hope of anything but getting away from the old one. He found fish plentiful, and with his bow and arrows he secured an occasional squirrel or rabbit. After a time his matches gave out and he was obliged to jerk his meat in the sun and eat it without salt. Thimbleberries there were and blackberries, but the season waned and there were times when he made his dinner off nothing but the watercress that grew rank about the springs.

In the third week after leaving the Basques, Tomaso—footsore and weak from lack of food—was riding listlessly along on Ladronito, who had waxed fat as Tomaso had grown thin. They were following a trail through a long winding canyon for no other reason than that it led in the general direction they wished to go, and promised easy traveling. Ladronito was not too stupid to discover the aimlessness of the last few weeks of travel, and had grown obstinate about taking any trail that did not entirely suit his fancy. They had been traveling for some time in this fashion when Tomaso noticed that Ladronito had settled into the steady jog of a burro who had an object in view. After a little he heard the barking of a dog, and presently came upon a party of Piute Indians— men, women, and children—camped in a broad ravine beside a stream. They had come up from Ochala to hunt and fish and gather piñons for the winter. There were cakes baking before the fire and a savory smell of meat was in the air.

The Piutes understood very little Spanish, but they knew the look of a starving child, and when they had remedied that evil they were able to give him news of his father. Five days before they had passed a large band of sheep, branded with the star and crescent of the Temblors, on their way to Red Butte where they must shortly arrive.

They did not know just what route the sheep would take, but they could show him a shortcut by which he could reach the place about the same time as the flock. By this trail he could not miss his father, sup- posing Ramón had already started south. So Tomaso stayed in the camp of the piñon gatherers and got himself well varnished with the drip of the resinous boughs, and danced with the little Indians around the glowing heaps of roasting cones while their elders laughed and gambled in the firelight. And so glad was Tomaso of the Temblors to be with humankind again, and to have enough to eat every day, that tears rose in his eyes and sobs in his throat when the Piutes made him understand that he must go on his way. This was not unkindness, for the Indians' keen sense foreboded a storm, and they meant to have the child down and out of the hills before it began.

From the top of the hill from which the Indians pointed out the trail to him, Tomaso went down and down by winding ways, all day and part of the next until he came clear of the mountains into the foothills.

The hills had been green and gay when Tomaso had gone into them on the other side, five months before, but they were brown enough now, with only late asters or tarweed for blossoms. Then he had heard the soft note of the nesting quail, and seen the newly hatched broods disappear before his eyes as if they had melted into the ground. Now he saw them running, crest up, securely unafraid, in flocks of a dozen or more; and in early morning, lying rolled up in his blankets under a black sage bush, he watched them moving down narrow ravines to the water by hundreds, one flock following another with that peculiar motion of running quail until the trail itself seemed sliding down to the stream.

Now he began to travel northward through Querisa Valley, which is not so much a valley as a narrow tableland slipped in between the main ridge of the Sierras and one of the flanking ranges. Over the brown, treeless hills that rolled up from the center of the plain trudged Tomaso and the burro toward Red Butte, two days' journey to the north. But they were not alone—slinking, slyfooted and mischievous, three gray coyotes followed from point to point. All night, as many a night before, Tomaso heard them shriek and howl. He had heard his father and other shepherds say that no wild beast, least of all the wolf kind, can stand before the steadfast gaze of man; and no coyote has been known to attack a man moving, seldom indeed under any provocation. Nevertheless in the loneliness of the Querisa it gave him an uncomfortable feeling to watch their lurking forms. They deployed about him to right and left, sometimes reinforced, sometimes dropping far behind, but never leaving him quite unattended. They crossed the hills by trails unknown to him, and posted themselves in the most advantageous places to cut him off in any direction. By night they came so near that he could hear the snap of white teeth under snarling lips; then they would wheel off to yelp and howl in the ravine, and tell each other what clever things they would have done had he been a fawn, a deer, or an antelope and not of the man kind, unfit for food.

There was yet no sign of the storm predicted by the Piutes. The sky showed clear, big fleecy clouds hanging just beyond the crests of the ranges that shut him in, lifting lazily into view now and then but not changing otherwise all day. At night he could hear the coyotes talking to each other out of sight. Before he had fairly finished his supper they were trotting in constantly narrowing circles about his camp. It was a dark night lighted by the thinnest rim of a moon, and there was no sleep or rest in it for Tomaso. There was no wind on the floor of the valley, but overhead the clouds fled from it and the roar of it sounded loud from the wide-mouthed canyons, and in the near darkness the coyotes howled and howled. His fire of sagebrush flared up quickly and burned out, so Tomaso kept moving from one bush to another all night, with a burning brand, holding Ladronito's rope and dozing a little while the fires burned brightest. At dawn the coyotes left him finally, so he slept on, tired out, across Ladronito's rope until long after sunrise. The morning was hot and close with a filmy sky, and by the middle of the forenoon the wind came up, rolling the loose sand before it in a flying cloud that rose higher than the highest hills. But before it had quite cut them off from view Tomaso had glimpsed Red Butte standing across the valley to the north, its fine brick-dust red soil showing its color although thickly covered with alfilaria.

Early that morning while Tomaso was still asleep, Ramón Eschovar had come down with his sheep out of a wide gulley, feeding toward Red Butte. Now Red Butte is really not a butte, but the crater of a worn-out volcano, cone-shaped and hollow like a cup; and on the south side a great gap is blown out of the rim. Once inside its hollow—if the wind be from the north, as it generally is in the Querisa—no place is more safe and sheltered. When the wind came up, Ramón had drawn his flocks together and headed for the sheltered hollow of Red Butte.

Meantime Tomaso was fighting his way up in the teeth of the wind, almost overcome at times by its fury and the blinding sand. Great winds like this play up and down the mountain passes in the spring and fall, and generally bring a change of weather. Toward night the wind went down, but a chill went down the valley with it, and a long arm of gray cloud reached out from the mountain on the west, until the valley was completely bridged over and a light flurry of snow began to fall.

The sheep fires were lighted and the complaining flocks were huddled in the hollow of the Butte. The faithful dogs paced slowly round them and the restless bleating was hushed into the drowsy tinkle of bells. The snow had whitened all the hills and ceased to fall as Ramón made his last round, thinking how many months had passed and were to pass before he should see Agua Caliente and Tomaso. The dog at his heels snuffed and whined, and ran out to search into the darkness, uttering sharp barks that were more of inquiry than alarm. Ramón could see nothing yet but could hear the steps of a fourfooted beast coming directly up the slope. Then, a small tired voice crying, "Father! Father!" Ramón fell on his knees, frightened, wondering, peering into the darkness. Into the flickering circle of the campfire rode a tattered, shivering boy on a limping, footsore burro.

The new moon came out presently and saw all the Querisa white with snow, and in the shelter of Red Butte, tending a campfire, a man who watched and murmured broken words over a child sleeping in the hollow of his arm, while a thieving burro nosed unchecked among the camp supplies. Tomaso had found his father.

Revista Nueva Mexicana

LAWRENCE CLARK POWELL

SEEK ESSENCES, enduring things, touchstones, and symbols; try to re-create in prose what makes this country so increasingly meaningful and necessary to one. Altitude, distance, color, configuration, history, and culture—in them dwell the essential things, but they must be extracted. "Crack the rock if so you list, bring to light the amethyst." Costs nothing to try. Some have succeeded—Lummis, Lawrence, Long, La Farge, Horgan, Waters, the Fergussons—proving that it is possible. Stand books on the shelf, hang up maps, gaze in the turquoise ball, finger the fragment of red adobe from Pecos, reload the Blue Scripto, take a fresh yellow pad, then sit down and see what comes.

On that night in Santa Fe I read aloud from Haniel Long's unfinished book and found it good, the ripe work of a writer who waited six decades to write his first novel. This was the fourth visit in two years to Haniel and Alice Long, and again I brought offerings of tea and affection and the feather of a dove; and faintly, very faintly, I envied him his twenty-year head start and his quintessential masterpiece, published in 1936, the *Interlinear to Cabeza de Vaca*.

At dinner on a high point east of town we looked across the river valley to Los Alamos, wickedly winking with lights, while a cottontail nibbled grass outside the window and the flares of sunset reached the zenith.

"You can't do both," Long said. "Lead the administrative life and write."

"I'm trying. And also I want to teach. It's taken me twenty years to learn librarianship. Now I want to teach it."

"I taught for two decades at Carnegie Tech before we came here. I like to think my books continue the process."

"It was your books that brought me here. The wide world's your classroom now."

And to illustrate this, Long gave me a German translation of the *Interlinear*, to add to the French one he gave me a year ago.

Burma born, Harvard schooled, tall, lean, and gray, and suffering the same eye trouble as Huxley's, this man who founded Writers' Editions is humorous, quizzical, wise, and gentle, and I always leave him and his wife with a feeling of refreshment, redetermination, faith, and affection, and the anticipation of the riches which await a man in the decades between fifty and seventy, if he is prepared to recognize them.

The next day I entered the mission church at the Ranchos de Taos, one of the Southwest's two fairest shrines (the other being San Xavier). A party of nuns was being shown through by the priest, and they were having a jolly time, especially the youngest of the lot—a sister whose vitality, unquenched by her funereal habit, led her to peek under the red silk robe of an image to see what was beneath. I had not witnessed such spiritual vigor since Dublin.

The sundrenched fields of Taos were lush with alfalfa, goldenrod, and dandelion, exuding midsummer fragrance to the point of asphyxiation. I had been reading *The Man Who Killed the Deer*, and I wanted to see the Blue Lake of the Taoseños. The sign promised a route, but it proved to be only by trail. The road corkscrewed fifteen miles up the Arroyo Hondo, down which white water was foaming. At Twining, elevation 9,412, the road became traversible only by jeep. The air was sharp, and smoke from a campfire rose unwaveringly into an eggshell sky. The bald dome of Mt. Wheeler rose another few thousand feet higher. A trail-sign pointed to Lobo Peak, on whose aspened shoulder I had visited Frieda Lawrence in 1941.

Everywhere I went the new edition of the New Mexico State Guide was open on the seat beside me, full of facts and photos and a minimum of misleading information. I never could find the church of San Miguel del Bado as the Guide had described it, or it must have been stuccoed over what the book said was stone, but the side trip brought an even greater reward.

I had been earlier in Las Vegas, having come over the Sangres from Taos, through the Penitente villages of Picurís and Mora, traversing a high back country of few people and no people, of drizzle and shower and cloud-piled skies, past fields of corn and flowers and heavenly bluebirds, over the haunted route of Coronado, Armijo, and Los Tejanos, of Gregg and Kearny; and in the station there had seen mixed Santa Fe trains, none of which had quickened my pulse—cars, crews, passengers, all ordinary.

And then on this detour, having crossed the Pecos and reached the tiny station of Ribera, I saw a wondrous sight: the westbound Super Chief drawn up on a siding. That meant only one thing: its eastbound counterpart was due, and O Lord! there it was, coming round the turn, the long snake of silver Pullmans drawn by the monstrous red and yellow double diesel, pulling, pulling, with deep-throated, smoking exhausts, horning once for the passing, the engineer riding high on his throne, his gloved hand raised slightly in response to my enthusiastic wave, there at that orgasmic moment of midway meeting; and to crown it all, sight of an old friend, the Pullman car Coconino Princess, on which I had ridden before, coupled between Pine Meadow and Regal Junction, as fair a vision as these eyes have ever seen.

The westbound train gathered speed slowly and I lingered alongside it for several miles, its pony trucks clickety-clicking over the railpoints, until finally it pulled away from me, approaching Glorietta Pass and the descent to Las Vegas and Lamy. The engineer waved as I turned off to Pecos Pueblo, a ruin abandoned in 1838, now a state monument.

Rain began to fall again, darkening the red soil and the green piñons, and I got soaked while dashing in and out of the ruins of the church, which is dedicated to the same lady as my home town—Nuestra Señora la Reina de los Angeles. Without planning it I found myself traversing Pecos Village and once again following a river to its headwaters, while the car radio transmitted such sentimental songs as to make me long to learn the guitar—songs with apparently no other words than *corazon, amor, alma, y mujer*. Well, what else is there? *Libros*. I had not realized that this fabled river rises in the Sangres, and I preferred the mountain aspect of the stream, lined with a Cistercian monastery and a State Fish Hatchery and the strange modern hacienda of Arnold B. Friedman, to the lower Pecos country of Billy the Kid and worse.

This search for the source is a philosophical urge, as well as physiographical, a blind going upward to the beginning of things, while the world narrows in and all else is eliminated. This focus on the basic elements is purifying, therapeutic, electrifying, and this way of recharging by stripping away is a dedicatory one, well suited to this Angeleno who lives ordinarily in the midst of multiplicity. Such were my thoughts up where the Pecos rises.

LAWRENCE CLARK POWELL   227

East of the Sandias the road runs north to Golden and Madrid. What's in a name? Much—especially if the name is foreign and musical. When asked for the most musical words in English, regardless of meaning, a foreigner replied "cellar door." Thus the Sandias, to one ignorant of Spanish. The Watermelon Mountains? Well, yes, as long as the mind doesn't visualize the seedy fruit.

The Sandia Mountains. How different they appear when seen from the east, dark green and wooded all the way up, humped like a whale, without the bare face they present to Albuquerqueans. Southernmost of their sacred peaks, the range was called Turtle Mountain by the Pueblos. The turnoff to the crest was alluring, but I had miles to go before I parked, and the compass pointed north. Golden? Hardly. Madrid? A company coal town, obviously misnamed. The beauty of this lonely route lay in the piñon forest, and in the clouds that were just beginning to cap the sky.

At Cerrillos I came to an unexpected crossing of the railroad, the main line of the Santa Fe, and on a hunch I turned off and cruised through the village. I stopped by a group of natives on the porch of the grocery. "Any trains due?" I asked, briskly. Whereupon one of them lurched toward me, preceded by his boozy breath. "My friend," he pronounced, "there passes here one train every half hour," and he staggered back to his fellows. They laughed, as I drove on, crossed the tracks, and reconnoitered. Not a sound or sign of life, only shining rails. Then I spied a lank sack hanging from the trackside hook and a car parked alongside, with a woman sleeping in it. The mail train was due. I waited, and pretty soon heard the low hum of an approaching diesel. A full five minutes passed before it burst round the curve, heading northeast to Lamy and Las Vegas, and bore down on the station with overriding urgency. The Super Chief, no less. The sack was hooked in, and an equally thin one thrown off. The silver vision passed. Toroweap, Tierra Amarilla, Cloudcroft, but this time my Princess was coupled elsewhere. The woman got out, picked up the sack, drove off. I had witnessed the postmistress of Cerrillos at work.

I paid my first visit to the Museum on the outskirts of Santa Fe and saw an exhibition of contemporary arts and crafts of great beauty; silver and wood, turquoise and wool, the elements worked by hand with loving skill, the objects displayed in imaginative ways, to give one of the best museum experiences I have ever had.

City of the Holy Faith, huddle of abodes, cottonwooded, piñoned, ringed by ranges with ringing names: the Sangre de Cristos, the Sandias, the Jemez. Day's end and the mountains were blue black; again a lone rabbit, this time a big-eared jack, nibbling and sniffing his way across the somnolent landscape, as I looked north to the last light on Truchas, knowing that the morrow would find me on upland slopes.

The morrow was Sunday, and I saw people in their best, as once again I left the highway and took a dirt road to Chimayó and beyond, a gentle climb against the flow of water, past fields and flowers and burdened orchards. "Cherries, cherries," cried the children, from where they crouched by the roadside, holding out handfuls of the little red fruit.

All the beautiful choices were mine, whether to seek the fabled *santos* in the Santuario of Chimayó or to see the Valley of Cordova, where Joseph Krumgold made *And Now Miguel*, that almost unbearably beautiful documentary film of sheepherding and a small boy's dream. One must always choose among several, and Truchas was my choice, an ancient village lying exposed on a hogback, inanimate on this Sunday morning, yet eternally alive, as the ghost towns of Arizona are not. Metals were not the reason for Truchas's naked site. The villagers built there originally for defense against their enemies, descending to the fields, or driving their sheep to mountain meadows.

I crawled along the spinal street, seeing a crocheted peacock in a window, potted geraniums everywhere, a rainbow-painted wall and matching eaves (someone was crazy for color), stacked woodpiles, and I breathed piñon smoke from cooking stoves.

Once again choice was necessary, and I bore north over piney slopes, instead of climbing higher toward the Truchas Peaks and the next highest point in New Mexico (Wheeler Peak, 13,151 feet; North Truchas Peak, 13,110 feet). I came at last to the *cor cordium* of Spanish New Mexico, the ancient village of Las Trampas. It was noon and the priest had locked the church and gone to lunch. So had everyone. The pueblo-like plaza was deserted, except for a car with Montana plates, but I could feel eyes on me as I prowled around the classic church of Santo Tomás del Rio de las Trampas, coming on a store of wooden crosses piled against the rear wall, evidence that this was indeed deep penitente country.

Leaving the village and descending toward Peñasco on the Rio Pueblo, I met a rodeo of pickup trucks and young men in white shirts, and a short distance beyond I saw a girl in a red dress disappearing through the piñons.

In Taos again was the ubiquitous smell of burning piñon, recalling Peattie's words in his book on trees: "They say that those who, like Kit Carson, had once known the bells, the women and the pinyon smoke of Taos could never stay away—come Kiowa, come Sioux, come Kansas blizzard or calabozo."

El Crepusculo carried news of the death in San Diego of Bert Phillips, one of Taos's founding artists, and of the visit of Frieda Lawrence's daughter Barbara while Frieda's husband Angie was in Italy. I found Frieda in the house on the plain at El Prado, thanks to the directions of Joe Montoya's son at the family service station, where he was being aided by a swarm of boys, each of whom performed one automotive chore in slow motion, a pleasant change from metropolitan "minute men" service. I had not seen Frieda in five years, and found her still a fountain of friendly vitality. If Swift and Pope and the other bachelor misanthropes could have known a woman like Frieda, English literature would have been different, in the way it differed through what she gave Lawrence; and as we sat over tea and biscuits and spun the thread of talk clear back to the fateful day she first saw him in flannels and blazer and red beard, launching cockleshell boats for her children, I knew that this was basic to all literary history, that literature is made by men *and* women, a fact best understood by French critics.

South of Eagle Nest, State Highway 38 takes off to the east, giving promise, on the map, of a graded road over the mountains to Mora. The promise was not kept. What appeared on paper to be a beautiful back road was actually a deteriorating set of ruts, suited only to truck or jeep. I was driving a Chevrolet coupé, albeit a powerful eight-cylinder job, and with the automatic transmission which, contrary to popular belief, is excellent for slow driving over wretched roads, because of the uniform flow of power that can be maintained down to standstill and start again. And the car was high-bedded enough to clear the boulders; so it went, but just.

The road began alluringly enough along the adobe edges of sloping meadows. Still I had an eye on the sky. It was beginning to pile up with clouds that would break with rain before the day was ended, and I didn't want to be on 'dobe when they did.

There was no sign of life, even at the occasional ranches. The highway markers were rusted and illegible, and there was an increasing number of *trancas*, gated fences, requiring all my strength to manipulate. My eyes lifted to the blue mesa toward which the road climbed. Black Lake lay to the right, a natural *ciénaga* edged with deep grass and herds of fattening Herefords. This was the last place to turn back, but I did not know it, and pressed on ignorantly past the point of no return.

Suddenly the road narrowed and grew rockier. I drove at five miles an hour, grunting and sweating, in shorts and sneakers, thankful that my arms were stronger than my foresight, and really very happy not to be on Wilshire Boulevard. My comfort was a fresh set of tire tracks; otherwise I would not have known which choice to make when the road forked, as it did again and again.

Gaining the mesa at last I paused and looked back to the northernmost Sangres in the distance—Wheeler, Pueblo, and Lobos peaks, those bare "cloud-capp'd towers"—wondering how long I had before the rain came, and if there were *caliche* ahead, then turned my back on 'em and resumed my forward motion. The "road" rutted rockily through ponderosas and Engelmanns, then turned into a bouldered trough, down which I caromed toward what the map called Coyote Creek. It seemed to flow into the Guadalupita Valley, eventually to Mora and what, by contrast, would be civilization. This was the very opposite of the experience of seeking the headwaters of the Pecos and the Hondo: I longed to leave the headwaters, my muscles rigid under the hot flow of sweat, compelled to control my desire to hurry and beat the rain, and instead to crawl, bump, bounce, creep, and slither, holding horsepower and heartbeat in check. It had rained the day before, and the road was pooled and treacherous.

Then the trough tossed me into a clearing— a sawmill, with promise of human beings, of whom I had not seen one since Eagle Nest three hours before. It was a big establishment, with many sheds and cabins and parked trucks, and piles of trimmings. But no saw buzzed. No voice spoke. There was no stockpile of logs.

Nada. Nadi. Ninguno. En ninguna parte. The quintessence of nothingness. God, but it was eerie, like something out of Poe or Melville. I whistled. Echo answered. The tracks ended at still another fenced gate, leading to a ford over the creek. I parked and went around and faced a sign, and read, ABSOLUTELY NO TRESPASSING. Too late. I had already trespassed. Was this Highway 38, a public thoroughfare of the sovereign state of New Mexico, or was it a private road of the woodcutters? Had I taken a wrong turn up on the mesa?

And then I smelled and saw smoke, coming from a cabin chimney at the far end of the clearing. I trudged over spongy sawdust earth and called *Holla!* Two heads popped out of two windows, like boxed jacks, one red, one black. Grown boys, they belonged to, their mouths full of food, their eyes of astonishment.

"Where am I?" I asked. "Can I get out?"

They laughed and came outdoors. El Rojo was an Anglo, El Moro, a *hijo de país* who had stumps for hands.

"This is the sawmill of the Ortega Brothers," said Red, and Blackie added, "Where you from?"

"From Eagle Nest, Black Lake, and down the road to hell," I replied.

Again they laughed. "The worst is over," they assured me.

"Through the gate to Mora?"

"Sure, but don't be in a hurry. Those rocks are hungry."

"Where is everyone?" I asked.

"Logging. We just brought in a load and stopped for lunch."

"I have sweat the hunger out of me," I said.

"Where do you live?" they asked.

"In the City of Angels," I replied, "and I bring you blessings from Nuestra Señora."

They crossed themselves automatically, thinking perhaps I was a priest, garbed for a swim, and as I went back to my car, I heard them banging around in their cabin, whooping like Indians.

"The worst is over" was a way of speaking. The "road" forded and reforded Coyote Creek (a lovely stream under other conditions), shelving high along the bank on one side and then the other, rain-pooled, rocky, ribbon-narrow, dropping me fast with thunder at my back, and the only good omen a flight of blue birds across the very hood of the car.

The canyon kept widening, however, and the flow of sweat had slackened, my muscles relaxed, and I came at last to an angel—a woman in a white dress who vanished into her cabin as I drove up. In the window was the face of her daughter, who spoke sweetly in the grave manner of the country, when I asked her where I was.

"Guadalupita Valley," she said. "You bring rain with you. Gracias, señor."

"The road is better?"

"Truly a fine road hereafter."

"Thank you, thank you!" I said, as if she were personally responsible for this engineering miracle.

The rain caught up with me as I reached Guadalupita store and stopped to drink a cold bottle of soda pop, utterly relaxed as the fall turned to hail, then back to rain and finally to drip, cool on my hot skin. I snapped on the car radio and it crackled hopelessly with static.

The valley continued to widen as I neared Mora. West northwest the triple peaks of Truchas formed the horizon. Beyond the eastern hills lay plains and rivers, the Ozarks, the Appalachians—pallid country, all of it. My compass swung west southwest.

I had not liked Mora on my first visit, and I liked it even less this time, sensing there a focus of evil forces, personified by a horseman leading another horse, an Anglo of such debauched visage as to chill my blood.

Rolling down the road to Vegas I had an exciting glimpse of an all but naked girl in a roadside *acequia*, and I thought of Frank Waters's *People of the Valley*, laid in this very region, with its beautiful episode of María and the soldier at the pool; and I was uncertain as to which is the more memorable and lasting, literature or life.

Flying back to Albuquerque in a Corco Beechcraft, I experienced a feeling of flight not possible in a large plane. We blew off The Hill's landing strip like a leaf in the wind, and floated out over the valley of the Rio Grande, as the mesa fell away steeply beneath us. I sat alongside the pilot, three other passengers in the seat behind us, and he pointed out the pueblos as we passed over them, following the serpentine source of life, matrix of New Mexican history and culture, fed by snow and spring, the grand configuration now visible in a glance, comprehensible in its symbiotic parts.

Rain and the Beechcraft fell together on the airport at Albuquerque, and I stood around on the edge of the cool curtain while waiting for a westbound plane. Belted down in TWA's Flight 82, then circling north over the city, I had a last sight of the Sandias and a final good omen, not one but two perfect rainbows—*circo iris, arcobaleno, arc-en-ciel, regenbogen, rainbow*, take your choice, all beautiful, all blessed—arching from Bernalillo to where Highway 66 breached the range.

Biographical Notes

BERNICE AMES was born in Corry, Pennsylvania, and received the B.A. from Wilson College. In 1967 she was the recipient of the James Joyce Award, and in 1971 the Cecil Hemley Award, of the Poetry Society of America. Her books of poems include *Where the Light Bends* (1955), *In Syllables of Stars* (1958), and *Antelope Bread* (1966). She divides her time between Los Angeles and the country near Flagstaff.

MARY AUSTIN was born in Illinois and schooled there. When she was eighteen her family moved to California, where she lived for many years in the sagebrush land east of the Sierra Nevada. Here she wrote her first and most popular book, *The Land of Little Rain* (1903). In 1918 she moved to Santa Fe, where in 1923 she built her famous Casa Querida, Beloved House. Here, among many other books of both fiction and nonfiction, she wrote her second classic, *The Land of Journey's Ending*. Her autobiography, *Earth Horizon*, was published in 1932. She died in 1934.

WILLIAM E. BARRETT was born in New York City. He is the author of some two dozen books, of which probably one of the best known, because of the immensely popular film that was made from it, is *Lilies of the Field*. He lives in San Francisco.

ROY BEDICHEK was born in a log cabin in the Sangamon Valley of Illinois, fifty miles west of Springfield. When he was five years old his mother brought him to Falls County, Texas, where his father had homesteaded on land near Eddy. In 1897 he entered the University of Texas, with which, except for a few years just after his graduation, he was identified for a lifetime. But his four books—*Adventures with a Texas Naturalist, Karankaway Country, Educational Competition,* and *The Sense of Smell*—were all written after his retirement as director of the university's Interscholastic League. Two of them, *Karankaway Country* and *Educational Competition,* won the Carr P. Collins Award of the Texas Institute of Letters for their years. He died in 1959, just before friends were to come for him to go for a walk in the woods.

WILLIAM BURFORD was born in Shreveport, Louisiana. He has taught at Southern Methodist University, Johns Hopkins, the University of Texas, the University of Montana, and Texas Christian University. He has been a Fulbright Fellow and has been awarded numerous prizes for his poetry. His books of poems include *Man Now, A World, A Beginning,* and *Face of the Earth (Faccia della Terra),* a bilingual selection of poems in Italian and English, published in Bologna. He lives in Fort Worth, Texas.

ROBERT BURLINGAME was born in Pratt, Kansas, but has been a resident of the Southwest since 1945 and of El Paso since 1954. He was a Fulbright scholar at the University of London. His book of poems, *This Way We Walk,* was published in 1964. He is a member of the English faculty at the University of Texas at El Paso.

WITTER BYNNER was born in Brooklyn, New York. After the success of his first book of poems, *Young Harvard* (1907), he lived and wrote for a decade in Cornish, New Hampshire. Then, after a year teaching at the University of California, he traveled in the Orient, where he became much interested in Chinese poetry. His translation, with Dr. Kiang Kang-hu, of the poems in *The Jade Mountain* (1929) was the first volume of Chinese verse to be translated in full by an American poet. The later years of his life were spent in Santa Fe, New Mexico, and Chapala, Mexico. He was the author of many books of poetry, biography, and philosophical interpretation. He died in 1968.

WILSON CLOUGH was born in New Brunswick, New Jersey. After receiving the B.A. from Union College, New York, he attended the University of Montpelier, France, and then the University of Colorado, from which he received the M.A. degree. He also received the Litt. D. from Union College and the LL.D. from the University of Wyoming, where he taught for many years and in 1961 became Professor Emeritus in the School of American Studies. In addition to his two volumes of poems, *Brief Oasis* (1954) and *We, Borne Along* (1950), his books include a *History of the University of Wyoming, Intellectual Origins of American National Thought,* and *Our Long Heritage.*

BORDEN DEAL was born in Mississippi. He has served as writer-in-residence at Transylvania University in Lexington, Kentucky, and has been the recipient of Guggenheim and MacDowell Colony fellowships. He is the author of sixteen novels, the most recent of which is *The Other Room.* He lives in Osprey, Florida.

DAVID CORNEL DEJONG was born in the Netherlands and came to the United States at the age of thirteen. He graduated from Calvin College, Michigan, and did graduate work at Duke and Brown. For many years he taught creative writing at the University of Rhode Island. He wrote eight novels, a volume of poems, two books of short stories, and an autobiography, *With a Dutch Accent.* He died in 1971.

J. FRANK DOBIE, born in the brush country south of San Antonio, was the undisputed dean of Texas letters, of whom Lawrence Clark Powell has written, "His score of books about the region represent the life and literature, the legends, lore, and natural history of the land." His *Coronado's Children* first brought him national recognition. His own favorite among his books was *Tongues of the Monte.* His *Guide to Life and Literature of the Southwest* is still used in courses of which his own at the University of Texas was the prototype. He never wrote a complete autobiography, but a group of his essays was collected after his death in 1964 by his widow and published as *Something of Myself.*

RICHARD DOKEY lives in Lodi, California. His story "Sanchez" has been included in two anthologies of Chicano literature, both published in 1971: *The World of the Chicano,* edited by Edward W. Ludwig and James Santibanez, and *The Chicano: From Caricature to Self-Portrait,* edited by Edward Simmen.

CHARLES EDWARD EATON was born in Winston-Salem, North Carolina, and educated at the University of North Carolina, Princeton, and Harvard. After teaching creative writing at the University of Missouri for two years, he was for four years Vice Consul at the American Embassy in Rio de Janeiro. Upon his return to this country he taught creative writing at the University of Carolina for several years. *The Shadow of the Swimmer*, his second volume of poetry, won the Ridgely Torrence Memorial Award, and his third volume, *The Greenhouse in the Garden*, was a final nominee for the National Book Award. He is the author of two volumes of stories and five of poems. He divides his time between Chapel Hill, North Carolina, and Woodbury, Connecticut.

JOHN GOULD FLETCHER was born in Arkansas. He was much influenced by southern traditions, although for twenty-five years he lived mainly in Europe, where he became a leader of the Imagists. Later he returned to Arkansas and in his work to the American scene, becoming a leading Agrarian. He won a Pulitzer Prize for his *Selected Poems* (1938). He wrote nine other volumes of poems and five prose works, including his autobiography, *Life Is My Song* (1937). He died in 1950.

WILLIAM GOYEN was born in Trinity, Texas, and attended Rice University. His early years in Texas furnished him with the background for his first novel, *The House of Breath* (1950), of which "Christy" became a part, and of other novels and stories, including his most recent novel, *Come, the Restorer. The House of Breath* has twice been a play, has been translated into several languages, and in 1975 will be reprinted by Random House. Its author is presently living and writing in New York.

ALBERT GUÉRARD was born in Paris and came to America to teach in 1906. For fifty-three years he taught, lectured, and wrote in America, most of that time as a professor at Stanford University, although he also taught at Williams College, Rice University (then Institute), and Brandeis University, as well as at half a dozen other universities during various summers. When Brandeis awarded him the honorary degree of Doctor of Letters, the citation called him "a civilized rebel, a sensitive nonconformist, a genuine Renaissance man, a genuine lover of people, a blend of Gallic wit and American pragmatism." Among his books were *French Prophets of Yesterday, Personal Equation, Testament of a Liberal, Bottle in the Sea,* and *Fossils and Presences.* He died in 1959.

JAMES HAINING lives in Quincy, Illinois, where he heads the Salt Lick Press and publishes the magazine of the same name.

PAUL HORGAN was born in Buffalo, New York, and grew up in New Mexico. He is the author of some thirty-five books, of which perhaps the best known are his first novel, *The Fault of Angels,* which won the Harper Prize, and his major historical work, *Great River: The Rio Grande in North American History,* which won the Pulitzer Prize, the Bancroft Prize, and the Carr P. Collins Award of the Texas Institute of Letters. He is professor emeritus and author in residence at Wesleyan University in Middletown, Connecticut.

ERNEST KROLL was born in New York City and received the B.A. degree from Columbia University. While at Columbia he studied Japanese, took a strong interest in Oriental culture, and received a grant for study in Japan. During World War II he was a Japanese language officer in the U.S. Navy. After the war he became an information and editorial specialist for the Department of State. He is the author of three books of poems: *Cape Horn and Other Poems* (1952), *The Pauses of the Eye* (1955), and *Fifty Fraxioms* (1973).

HANIEL LONG was born in Rangoon, where his father was a Methodist missionary, and grew up in Pittsburgh, where he taught literature for twenty years at Carnegie Institute of Technology. In 1929 he moved to Santa Fe, where he spent the remaining twenty-seven years of his life. Of his many books the best known is *Interlinear to Cabeza de Vaca,* which has had editions in Italian, French, and German as well as several in English. He was the dominant force in Writers' Editions, a cooperative publishing group in Santa Fe which published seventeen books before World War II cut off its supply of paper. Long died in Santa Fe in 1956.

STEPHEN MALIN is a native of Pennsylvania. As an undergraduate at Pennsylvania State University, he worked in Joseph Leonard Grucci's poetry workshop. He has taught speech and drama at Memphis State University in Tennessee, having left there only for a stay in England on a research grant. His work was included in the anthology *Poetry Southwest 1950-1970*.

ALICE MARRIOTT was born in Wilmette, Illinois. She attended the University of Oklahoma, where she was the first woman to be granted a degree in anthropology. She has devoted many years to the study of the American Indian, past and present. She is a Fellow of the American Anthropological Association and a Fellow of the American Association for the Advancement of Science. She served for years as a specialist with the Indian Arts and Crafts Board of the Department of the Interior. She has written a number of books, including *The Ten Grandmothers*, an ethnological study of the Kiowa Indians; *Maria: The Potter of San Ildefonso*; and, with Carol Rachlin, *American Indian Mythology*. She lives in Oklahoma City, where she and Miss Rachlin have established Southwest Research Associates. They are also writers in residence at Central State College in Edmond, Oklahoma.

WILLARD MARSH was born in Oakland, California. He received the M.A. degree at the Writing Center of the University of Iowa. His stories have appeared in *Prize Stories 1957: The O. Henry Awards* and in the Foley *Best American Short Stories* volumes for 1953 and 1961. His novel *Week with No Friday* was published in 1956. His volume of short stories, *Beachhead in Bohemia*, published in 1969, won the Jesse H. Jones Award of the Texas Institute of Letters for the best Texas book of fiction of that year.

JOYCE CAROL OATES was born and grew up in the country outside Lockport, New York. Novelist, poet, playwright, critic, and short story writer, she has published nineteen books in half as many years. Her novel *Them* won the National Book Award in 1970. She is an associate professor of English at the University of Windsor in Ontario, Canada.

MAURICE OGDEN was born in Oklahoma and received his education in that state. He has alternated his writing activity, much of it in the field of science fiction, with jobs as steelworker, radio announcer, electronics and computer worker, and teacher. His ballad, *Hangman*, was produced as a one-reel full-color film. "Freeway to Wherever" was reprinted in *Prize Stories 1960: The O. Henry Awards*.

CHARLES OLIVER was born in Van Buren, Arkansas. He attended the universities of Tulsa, Arkansas, and Oklahoma and taught at Northeastern State College in Tahlequah, Oklahoma, before coming in 1969 to Southern Methodist University, where he has been a member of the English faculty since that time. One of his stories won the John H. McGinnis Memorial Award for 1974. He is represented in *The Bicentennial Collection of Texas Short Stories*.

LAURENCE PERRINE was born in Toronto and brought up in Cleveland. He received the B.A. and M.A. from Oberlin and the Ph.D. from Yale. Since 1946 he has taught at Southern Methodist University, where he is now Frensley Professor of English Literature. Among his numerous works the one for which he is probably best known, *Sound and Sense: An Introduction to Poetry*, is perhaps the most widely used text in its field. "The Poet and the Laboratory" will be included in a book of his essays on poetry to be published by Newbury House.

LAWRENCE CLARK POWELL was born in Washington, D.C., but while he was still a child his family moved to South Pasadena, California. He attended Occidental College, where he received the B.A., and then went to France, where he obtained the doctorate at the University of Dijon. He became head of the UCLA Library and director of the William Andrews Clark Memorial Library, and then founding dean of the UCLA School of Library Service. He has written over a dozen books, most of them *about* books, the most recent being *Southwest Classics* (1974). He is now living in Tucson and teaching in the Graduate Library School of the University of Arizona.

NORMAN H. RUSSELL lives in Edmond, Oklahoma, where he is a professor of biology at Central State College. His Indian poems owe much to his being one-eighth Cherokee, but his research in ecology and botany has given him, he states, the experience he needed to write them. He has published two books of poems, *At the Zoo* (1969) and *indian thoughts: the small songs of god* (1972).

ARTHUR M. SAMPLEY was born in Leander, Texas and received the B.A., M.A., and Ph.D. degrees from the University of Texas. He is Distinguished Professor of English Literature at North Texas State University, where he has also served as Director of Libraries, Dean of Arts and Sciences, and Vice President. He is the author of four volumes of verse: *This Is Our Time* (1943), *Of the Strong and the Fleet* (1947), *Furrow with Blackbirds* (1951), and *Selected Poems 1937-1971* (1971). The last three of these volumes received the Texas Institute of Letters Award for the best Texas book of poems for the years in which they were published.

BILL D. SCHUL lives in Winfield, Kansas. He is the author of *Hear Me, Barabbas* and *Let Me Do This Thing*, both published in 1969, and articles on science and social problems in over a hundred magazines. He was a member of the 1970 and 1971 White House Conferences on Children and Youth and served on the President's Committee on Juvenile Delinquency and Youth Crime and the National 7th Step Foundation.

DAVID SEARCY is a graduate of Southern Methodist University. He lives in Dallas and commutes to Seven Points, in East Texas, where he is editor of the *Cedar Creek Pilot*.

WILLIAM STAFFORD was born in Kansas. His second book of poems, *Traveling through the Dark* (1962), won a National Book Award. His other book titles are *West of Your City* (1960), *The Rescued Year* (1966), *Allegiances* (1970), and *Someday, Maybe* (1973). After a stint as Consultant in Poetry in English to the Library of Congress, he is back teaching at Lewis and Clark College in Oregon.

JESSE STUART is a native of Greenup County, Kentucky, where he still lives in W-Hollow in a house that includes the log cabin in which he lived as a boy. He is one of America's most prolific writers, with some forty books, over four hundred published short stories, and over two thousand published poems to his credit. His second book, *Man with a Bull Tongue Plow*, made him famous. His novel *Taps for Private Tussie* was chosen a Masterpiece of World Literature and won the Thomas Jefferson Memorial Award. He won an Academy of Arts and Sciences Award for his book of short stories *Men of the Mountains*. He has been a teacher in Kentucky and as far away from W-Hollow as Cairo, where he taught American literature at the American University.

JOHN TAYLOR teaches at Washington and Jefferson College in Washington, Pennsylvania. His book, *The Soap Duckets*, was published in 1965.

MARSHALL TERRY was born in Cleveland, Ohio. He attended Amherst and Kenyon and received the M.A. from Southern Methodist University, where he is now chairman of the Department of English. He is the author of two novels, *Old Liberty* and *Tom Northway*. The latter was cowinner of the Jesse H. Jones Award of the Texas Institute of Letters.

ROBERT TRAMMELL was born in Dallas and is a graduate of Southern Methodist University. He is now living in New York. His first book of poems, *Famous Men*, was published in 1971.

WALTER PRESCOTT WEBB, a native of Texas, was one of America's most distinguished historians. He was Harkness Lecturer in American History at London University, Harmsworth Professor of American History at Oxford, and from 1933 on, Professor of History at the University of Texas. In 1958 he was president of the American Historical Association. His *The Great Plains* received the Loubat Prize of Columbia University. *The Texas Rangers* was published in 1935, *Divided We Stand* in 1937, and his major work, *The Great Frontier*, in 1952. He died in 1963.